Begin Here →

•Begin Here

Reading Asian North American

Autobiographies of Childhood

Rocío G. Davis

University of Hawai'i Press
Honolulu

© 2007 University of Hawai'i Press
All rights reserved
Printed in the United States of America
12 11 10 09 08 07   6 5 4 3 2 1

Library of Congress Cataloging-in-Publication Data
Davis, Rocío G.
    Begin here : reading Asian North American autobiographies
of childhood / Rocío G. Davis
        p. cm.
    Includes bibliographical references and index.
    ISBN-13: 978-0-8248-3092-2 (cloth : acid-free paper)
    ISBN-10: 0-8248-3092-X (cloth : acid-free paper)
    1. Asian Americans—Biography—History and criticism.
2. Asians—Canada—Biography—History and criticism. 3. Asian
American children—Biography—History and criticism. 4. Children—
United States—Biography—History and criticism. 5. Children—
Canada—Biography—History and criticism. 6. Autobiography—
Asian American authors. 7. Asian Americans in literature.
8. Children in literature. 9. Asian Americans—Social conditions.
10. Asians—Canada—Social conditions. I. Title.
    E184.A75D38 2006
    305.23092'39507—dc22
                                        2006022571

University of Hawai'i Press books are printed on acid-free
paper and meet the guidelines for permanence and durability
of the Council on Library Resources.

Designed by University of Hawai'i Press production staff
Printed by The Maple-Vail Book Manufacturing Group

To my teachers, Joseph A. Galdon
and Doreen G. Fernandez.
And to kindred spirits—here,
there, and everywhere.

Like a good mystery novel, I thought to myself, one's life should always be read twice, once for the experience, then once again for astonishment.
    —Wayson Choy, *Paper Shadows*

Contents

Acknowledgments

My gratitude goes, in the first place, to the persons in the Modern Languages Department of the University of Navarra for their daily doses of companionship, encouragement, and laughter: Rosalia Baena, Andrew Breeze, Ana Delgado, Carmen Poher, and Pilar Saiz. I would also like to thank the College of Arts and Letters for their continued support over the years. In particular, I thank the Comisión de Investigación of the University of Navarra, whose funding has made this book possible. Many of the ideas in this book have evolved from seminar sessions with the members of our PIUNA research group: thank you.

A grant from the Centre of Women's Studies and Gender Relations of the University of British Columbia allowed me to do research on Asian Canadian autobiographies in 2005. I thank the Centre's director, Sneja Gunew, for conversations and videos. I'm also grateful to Valerie Raoul and the other scholars and students who made my stay a delightful learning experience. Bill and Peggy New and Laurie and Treva Ricou made it a very enriching incursion into Canadian history, literature, and flora. Very special thanks to Susanna Egan for hours of conversation and a continuing friendship. I'm especially grateful for that wonderful birthday dinner with a terrific group of scholars on autobiography: Gabrielle Helms, Laurie McNeil, and Manuela Constantino.

I would also like to thank the community of scholars and friends who patiently read my drafts, sent me books or articles, answered listserv questions, and simply listened when I spoke about "that book on autobiographies of childhood." Thanks to Santi Aurell, Rosalia Baena, Bubbles Bandojo, Ana Delgado, Floyd Cheung, Monica Chiu, Nancy Cirillo, Melinda de Jesús, Dolores de Manuel, Marilés Ebro, Susanna Egan, Heinz Fenkl, Dorothea Fischer-Hornung and the MESEA folks, Nona Flores, Claire Huang, Sue-Im Lee, Pilar Leon, Shirley Lim, Marie Lo, Sämi Ludwig, Seiwoong Oh, Alicia Otano, Raul Rodrigo, Lyra Rufino-Maceda, Pilar Saiz, Danielle Schaub, Paul Spickard, Gita Rajan, Linda

Vavra, Pablo Vázquez, Donna Wong, Sau-ling Wong, and Zhou Xiaojing. Without you, this book would not have happened.

My thanks to Masako Ikeda for her enthusiasm for this book from the start, and to the readers of the manuscript for their support and suggestions.

As always, my gratitude to my family in Manila and Pamplona, especially to my mom, who makes everyone read my books. Finally, I want to thank the Trigo kids—Miguel, Josemaría, Bea, Tommy, Javi, Isabel, Patricia, Catalina, and Gabi—for the privilege of sharing their childhoods and the De Langes—Nachi, Angela, Jaime, Gab, Cio, and Miguel—who, even from across the sea, make me a part of theirs.

Note: Earlier versions of sections of this book have been published in the journals *Prose Studies, Children's Literature Association Quarterly, MELUS,* and *The Lion and the Unicorn,* and the volume *Transnational Asian American Literature: Sites and Transits,* edited by Shirley Geok-lin Lim, John Blair Gamber, Stephen Hong Sohn, and Gina Valentino.

Introduction

Revisiting the Childhood

In the final chapter of *Farewell to Manzanar,* Jeanne Wakatsuki Houston travels back to the internment camp she had lived in as a child, this time with her husband and three children, in an act of reconciliation and recovery. Manzanar, which in the summer of 1942 was "the biggest city between Reno and Los Angeles" (135), is now deserted. As she looks around at the ruin that had been her home during the war years, she contrasts her conflicted feelings with those of her children, who run around oblivious to the multiple stories of their own past buried in that desert. For Houston, the trip and the actual writing of her autobiography are occasions of historical, cultural, and personal processes of recovery: "until this trip I had not been able to admit that my own life really began there. . . . Much more than a remembered place, it had become a state of mind. Now, having seen it, I no longer wanted to lose it or to have those years erased" (140). The act of writing an autobiography of her childhood in the camp, as well as the early years after leaving it, becomes an important literary and cultural gesture that resonates as genre and as a contribution to the creation of cultural memory.

What Houston enacts in her text lies at the center of my critical perspective on the writing of Asian American and Asian Canadian autobiographies of childhood. The role of autobiography in ethnic writing continually obliges us to read through the strategies the authors engage in their life writing projects, to accommodate both literary and cultural aims.[1] This study limns the forms that this process takes in Asian American and Asian Canadian writing. Considering the progressive development of life writing and the politics of identity formation in this century, writers and critics have become increasingly conscious of the play of the autobiographical act itself.[2] I argue that Asian North American memoirs of childhood are challenging the construction and performative potential of the national experience, particularly in the experiential categories of epistemology and phenomenology.[3] This understanding has important implications for ethnic life writing, which has consistently challenged and widened the boundaries of traditional autobiography by negotiating narrative techniques, experimenting with genre, and raising increasingly complex questions about self-representation and the construction of cultural memory. Here, I trace a crucial transition in the development of the autobiographical subgenre defined as the "Childhood" by Richard N. Coe and address its increasingly creative and subversive appropriation by Asian North American writers. I examine the artistic project of Asian American and Asian Canadian writers—from Phan You Lee and Ilhan New to Jade Snow Wong, Wayson Choy, Rae Yang, Michael Kwan, Lynda Barry, Kien Nguyen, and Luong Ung—who choose to deploy narratives of their childhood years as literary acts that articulate their individual processes of self-identification and negotiation of cultural and/or national affiliation.

The title of this book gestures toward the critical process I see enacted in Asian North American Childhoods. Coe notes, "Childhood revisited is childhood *recreated,* and recreated in terms of art" (*When the Grass* 84).[4] The statement "begin here" signifies on generic, thematic, and discursive levels. It reminds us of Georges Gusdorf's concept of autobiography as "a second reading of experience, and it is truer than the first because it adds to experience itself consciousness of it" (38) and echoes Paul John Eakin's idea of life writing as a process of "narratively constituted identity" (*How Our Lives* 139). The formulation signals the specificity of the Childhood, a contemplative text that narrativizes processes of self-awareness. The writing of the text itself may constitute that new beginning, when the writer is enabled to produce the story of his or her own life, a vital metaliterary gesture. Further, the genre problematizes two mutually enhancing processes—a simultaneous awakening of temporal and spatial consciousness; "here" and "now" become axiomatic of the subject's itinerary of selfhood and function as a frame for understanding and claiming the past. As Rosemary Lloyd points out, some form of justification establishes the starting point in memoir, just as the search for an opening, "the act of recapturing the first memory, or isolating the moment when the child first becomes aware of its identity" frames the narrative act (41). Reliving early memories or events that lead the subject to contemplate him- or herself as an individual heightens the performative aspects of autobiography as it foregrounds the manner in which personal circumstances and cultural contingencies function in the process of self-inscription.

My concern in this project is twofold: first, I want to negotiate the manner in which Asian North American writers rewrite the inherited scripts of the Childhood, as defined by Coe in his germinal study, *When the Grass Was Taller: Autobiography and the Experience of Childhood.* I read the texts as generic engagements that dialogue with the manner in which North American autobiography is being written and read, and analyze methodological approaches to this form of literary production. Second, I examine these texts' performative potential within a wider project of creating a reader and a community as a tool for the production and preservation of cultural memory. I argue that these texts function importantly in the intersecting projects of reclaiming history and building community. These two purposes overlap significantly and lead us to understand the need to continually address the cultural work enacted by these *literary* texts, as well as their specific aesthetic projects as mutually enhancing and intertwined purposes. To address only the cultural project of writers is to elide important aesthetic choices and ignore the carefully wrought formal investment of the authors who are clearly writing in a context of literary and cultural criticism.[5] This project is closely related to my earlier work on Asian American appropriations of established Euro-American genres such as the short story cycle and, in particular, to a recent collected volume, edited by Sue-Im Lee and myself, titled *Literary Gestures: The Aesthetic in Asian American Writing.*[6] This collection proposes a revised perspective on Asian American literary criticism, one that transcends the currently fashionable dominance of sociological and cultural materialist approaches to engage writers' formal and aesthetic choices as part of a responsible and holistic analysis. Crucially, we argue, though materialist and political examinations of race, gender, history, and nation need not exclude a literary perspective, this balance has not been successfully maintained in recent criticism. As Sue-Im Lee points out: "Asian American literary criticism at large has been slow to extend the analysis of the constructedness of human-made categories and institutions to include the examination of Asian American literary works as aesthetic objects—objects that are constituted by and through deliberate choices in form, genres, traditions, and conventions" (2).

The concerns that have guided my earlier work continue to motivate this project: to foreground literary perspectives in order to avoid the dangerous pitfall of allowing a body of literature susceptible to political, social, or materialist readings to be considered exclusively from that perspective. The literary quality of Asian North American writing, because of its highly racialized and political nature, is constantly in danger of being elided in favor of those concerns. Asian North American autobiography, because of the genre's relation with history and personal story, is in even more danger of losing its perspective. I contend that a primarily ethnographic perspective denies these texts both their formal and aesthetic complexity, the existence of a dialogue with established cultural forms, and importantly, their power to *act upon* and *transform* genre itself. As Marianne Gullestad notes, life stories are constructed from the cultural contexts in which lives are lived, and autobiographies allow us to examine how cultural resources, conventions, and histories are deployed in the recreation of that life: "a life story is shaped not only by the material facts of social existence, but also by deeply embedded notions and expectations of what is a culturally normal life, as well as by conscious and unconscious rules about what constitutes a good story" (12). To use a well-known example, any responsible reading of the reception of Maxine Hong Kingston's *The Woman Warrior* not only reveals an important intervention in the definition of Chinese America and what it means to be Chinese American but, perhaps more importantly, it unveils the challenges that this text produced to contemporary criticism on autobiography in general.[7] It obliged us to rethink feminist, postmodern, avantgarde, or ethnic perceptions and enactments of the autobiographical mode. To a large extent, we can affirm that after Kingston, American autobiography was never the same. Formal and aesthetic issues have become protagonists of the autobiographical act, serving as ways of signifying. We no longer ask only *what* the text is about, but are equally concerned with *how* processes of self-representation are articulated.

For these reasons, I consider how these autobiographies of childhood dialogue with other texts of the same genre and as interventions in American literary history. I focus on these autobiographies as *writerly* acts and, simultaneously, I also consider the reality of a larger project—the production of cultural memory and the creation and/or preservation of a community of readers. From a generic perspective, life writing narrativizes memory, reflection, and imagination, as the autobiographer configures his or her past into a shape that takes its formal design from established modes. But because the content of the narration in the context of Asian North American writing necessarily involves racial negotiation, social experience, and political engagement, the narrative becomes "history"—the public story of a past shared with others and assumed to have actually occurred. Important for our purposes, these stories promote that history and prevent its erasure by means of the physical existence of the text. Albert Stone refers to this process when he conceives of life writing "not simply as a literary convention but more broadly as a cultural activity" (2).[8] By presenting a reasoned theoretical approach and reading the texts to unveil what they operate on both aesthetic and cultural levels, I offer a new perspective on the intersection between formal and cultural designs within the context of Asian North American writing.

By reading these texts in this manner, I suggest that these autobiographies intervene significantly in our critical conception of both genre and ideas of reception. More important, when crucial events of history itself—war, diaspora, the civil rights movement, among others—are part of the context of these works, the genre becomes a doubly valuable historical document.[9] Or, as Shirley Neuman puts it, "An adequate poetics of autobiography, I would suggest, would acknowledge that subjects are constructed by discourse but it would *also* acknowledge that subjects construct discourse" (223). Similarly, I argue, there is a history that shapes individual autobiographies—a history of a literary and cultural tradition—that, in its turn, influences the shapes taken by later auto-biographies. Interestingly, life writing acknowledges the multiplicity of histo-ries as strongly as the intersection of histories, where the differences between the subjects and texts invite plural identification. These autobiographies of childhood thus execute important historical projects, as Kate Douglas has sug-gested in her work on Australian and British Childhoods, noting that these texts are "used to write particular childhoods into history" (12).

In the context of Asian North American writing, these Childhoods oblige us to rethink accepted Western concepts of childhood and identification as "American" or "Canadian" subjects, nuancing essentialist notions of the univer-sal child. As Sidonie Smith and Julia Watson argue, when reading autobiogra-phy we must examine how "larger historical and cultural conjunctions and shifts bear upon the composing and publication of a particular narrative" (166). For this reason, the literary, cultural, and political circumstances that surround the writing and publication of these texts help us understand why they are writ-ten, how they are shaped, and how they are read.

This position structures my arguments as I strive to identify the way in which generic choice has influenced how Asian American and Asian Canadian writers tell their stories to develop cultural memory. I ground my interpretative strategies on a minimum of theoretical positions, preferring to read the texts themselves, an approach that allows me to negotiate the ways in which generic choices produce cultural meaning without limiting myself to prescriptive modes and systems.[10] This book thus interrogates the literary strategies and cultural significance of Asian North American autobiographies of childhood and considers the ways these texts are produced and read.

First, I analyze how these Asian American authors address and rewrite the paradigms of the Euro-American Childhood, as defined by Coe, to engage their own historical and cultural specificities. I explore how these Childhoods can be examined in terms of the negotiation of narrative perspective, style, meta-phors, language, and structure to explore to what extent these texts dialogue with an existing Asian North American autobiographical tradition. Specifi-cally, for example, although most of the texts under consideration are written in traditional chronological order, some employ inventive narrative strategies to expand meaning and enrich our reading process: Hilary Tham's Childhood blends prose and verse; Sing Lim and Shichan Takashima merge drawing with text; Jade Snow Wong uses a subversive third person in *Fifth Chinese Daughter* to speak of herself; Lynda Barry designs comics.

Second, I am interested in showing how these autobiographies produce and develop a reader and a community where texts like these can flourish and, in turn, produce more writing. Issues of autobiographical mediation on histor-ical, racial, ethnic, cultural, and gender issues in the context of questions of identity and agency for their writers also direct my critical analysis. By attending to the formal strategies of these Asian North American Childhoods, we discern clear community-building strategies and identify a powerful means to address the intersection of literary genre and cultural position that allow us to understand the renewed sociocultural construction of childhood in contemporary American and Canadian societies.

This analysis develops following a thematic perspective, which helps unveil the writers' diverse formal strategies. Though I have two separate aims in this project, I recognize that it is impossible and, indeed, counterproductive to divorce formal from cultural perspectives, and the book's structure reflects that happy difficulty. The first chapter explores the theoretical definitions and positions I use as the basis for my reading of the texts. Subsequent chapters offer close readings that negotiate writerly strategies as well as cultural or community aims. I have chosen to order the texts according to their central thematic components, which reveal important narrative similarities, rather than chronologically. This organization allows me to reproduce the macrostructure of the immigrant narrative of Americanization, the most common thread that links these texts, emphasizing the metacritical component of forms of analysis. Each chapter title highlights both the thematic and formal reading approach used. Chapters 2 and 3, "The Asian Childhood: Writing Beginnings" and "Cultural Revolutions and Takeovers: War as Structure," center on narratives set in Asia, which challenge accepted notions of the past of the "American" or "Canadian" subject and enact important processes of history making and community building. "The Liminal Childhood: Biraciality as Narrative Position" (chapter 4) focuses on an important paradigm in Asian North American narratives, biraciality, and the creation of the mixed-race subject and community. Chapter 5, "Citizens or Denizens: Inscribing the Tropes of Asian North Americanization," explores the experience of immigration and the existence of segregated spaces such as Chinatown or the internment camps as tropes or metaphors for the arduous process of North Americanization. Chapter 6, "In North America: Formulating Experience," explores the possibilities for new formal and structural representations of the Asian North American model of selfhood. The final chapter, "The Childhood for Children: The Cultural Experience of the Early Reader," discusses the articulation of this genre of life writing as children's literature to read the ways in which writers participate in the formation of American and Canadian children's imagination and perception of cultural realities. The ultimate aim of this project entails reading the strategies of these Asian North American writers to show how literary acts significantly intersect with wider social concerns, the creation of a community, and the enhancement of its forgotten or disenfranchised history.

Chapter 1

● **To Begin Here**

In his germinal text, *When the Grass Was Taller: Autobiography and the Experience of Childhood,* as in subsequent articles that elaborate on specific issues, Richard N. Coe presents a review of more than six hundred accounts of childhood written in six major European languages over the last 150 years.[1] The existence of a multiplicity of texts justifies Coe's classification of this type of writing as an autonomous subgenre of autobiography, with its own internal rules and structures and a specific name, the "Childhood." The study is admirably comprehensive and continues to be a touchstone for any discussion on memoirs of childhood. Any deficit we note today in his scope needs to be counterbalanced by a recognition of his innovative work in autobiography criticism in the early 1980s, when feminist and ethnic theories were only beginning to influence readings of life writing. Coe defines the genre as *"an extended piece of writing, a conscious deliberately executed literary artifact, usually in prose* (and thus intimately related to the novel) *but not excluding occasional experiments in verse, in which the most substantial portion of the material is directly autobiographical, and whose structure reflects step by step the development of the writer's self; beginning often, but not invariably, with the first light of consciousness, and concluding, quite specifically, with the attainment of a precise degree of maturity"* (8–9, italics in original).

The Childhood strives to exhibit the gradual construction of a preadult self, opening as near the beginning as possible and with the maximum attempt at "poetic truth"—which, though difficult to verify, remains the only acceptable criterion (*When the Grass* 2). Coe notes that the typical Childhood ends not at the point of the author's final and positive integration as a member of society, but at a point of total awareness of self as an entity and especially as a writer who will produce, as evidence of a mature poet-identity, *this* Childhood. I have identified more than fifty Asian North American autobiographies that center primarily on the author's childhood. This number validates the imperative to evaluate the paradigms that Coe sets out, expanding and rearticulating them in order to evince the specificities of the Asian North American experience and narrativization of childhood.

The manner in which Asian North American writers appropriate and subvert traditional literary genres in order to enact particular subjectivities makes a detailed study of their writerly strategies exigent. My purpose involves examining the artistic project of these writers, rather than their political or social approaches to transglobalization or diaspora. Though Asian North American writing must be read within specific historical and social contexts, its engagement with and revision of traditional Euro-American literary genres strategically rearticulates their subject positions and challenges dominant ideologies. As I have argued in more detail elsewhere, we must move beyond an analytical model of merely reading the surface of texts for potential meanings and unravel what the texts allow us to do within the contexts of larger questions of literary performance.[2]

Genre definition directs the act of reading and writing and provides readers and writers with interpretations that enable them to share the process of meaning. Generic choices influence the sources of signification and the readers' reception of the ideological issues and concerns embedded in the narrative enactment. Todorov's notion of genres functioning—consciously or unconsciously—as "horizons of expectation" for readers and as "models for writing" for authors attests to the crucial historical existence of the genres and the cultural work they execute (163). The Childhood, which Coe considers "an ideal form destined never to be fully realized: the ideal being to tell a total truth about a previous self which, in reality, can never be more than half-remembered" (*When the Grass* 2–3), struggles to approach this ideal. By appropriating an established autobiographical genre, Asian North Americans enter American and Canadian literary institutions and explore the possibilities of social mobilization and community service. Elizabeth Bruss suggests "we can speculate on what cultural conditions promote an emphasis on individual identity, but conceptions of individual identity are articulated, extended, and developed through an institution like autobiography" (5), a position that stresses the cultural work enacted by the choice of genre. Also, when writers choose to engage autobiographies of childhood and readers choose to read them, we enter into a dialogue motivated precisely by the generic label of the text.

Importantly, I emphasize that these are *literary* texts by analyzing them as strategic interventions in the history of North American autobiography and in the context of the Asian North American bildungsroman. Patricia Chu has analyzed the nuances of the Asian American bildungsroman to show how Asian American writers "rewrite the genre to register their vexed and unstable positions in America. . . . Finding themselves without a clear place in American society, these writers have made the struggle for authorship, and for the founding of a new literary tradition, central tropes for the more fundamental tasks of claiming and constructing Asian American subjectivity" (6). This discussion applies well to the points I make about authorial practices and genre negotiation in the context of ethnic writing. As Betty Bergland notes, what is at stake here is not only how ethnic subjects name themselves and present their own histories, but how these evolving cultures will be represented and understood, a charge that revolves around the autobiographical subject, the "I" who speaks ("Representing Ethnicity" 77–78). Because of the indeterminate place of Asians in American and Canadian inscriptions of history, Asian North American writers who deploy the Childhood take advantage of an established genre, but expand its possibilities to limn particular forms of belonging and knowledge. Donald Goellnicht emphasizes this idea when he claims that "one of the most powerful and productive aspects of life writing by marginalized peoples is its ability to challenge, destabilize, and subvert traditional generic conventions" ("Blurring Boundaries" 344). This affirmation supports the notion that a reconstruction of the Childhood is necessarily inflected by the relationship between creative writing and immigrant or ethnic configurations of subjectivity and national affiliation.

Criticism has arrived at a point where the problematic and shifting modes of ethnic autobiographies may be addressed fruitfully. Indeed, after the 1960s civil rights movement, with its revisioning of traditional autobiography theory from the perspective of feminist and ethnic studies, we can look back and discern many of the subversive literary and political strategies in even the earliest texts. Contemporary cultural and diasporic studies, as well as ethnic literary theory, have managed to redress the presumptive predominance of Euro-American critical paradigms.

Both Betty Bergland and William Boelhower's work on ethnic and immigrant autobiographies may be productively deployed in this context. Their contrapuntal scholarship stresses the corrective agenda of ethnic studies to demystify Euro-American theory's exclusivism, particularly its universalizing and prescriptive prerogative that set the White male as normative subject, and successful integration into mainstream society as the prescribed conclusion. Bergland's exploration of postmodern autobiography successfully contextualizes ethnic life writing within American literature and suggests innovative approaches to this multiply positioned genre. She argues that autobiographies of ethnic groups in the United States "provide a key and meaningful site for examining the politics of culture and identity past and present. Collectively, representations of diverse histories, memories, and identities challenge any simplistic, unified, or dualistic map of the American society" ("Representing Ethnicity" 70). This strategy interrogates the tradition of American autobiography, which tends to posit the trajectory of successful socialization of its subject, usually a White male, in his process of identification with the norms of society. In cases where the subject did not identify, as with Henry Adams, it was precisely through this idiosyncrasy that the norm was maintained. Oftentimes, the "necessary" socialization was not completed at the end of these autobiographies, and this lack of closure tended to be problematic, questioning, in turn, the very notion of the subject's "American-ness."

The nature of the speaking subject remains a critical arena for continued discussions on life writing because the subjects represented in these autobiographies are constructed ethnically and positioned historically in changing worlds and shifting discourses. Boelhower's approach to ethnic autobiography draws upon poststructuralism and semiotics to explore the structure of ethnic narratives. He argues that the fundamental issue in ethnic life writing becomes the occasion of ethnic subjects' appropriation of the primary American mode of self-representation that entitles them to tell their own histories, name themselves, and depict alternative versions of American culture and society. He points out that "the specialty of ethnic autobiographical signification, its unique semiotic jeu, largely consists in consciously reelaborating or simply rewriting the received behavioral script of the rhetorically well-defined American self" ("Making of Ethnic Autobiography" 125). Insofar as ethnicity is an intrinsic component of identity and self-representation in American society, the discourse of ethnic life writing becomes a powerful mode of cultural criticism. Ethnicity itself is not a stable category and must be reinvented, reinterpreted, and rewritten in each generation by each individual of each ethnicity. The dynamic and processual character of ethnic identification and representation leads the autobiographer to be more "at ease among the chaos of signs" than most people, which suggests to Boelhower that ethnic autobiography might be "the most suitable vehicle for new and exquisitely modern versions of the American self" and "a lens for interpreting the complex structural tensions" (139) of America's narrative of itself. Furthermore, when ethnic subjects write autobiography, they control the representation of the American or Canadian subject, instead of allowing themselves to be passively represented by the received scripts of the dominant culture.

From our renewed appreciation of the constructedness and performative potential of life writing—where *saying* something is also *doing* something—we need to appraise, albeit briefly, the authors' choice of this particular autobiographical form.[3] When considering Asian North American life writing in general, we are usually influenced by the notion that an autobiography must adhere to two general formal models: a chronological pattern structured by the external events in the author's life, or an interpretative pattern based on an exposition of the writer's creative imagination and inner life, often within the text itself. The first type is the most numerous, from Etsu Sugimoto's *A Daughter of the Samurai* to Wayson Choy's *Paper Shadows*. Examples of the second approach include Kingston's *The Woman Warrior*, Michael Ondaatje's *Running in the Family,* Fred Wah's *Diamond Grill,* and Lynda Barry's *One Hundred Demons,* where generic experimentation forms part of the autobiographical act. Thematic approaches tend to follow a relatively set pattern: texts may generally be classified into a) ethnographic accounts that focus on life in an Asian country and in a particular (usually highly dramatic) time, where the life of the individual is often subsumed within a cultural experience that he or she narrates authoritatively to the reader; b) stories of immigration and life in North America, which involve the decision to assimilate or adapt or not; and c) descriptions of life in the United States or Canada and a personal engagement with the shifting forms of ethnic identity.

In this context, the Childhood offers possibilities that other forms of autobiography do not. First, narrating the period of childhood becomes a highly symbolic device for negotiating cultural contingencies and personal choices, constitutive elements of ethnic literature in general. Peter Coveney, in his germinal work, *The Image of Childhood,* comments on the advantages of the child's voice and perspective in texts that center on the artistic consequences of ambivalent sociocultural affiliations in the modern world: "in childhood lay the perfect image of insecurity and isolation, of fear and bewilderment, of vulnerability and potential violation" (32). Moreover, as Coe points out, childhood constitutes an alternative dimension, which cannot be conveyed by the utilitarian logic of the responsible adult; not "accuracy" but "truth"—an inner, symbolic truth—becomes the only acceptable criterion (*When the Grass* 2). Therefore, the adult writer takes advantage of the remembering, the imagining, and the retelling of these "truths" from the child's perspective to focus the experience of personal and communal processes of identity from the very beginning.[4]

Second, the narrative conclusion typical of the Childhood, at the point of a new maturity or on the verge of a new beginning, makes the text highly suggestive and intriguing. Because of the referential possibilities of the form, Wordsworth's notion of the child as father of the man is significantly deployed in this context: an autobiography is always constructed to explain a present circumstance—the narration of the "then" is organized and nuanced by the reality of the "now." Also, we understand that life writing "is a dialogue not only between writer and reader, but also between the narrator and his or her former selves," as through the earliest perceptions of the world one acquires the founding ideas, images, and metaphors that will structure creativity and autobiographical performance (Gullestad 22). In particular, Childhoods set outside the United States or Canada explain in particular ways the present self and reassert how the past (and often the present) needs to be known and understood through narrative. In a sense, reading a Childhood involves asking pressing questions about the act of construction (or reconstruction) of the self-in-narrative. Significantly, these texts exhibit metadiscursive qualities and draw attention to their linguistic stratagem and fictive nature, "using the narrator as an inscribed figure within the text whose manipulation calls attention to authority structures, of encouraging the reader to self-consciously participate in the production of meaning" (Fischer, "Ethnicity and the Post-modern Arts" 232). This particular genre of life writing therefore serves as a highly effective vehicle for two fundamental concerns of ethnic self-inscription: the performance of selfhood and how meaning itself evolves. Gullestad asserts that knowledge about childhood is always *mediated knowledge,* which references the distance between the lived childhood and its narrative reconstruction (22–23). Finally, ethnic autobiographers, particularly of non-North-American-set Childhoods, may also be engaged in a didactic project—the reader accompanies the writer as his or her self-as-child learns about heritage culture and experiences historical events, fashioning a seemingly artless insider perspective that is, nonetheless, complexly layered.

The appropriation of an established form by writers with renewed creative and imaginative sensibilities heightens the literary experience by renovating the content and cultural paradigms of an established genre. In Asian North American studies, autobiography functions as a transformative device and demonstrates how a traditional literary form converted into a transnational literary phenomenon transcends geographic, cultural, ethnic, and even linguistic boundaries. Importantly, ethnic American autobiographies have repeatedly challenged the generic scripts ostensibly required by Euro-American autobiography.

One of Coe's most important paradigms—a concept that acts as a cognitive device in the life writing of particular groups—issues from his observation that, given a sufficient number of autobiographies of childhood, features common to particular cultural formations become evident. Coe designates these elements "myths of childhood," a trope that defines recurrent preoccupations and obsessions that seem to operate as symbolic embodiments of experiences and acquire the status of myth in its modern, post-Jungian sense ("Reminiscences of Childhood" 2). As a product of a racial or a cultural subconscious, a myth of childhood incarnates anxieties, or drives, or urges too deeply buried to be clearly and rationally apprehended by the individual but that, when analyzed, demonstrate a positive and deterministic relationship between the social, cultural, and religious environment surrounding the child and the subsequent creative recall of those experiences.[5] By analyzing these myths, Coe suggests, we can trace a path "from the merely contingent to the genuinely significant in any particular recall of the child-self" ("Portrait of the Artist" 129). Interestingly, Coe signals the specific myths of national Childhoods: the idea of education for the English child, language for the French, the recall of the mother in the case of Russian Childhoods, etc. The point that relates to our discussion is his notion of the Third-World child, whose myth is that "of the white presence," and the North American child, whose autobiographical writing, Coe claims, foregrounds community (130). This formulation becomes problematic in the case of the Asian North American Childhood, requiring critical reexamination. Indeed, even as I read these texts together, I am aware of the crucial differences that mark the formulation of "American" and "Canadian" childhoods, as the immigrant histories, community development, racial policies, cultural evolvement, and literary traditions are quite distinct.

Translating Coe's Euro-American focus to negotiate Asian North American exercises in life writing involves a complex operation. The transaction between formal and cultural modes produces texts that challenge inherited ideas of autobiographical structure and content. Further, these narratives clearly serve a significant didactic purpose, as Traise Yamamoto explains, because they implicitly gesture "toward the shift . . . from uncritical, naïve notions of the American ideals of democracy and respect for the individual to a perspicacious awareness of the failures and limits of those ideals" (125). The conversions enacted in these texts, rather than solely centering on the Asian North American child's awareness of his or her history and cultural development, lie simultaneously in "the hoped-for effect, the conversion of white American awareness" (125–126). The increasingly dialogic nature of life writing reflects a multivoiced cultural situation that allows the subject to control and exploit the tensions between personal and communal discourse within the text and signify on a discursive level. As Fischer argues, we must consider a concept of the self as pluralistic, multidimensional, and multifaceted, and one that might be a "crucible for a wider social ethos of pluralism" ("Ethnicity and the Post-modern Arts" 195).

Issues of ethnic representation direct the autobiographical strategies employed by these writers and the manner in which each text performs the writer's process of self-awareness. As life writing has become more self-reflexive, the mediated quality of these narratives leads the reader ultimately to witness the process that led to the writing of this book. Similarities or differences between the writer and the reader constitute the dialectic of signification in these texts, emphasizing the constructedness and performativity of ethnic representation. The autobiographer, therefore, is not merely "an actor who follows ideological scripts, but also an agent who reads them in order to insert him/herself into them—or not" (Paul Smith xxxiv–xxxv). The engagement with the act of narrative evolves into a strategy that blends subjectivity and history, stresses individual sensibility, and challenges contextual authority. As Yamamoto explains regarding Japanese American women's narratives, "what is at stake here is not simply the question of whether the autobiographical form, as though it had a life of its own, empowers or disempowers its practitioners. At issue are crucial acts of discursive agency and the (re)appropriation of representational power, both of which are directly related to whether one reads these autobiographies as the introspective impulses of self-contemplation" (106–107).

Today, we no longer accept the pervasive privileging of White androcentric autobiographical scripts in American and Canadian theory because of the important work of feminist, ethnic, and disability studies, among others. We do acknowledge that the subversive potential of Asian North American autobiographies in general and of Childhoods in particular lie in the articulation and representation of the American or Canadian subject. Asian North American writers are transforming the constituent characteristics of the Childhood through two complementary processes. First, by challenging Coe's proposal of the "myth of childhood" for Asian North American writers. I argue that the Asian North American myth of childhood is, rather than merely the White presence or community, the definition of America or of Canada itself, which involves the negotiation of White hegemony and, further, of the literary traditions that govern the writing of the self. This renewed formulation accommodates those Childhoods set outside the United States or Canada. The concept of North America, and its corresponding "Dream," on some occasions, becomes constitutive of the Asian child's perception of sociocultural and spatial location. Yet the subject who inscribes the Childhood—the Asian North American adult—critically deploys the process of Americanization in the act of writing itself. Second, a complex mesh of three processes that stem from a rearticulation of Coe's "myth of childhood" but that signify differently on a discursive level include: a) a revised process of subjectivity involving differentiation rather than identification with the mainstream and situating the subject in multiple discourses; b) renewed approaches to national and ethnic affiliation, which include overt connections to the diaspora and reactions to racial discrimination and separation in America and Canada; and c) truncated or unsuccessful socialization, rather than the successful socialization typical of the Euro-American model. I provide here a brief description of these ideas, which will be developed in more detail later in the book.

Representing Processes of Subjectivity

In general, autobiography centers on development and change in the subject's life, narrating the events, choices, and transformations constitutive of the self's evolution. Caroline Barros posits that "change" is the "operative *metaphor* in autobiographical discourse," presented as "*transformative,* a significant mutation in the characteristic qualities and societal relationships of the principal persona. Autobiography offers these various metamorphoses emplotted, bounded, and framed by its language and inscribed in its configurations of words and images" (2). Poststructuralist theories present the subject as an illusory being, fragmented, unstable, whose existence depends on structures beyond the individual: language, ideology, or discourse. As such, when we speak of the "subject," we allude to two realities simultaneously. As a noun, the term refers to an individual conscious of his or her identity and the processes of identity. As an adjective, it refers to the state of dependence that is imposed on the individual as we refer to him or her. Asian North American Childhoods construct subjectivity through a complicated mesh of dispositions, associations, and perceptions that are represented through a singular selection and ordering of the accounts of events and persons who have played important roles in the authors' distinct processes of selfhood. The writer's identity as a diasporic and immigrant subject, in the first place, is frequently formulated and developed according to Stuart Hall's terms, when he argues that diasporic identities are "'framed' by two axes or vectors, simultaneously operative: the vector of similarity and continuity; and the vector of difference and rupture; diasporic identity is a dialogue between these two axes" (226–227).[6] In Asian North American Childhoods, the axes of subjectivity and self-representation intersect or dialogue with those of narrative construction and textuality. The constructedness of the text highlights the writers' consciousness of the processes of meaning and memory, subjectivity and representation. As Sau-ling Wong notes, "From an intraethnic point of view, the writing of autobiography may be valued as a means of preserving memories of a vanishing way of life, and hence of celebrating cultural continuity and identity; in an interethnic perspective, however, the element of *display,* whether intentional or not, is unavoidable" ("Autobiography as Guided Chinatown" 264).

Bergland claims that the nature of the narrator remains a critical arena for discussion because "the autobiographical self must be understood as socially and historically constructed and multiply positioned in complex worlds and discourses" ("Postmodernism" 131). Asian North American Childhoods enact models of subjectivity that reflect contemporary sociological perspectives on ethnic selfhood as well as the evolution of those perspectives. This process involves the intersection of consciousness of location, the negotiation of language, race, and on many occasions, social status in the heritage country.

A chronological analysis of the texts reveals an ostensibly linear perspective on the question of subjectivity. The earliest Asian North American autobiographers may be considered, in the words of Elaine Kim, "ambassadors of goodwill," writers who sought to explain the East to the West in positive terms in an attempt to plead for tolerance, challenge stereotypes, and address the negative view of Asians in America (*Asian American Literature* 24–25). The first known Asian American Childhoods, Yan Phou Lee's *When I Was a Boy in China* and Ilhan New's *When I Was a Boy in Korea,* present primarily anthropological accounts of boyhoods in Asian countries (with detailed descriptions of traditions, meals, holidays, family life, etc.), which suggest that the writers hoped to enkindle understanding about their homelands and their people. There is little character development, scant personal testimony, or detailed description of immigration and adaptation. Also, the lack of personal references suggests a collective rather than a personal voice. These narratives, commissioned within the tradition of autobiographies of childhood, thus offer interesting readings on the early Asian American subject positionality and the nature of the American prerequisite for writing about Asians. In the late 1800s and early 1900s, Asian immigrants' writing was of interest primarily because of what it could reveal about countries of origin, rather than as accounts of subjects actively negotiating American society.[7]

After Lee and New, Asian American autobiographers of childhood began to explore more critically their processes of adaptation, a development that responds to an increasing awareness of the nuances of subjectivity. In the pluralistic American society, as Bergland suggests, we must critically examine the notion of "the humanist and essentialist self at the center of the autobiography and recognize the multiply situated subject in autobiography, socially and historically shaped. In such a context ethnic autobiographies provide a meaningful site for exploring multiple subjectivities with implications for the larger culture" ("Postmodernism and the Autobiographical Subject" 134). In subsequent chapters, I explore how autobiographers deploy specific tropes—images of cities or towns, language, food, music—to perform their evolving sense of subjecthood and assert narrative agency. I also analyze how the subject's location in intersecting discourses on race, ethnicity, class, and gender nuances their perception of that subjectivity and their manners of inscribing this often palimpsestic process.

National and Ethnic Identification and Affiliation

Revisionary models of transnational and transcultural affiliation that have arisen from writing that engages the immigrant and ethnic position have modified reductivist ideas of otherness, and the process of othering. I suggest that Asian North American Childhoods exemplify that new "intermittent time and interstitial space" (Bhabha 312) in literary studies. Many of these writers engage increasingly complex ways of understanding and articulating migrant and ethnic identity by choosing a transnational position, one that is neither purely assimilationist nor oppositional. More important, because we are dealing with literary texts, the Asian North American Childhood may be read as the ethnic subject's act of writing him- or herself into American and Canadian narratives about itself. As the child has always been the emblematic symbol of America and Canada and its most beloved literary character (think of Huckleberry Finn and Anne of Green Gables, for example), the performance of the Asian American child, or the Asian child who will become the Asian North American adult, complicates issues in the discourse of nationalism and affiliation. In this context, Boelhower's approach to ethnic autobiography stresses historical contexts as well as the socially constructed dimensions of the cultural discourses adopted by immigrants and their children. Specifically, he notes the macrotext of immigrant autobiography that revolves around the contrapositioning of the Old World and the New World, and the idea of the American Dream embedded in dominant cultural discourses. Boelhower explains that the process of transculturality becomes a metaphor for the contemporary, postmodern condition, and he argues that "the more one's local ethnic encyclopedia is disestablished, the more its semiotic nowhere becomes a cultural everywhere, with the ethnic subject now forced into a floating practice of genealogical ordering and interrogation. It is easy to see why ethnicity remains a perennial cultural option in American culture" ("Making of Ethnic Autobiography" 137). When the spaces represented in the text are located outside North America, the implications for national and cultural allegiances become more complex.

Many Asian North American Childhoods are set outside the continent and have departure from the original country or arrival to North America as the conclusion to their narratives. Younghill Kang's *The Grass Roof,* Richard Kim's *Lost Names,* Heinz Insu Fenkl's *Memories of My Ghost Brother,* Kazuko Kuramoto's *Manchurian Legacy,* Loung Ung's *First They Killed My Father,* Michael David Kwan's *Things That Must Not Be Forgotten,* and Kien Nguyen's *The Unwanted,* among others, end with a disruptive point that solicits and authorizes multilayered interpretative possibilities. First, they validate a non-American childhood setting for the Asian American subject. This particular aspect, an important gesture in the rewriting of the official scripts of the American or Canadian experience of childhood, challenges hegemonic notions of the location of the childhood experience of the (Asian)American/Canadian subject. Narrating non-American-set experiences reconfigures North America's image of its children, or at least of its citizens' pasts.

Second, I argue that these Childhoods, in particular, challenge the myth of North America by forging a palimpsestic itinerary of location and affiliation. If, as Coe asserts, the writing of the Childhood is the writer's attempt to find an order or pattern, then setting the childhood away from the United States or Canada and privileging an Asian life is noteworthy. Because the writer of the

Childhood identifies with North America or being American/Canadian, this project expands and complicates the traditional fixed representation of the American or Canadian child's awareness of position.

Third, and most important, it posits North Americanization as a process, rather than as a fixed disposition or merely an inherited patrimony. Asian North American Childhoods set outside the United States or Canada, therefore, articulate itineraries of affiliation in a way that the Euro-American texts Coe reads do not, as they stress trajectories and transitivity rather than static or endowed identification. In different ways, these children demonstrate a distinctive ambivalence in their inscriptions of their homelands, perhaps because of the adult writers' consciousness of the transitional role of that place and the culture it nurtures. The representation of familial, social, and communal life is modulated by the instability of that system in the narrator's life.

Often, the desire to participate in American or Canadian society is countered by marginalization, a history of racial discrimination, heightening the child's sense of indeterminacy in a nation from whose history he or she has been written out and from whose present children like him or her appear to be excluded. Interestingly, much of the difficulty for many of these Asian North American children lies in the gap between their perceptions of themselves and their encounter with the gaze of the mainstream/White observer. Asian North American children's features consistently identify them as mere denizens, rather than the citizens they are often proud to be. Bhabha's optimism regarding what he calls "interstitial spaces" because they "initiate new signs of identity, and innovate sites of collaboration, and contestation, in the act of defining the idea of society itself" (1–2), becomes vulnerable to revision in this context.

In narratives that describe the child's process of learning about and attempts to integrate into American society, issues of racism, awareness of difference, and the desire to belong persist. The question of naming becomes highly symbolic in this context, serving in many cases as a central narrative trope. In a diverse society, names become signifiers of more than merely individual or familial identity and gesture toward membership in a particular racial, ethnic, and/or cultural group. As Daniel Nakashima explains, the combination of words that constitutes a personal name can become a contested site for the negotiation of the private and the public selves: "what one calls oneself, personally as well as ethnically, is thus a site of political struggle, where conventional racial classifications can be transgressed, accepted, or ignored" (113).

Richard Kim's Childhood, for example, demonstrates how Japanese colonization used the erasure of Korean names to attempt to eradicate a culture. The names given at birth to many of the autobiographers reflect their cultural heritage or their bicultural positions. Jade Snow Wong's name links her to her siblings; Monica Sone's full name is Kazuko Monica, the Japanese name meaning "peace" and the English name from Saint Monica, the mother of Saint Augustine. She is called Kazuko at home but later privileges her second name. Biracial Heinz Insu Fenkl is called Insu by his Korean mother and Heinz by his German American father, after whom he is named. The names he uses on different occasions, therefore, correspond to diverse spaces he occupies. Yoshiko Uchida perceives the difficulty of having a "foreign" name as she becomes aware of difference in America. She comprehends that the identifying markers of ethnic affiliation—name and facial features—differentiate her from other children, an alienation she struggles against: teachers cannot pronounce her name properly, even when she shortens it to "Yoshi" and she wishes to have blonde hair, blue eyes, and a name like Mary Ann Brown or Betty Johnson (*The Invisible Thread* 13–14). Her sister's name evolves smoothly from Keiko to Kay as they struggle for acceptance. Wayson Choy's appellative evolution is typical: he is named "Choy Way Sun, soon to be called by his English nickname, 'Sonny,' because his parents had been fond of Al Jolson's rendition of 'Sonny Boy,' and because, as a child, he had a sunny disposition" (*Paper Shadows* 17). As an adult, his name is further modified to Wayson.

For immigrant children, a name change can be more traumatic. In M. Elaine Mar's *Paper Daughter,* Mar Man Yee is informed by her aunt, soon after she immigrates to the United States, that she needs an American name "to fit in." The child panics: "Mother won't be able to say my name if it's American . . . I don't know English either. How will I know my name?" (61). The ritual of endowing a Mexican American aunt the honor of choosing her name is meaningless to the child, who construes the name change as a shift away from selfhood. When they choose the name, she struggles to pronounce it—"Eee-laine. . . . I repeated the sound. So that's who I was. My life cleaved in two" (62).[8] Naming, and being denoted by a name, for these Asian North American subjects, is their primary mode of representation in Western society. When the name is rejected as too foreign, it alienates the children from their peers; but a name shift for the sake of adaptation often has more insidious consequences on the child's evolving sense of self-in-place.

Acknowledging Bakhtin's view that the representation of the person is always chronotopic—situated temporally and spatially—the subjects of autobiography must be read in the context, or contexts, in which they live. As Fischer points out, ethnic autobiographies become highly metadiscursive and draw attention to their performative nature and possibilities, and in particular, encourage the reader to share in the production of meaning; this strategy "is not merely descriptive of how ethnicity is experienced, but more importantly is an ethical device attempting to activate in the reader a desire for *communitas* with others, while preserving rather than effacing differences" ("Ethnicity and the Post-modern Arts" 232–233). Representation of ethnic affiliation in these autobiographical texts sanctions Fischer's observation that "ethnicity is something reinvented and reinterpreted in each generation by each individual and that it is often something quite puzzling to the individual, something over which he or she lacks control. Ethnicity is not something that is simply passed on from generation to generation, taught and learned; it is something dynamic, often unsuccessfully repressed or avoided" (195). More important, in the context of the specificities of the Childhood, the dynamics of the processes involved in Asian North American children's awareness of national or cultural affiliation enacts a version of memory that is or ought to be "future, not past, oriented" (201).

Socialization

Patricia Chu, writing on the Asian American bildungsroman, argues that Asian American subjectivity should be seen as "a dialectic between two mutually constitutive aspects of ethnicity, the Asian and the American." She reads these two components of an Asian American's culture and identity not in the framework of earlier conceptions of the "dual personality" model, but "as organically connected but requiring different rhetorical gestures. To be Asian *American,* one claims Americanness but reshapes conventional narratives of American subject formation; given national narratives that position Asian Americans as ethnic, racialized outsiders in America, Asian American authors respond by imaginatively inhabiting and transforming such stories" (6). Thus, she explains that "Asian American subjectivities in these texts are characterized by the emergence of a critical ethnic intelligence that deploys and interrogates traditional narratives of Americanization" (6–7). In this context, Sau-ling Wong points out that one of the most "thoroughly naturalized scripts in the United States is the idea of cultural conflicts as the inevitable result of immigration: the forward-looking, freedom-loving American-born child, acting out what amounts to an immutable law of physics, contends with the tradition-bound, tyrannical foreign-born parents. The canonical dénouement of the drama is assimilation; the child, after waging appropriate struggle not only against the deputies of unreason but against his/her own incomprehension, finally puts aside outdated ethnic differences and wins his/her place in the larger society of free agents" ("Autobiography as Guided Chinatown" 277).

The critical intelligence Chu refers to also contests uncritical conceptions of American autobiography as narratives of successful socialization by presenting a model that negotiates alternative approaches to the representation of the "American" self. As Lisa Lowe argues, "The making of Asian American culture includes practices that are partly inherited, partly modified, as well as partly invented; Asian American culture also includes the practices that emerge in relation to the dominant representations that deny or subordinate Asian and Asian American cultures as 'other'" (65). Asian North American autobiographies thus perform a vital task: by recontextualizing the forms and themes of traditional North American autobiography, they enact alternative modes of being and identifying as American or Canadian through itineraries marked by separation and difference, rather than by integration.

This strategy interrogates the tradition of North American autobiography, and in particular, its paradigm of the trajectory of successful socialization of its subject. Often, the "necessary" socialization is not completed at the end of these autobiographies, leading to a problematic lack of closure that questions, in turn, the very notion of the subject's "American-ness" or "Canadian-ness." Importantly, the nature of the speaking subject remains a critical arena for continued discussions on life writing because the subjects represented in these autobiographies are constructed ethnically and positioned historically in changing worlds and shifting discourses.

Notable, for example, are the different epistemological issues related to American model minority discourse in the United States and Canadian visible minority discourse, which shape their subjects' self-perception in diverse ways.[9] Some of texts subvert the pervasive "model minority" concept, which developed out of U.S. racial discourse in the 1960s and extended to Canada, by challenging the conclusion with successful socialization expected of the autobiographical genre and the scholarly and economic achievements predicted upon Asians, due to their family values that emphasize work and honor. The experiences that mark each individual child's itinerary of socialization begins with highly personal experiences that are later reconfigured and inflected in the larger context of social obligation and interaction. As with mainstream American children, experiences that may be classified as traumatic cloud a number of these Childhoods to differing degrees. Disability (blindness in Mehta's *Vedi* and *The Ledge between the Streams*), mental illness (anorexia in Liu's *Solitaire*), abuse (Mah's *Chinese Cinderella*), and war (Ung's *First They Killed My Father*, Reyes' *Child of Two Worlds*, Nguyen's *The Unwanted*, Accomando's *Love and Rutabaga*, and Kuramoto's *Manchurian Legacy*) shape the way the autobiographical subject acts in society and, importantly, enacts the Childhood.

Coe notes the experience of loss of religious faith as a pivotal experience in Euro-American Childhoods, but has little concern for the impingement of early political or social ideas. He explains that unless political situations "actually cause a rift within its own family, the child, comfortable in the heart of its 'small world,' is to all intents and purposes immune from political debate. . . . But the exception to this is to be found when the political history of a country or of a culture is so consistently tragic that it penetrates, as it were, into the communal subconscious—in which case, once again, it acquires the status of

"Myth" ("Childhood in the Shadows" 7–8). In Asian North American Child-hoods, on the contrary, political events in the heritage country often lead to immigration and experiences of institutionalized racism, and multicultural policies in the United States or Canada color the narratives. These children's awareness of politics gives their stories powerful historical energy and illustrates how certain American and Canadian subjects' pasts are strongly influenced by historical circumstances.

It would be limiting to argue that the Asian North American child's process of socialization is invariably negative. Indeed, several of these Childhoods end precisely with a version of successful socialization and a turn to art as a way of healing the difficult trajectory of the past. Clearly, the existence of the text of the Childhood itself, many of them established within the canon of Asian North American writing, already signals a measure of agency and success for the subject. The narratives by Ved Mehta, Michael Kwan, Wayson Choy, or M. Elaine Mar clearly posit the writers' comfortable integration in society. In some cases, extratextual information, such as Mehta's successful career as a journalist or Kwan's as a dramatist, allows readers to accept the notion of successful socialization. Yet many of these texts require the reader to look beyond the appearance of accomplishment to contemplate continuing difficulties. Specifically, for example, although the narratives by Yoshiko Uchida and Laurence Yep—the most prolific Asian American writers of children's literature—end positively with the illusion of the traditional triumphant socialization, the status the writers achieve and the positions they occupy remain contested terrains, evidenced extratextually by the recurring concerns of their literary production. We can therefore read these representations of autobiographical subjects as resistance to prescriptive norms of social conformity and prevailing discourses on the paradigms of the genre. The trajectory of socialization is thus performed in nuanced ways in the diverse texts, processes I explore in detail in the following chapters.

Creating a Reader: Processes of Cultural Memory

Though Coe insists that Childhood is primarily an intellectual quest for understanding the past (*When the Grass* 41), to address Asian North American Child-hoods effectively we need to attend to what this aesthetic project enacts in the present and for the future. Ethnic autobiographies generally operate specific contemporary cultural or historical purposes behind the personal story of the past. In this section, I describe briefly the project of Asian North American life writing, as limned by the relationship established in autobiography between the writer and reader and within the context of the creation of cultural memory. As noted earlier, the formal engagement with the Childhood suggests that writers may have a larger cultural purpose—which includes history making and community building—because of the important emancipatory work done by ethnic writing. The writers' aesthetic choice implies a cultural purpose that stems organically from the completed text, which becomes part of a dynamic body of writing within a community.

The task of the ethnic autobiographer is complex, subject to much contradicting scrutiny by ethnic or mainstream critics. In "Autobiography as Guided Chinatown Tour," Sau-ling Wong analyzes the controversy surrounding the classification of Kingston's *The Woman Warrior* and exposes the invalidity of many of the more widespread approaches. She points out the inconsistencies inherent in uncritical expectations of ethnic life writing as well as the Herculean task assigned to the autobiographer.

> Recognition of a preexisting external reality, however, imposes a special obligation on the ethnic American autobiographer: to provide a positive portrayal of the ethnic community through one's self-portrayal. At the very least, the autobiographer's work should be innocent of material that might be seized upon by unsympathetic outsiders to illustrate prevalent stereotypes of the ethnic group; the author should stress the diversity of experience within the group and the uniqueness and self-definition of the individual. Ideally, an ethnic autobiography should also be a history in microcosm of the community, especially of its sufferings, struggles, and triumphs over racism. In other words, an ethnic autobiographer should be an exemplar and spokesperson whose life will inspire the writer's own people as well as enlighten the ignorant about social truths. (258)

Wong recognizes the requirements put upon autobiographers, even as she acknowledges the importance of the task. The dynamics of this project, which includes the writing and reception by an implied audience, requires us to analyze in some detail the processes of reception and creation of cultural memory.

From the perspective of genre, autobiography seems to suggest an established and even comfortable relationship between the text and the reader. Writing within a defined genre and choosing to read a text that adheres to an ostensibly inviolable pact of knowable truth, authenticity, and sincerity implies that the relationship between the writer and reader should be unproblematic. The shifting nature of that relationship, I argue, is complicated in the context of ethnic writing, as in other nontraditional forms of autobiography, where issues of agency, community building, and cultural memory serve as the intertext of the actual writing. Indeed, a memoir of childhood is a dynamic project that is highly interactive and whose construction anticipates the encounter with an often clearly implied reader. Susanna Egan describes autobiography as an "'encounter of two lives' between the reader and writer of life and of 'life,' repeated both outside and inside the text" (3). She notes that autobiographers of diaspora, of which Asian North Americans are a crucial example, discriminate in their act of writing "among a plurality of possible positions, all incomplete and in continuous process, in order to recognize who speaks, who is spoken, and just who might be listening" (121). Readers are therefore closely implicated in the processes that create meaning: there is often clear textual evidence that writers are conscious of their implied readers, who are, in turn, aware of their role in validating, disseminating, or as the case may be, canonizing a given text as emblematic of an ethnic identity or position. "Many texts invite this self-consciousness," Egan argues, "explicitly constructing an ideal or desired reader" (121). She uses the image of the mirror as her central metaphor for life writing processes to stress "a combination of reflexive practices in autobiography" and to foreground "interaction between people, among genres, and between writers and readers of autobiography" (11–12).

In the same manner, Michael Fischer speaks of three autobiographical voices: the first one as a singular attempt to inscribe individual identity; the second as "structured through processes of mirroring and dialogic relations with cross-historical and cross-cultural others" and resonate "with various sorts of double voicings"; and the third as "depend[ing] upon explicit triangulations among multiple perspectival positionings and understandings" ("Autobiographical Voices" 79). Autobiography, in this context, becomes a powerful tool for literary constructions of identity and community building.

This dynamic interaction between the writer and the reader of autobiography acquires heightened significance in the context of ethnic texts that often posit renewed perspectives on identity and cultural validation. We therefore need to consider how the assumptions that an autobiographer makes about the nature and position of the audience are also subject to the reader's scrutiny (Bruss 13). The transformative character of life writing acts on the reader as well as on the writer. Readers who implicate themselves in the text are potentially altered by the experience because larger historical and social contexts are always present, nuancing perspectives on cultural issues. Just as important transformative processes take place in the act of writing one's memoirs, significant transformations are also enacted on the reader, from the perspective of social information and, I would also argue, aesthetic formation. Readers of Childhoods not only learn about events of the past, such as war in Asia, for example, but also engage the literary gestures that transform those experiences into art.

In the context of ethnic writing, as Linda Anderson points out about African American autobiography, many texts may be understood within a particular group's "emancipatory project" of self-definition as well as deployed to forge an identity for a particular group by "encoding a particular readership and . . . employing a discourse linking community and selfhood which is also, ultimately, a historical discourse" (107). While I do not suggest that Asian North American autobiographers of childhood necessarily privilege the documentary nature of their texts over their creative or interpretative character, I cannot ignore the important historical work that results from these texts. This social and historical project is realized precisely in the interpellation of the history of a community. As autobiography narrativizes personal life, it constructs a life within a community that shares a history, often one that challenges existing essentialist or universalizing modes of reading the past.[10]

The existence of an implied reader marks the narrativization of these Asian North American texts in clear ways. In a general sense, we can classify this reader into two main groups, which may occupy interacting/intersecting positions, corresponding to the writers' projects. On the one hand, autobiographers write for mainstream North America to explain their heritage culture from an insider's perspective and to write their own history into existing "official" versions. There is explicit disclosure of authorial intention of this in several cases: Jade Snow Wong, in her introduction to *Fifth Chinese Daughter*, says, "At a time when nothing had been published from a female Chinese American perspective, I wrote with the purpose of creating a better understanding of the Chinese culture on the part of the Americans" (vii). Also, the texts dialogue with issues that have shaped uncritical epistemological perspectives on Asian Americans—such as model minority discourse—and Asian Canadians—such as their position as visible minorities. On the other hand, autobiographers also write for the members of their communities to give them characters with whom to identify and in order to preserve a history in danger of obliteration. Many readers of Asian North American life writing identify with that community and view themselves as subjects fully committed to furthering cultural politics/policies and developing cultural knowledge in diverse forms.[11] Yoshiko Uchida states this metanarrative purpose to her fiction and memoirs when she explains that her writing is an attempt to pass on a legacy of ethnic appreciation to the Sansei—the third generation Japanese Americans—"to give them the kinds of books I'd never had as a child. The time was right, for now the world too, was changing. . . . I wanted to give the young Sansei a sense of continuity and knowledge of their own remarkable history. . . . I hoped all young Americans would read these books as well" (*The Invisible Thread* 131). This purpose is manifested more or less explicitly in a number of texts or interviews granted by the writers, who repeatedly demonstrate their commitment to a wider project of ethnic validation and the creation and preservation of cultural memory.

The fact that many of these books are well received attests to the existence of this reader who might certainly influence the multiplication of these texts.

As a brief statistical observation, I note that of the approximately fifty autobiographies I consider in this study, a corpus that begins chronologically in 1887 and ends in 2005, approximately two-thirds of the texts were written in the 1990s, when consciousness of Asian North American cultural identity had become established enough to require texts that would continue to explore this renewed national experience. Autobiography was the ideal tool for this kind of cultural work; the Childhood, in particular, because of the heightened symbolic meaning in the use of the child as the narrator/protagonist, effectively negotiates this crucial critical concern.

Gillian Whitlock, writing about the memoirs of postcolonial women, offers interesting perspectives on the increasing protagonism of the reader in the execution of life writing texts: "agency is too often seen as the prerogative of the writer, and yet one of the legacies of recent postcolonial criticism is the renewed sense of the agency of the reader, and the urgency of reading. . . . The reader, no less than the writer, has the power and authority to pursue the other stories, histories, knowledge and experience that remain suppressed, unwitnessed and unauthorized between the lines" (203). She asserts the central position of the reader in autobiographical writing, which she affirms is "engaged in an ongoing process of authorization in order to capture not its subject so much as its object: the reader" (3). The ostensible representation of a life, she continues, is only an illusion used to seduce the reader and to claim the privilege to speak to him or her about his or her own life. As Leigh Gilmore points out, for many women, "access to autobiography means access to the identity it constructs in a particular culture and for particular readerships" (qtd. in Whitlock 3). In this context, we need to explore precisely what it is that the authors enact and what forms of connection they seek to establish with the reader.

In short, I argue, these Asian North American Childhoods create a reader by interrogating an implied audience for culture and history, through a specific form that makes that interaction highly effective. In the encounter between text and reader, Gullestad observes, "readers create the text while interpreting it, and, to some extent, they find *their own truths* in the texts under study" (31). This idea requires us to unravel what the existence of a community of readers might mean in the context of Asian American literary and cultural discourse. You create a reader when you present texts that propose new perspectives on shared experiences through a specific genre. The earliest Asian North American autobiographies focused generally on Asia and the Asian experiences, mostly because the public that could consume this product was primarily mainstream America or Canada, a group largely ignorant about Asian realities and susceptible to Orientalist stereotypes. As time passed and the community grew, the increasing number of books began to redefine both the Asian North American subject and the reader of those life writing texts. Once again, the cultural status of Kingston's *The Woman Warrior* structures our perspectives on this process. Apart from being the first text to critically interrogate the notion of Chinese American-ness, *The Woman Warrior* launched a debate that effectively formulated this community in the Asian American imaginary. Interestingly, in my opinion, the particulars of the debate were less important than the *fact* of the debate. For the first time, mainstream American and Asian American scholars began to critically inquire about the nature of this "hyphenated" identity and the forms in which this identity could be inscribed. Kingston's "avant-garde" autobiography, to use Sau-ling Wong's phrase, also gestured toward a renewed postmodern, feminist aesthetic that decisively changed the way we write and read autobiography.

As the literary community began to attend to Kingston's text, consciousness about the cultural work these texts could enact grew. The autobiographical pact inherent to these texts also allowed for "authentic" cultural statements that often became part of the collective imaginary. In order to develop this collective imaginary, revisionary work began to be done on earlier autobiographies to see how they addressed the burgeoning Asian American community and, specifically, its developing sense of identity and negotiations with race, class, gender, and politics.[12] The community that received these texts became conscious of how these works supported the community by providing the narratives of cultural or collective memory that they needed to validate their history, their positions, and even their political agendas. In this context, questions that historian Carolyn Steedman asks about the making and writing of the modern self resound: "who uses these stories? *How* are they used, and to what ends?" (28).

To explore those questions, we need to return to the notion of life writing as, primarily and superlatively, the performance of memory. When the subject of autobiography tells a story, it is always about what is remembered and how it is remembered. Recent critical studies on autobiography suggest, as Sidonie Smith and Julia Watson do in *Reading Autobiography,* that "if we think about remembering not as an entirely privatized activity but as an activity situated in cultural politics, we can appreciate to what degree remembering is a collective activity" (19). Further,

> The collective nature of acts of remembering extends beyond the acknowledgement of social sites of memory, historical documents, and oral traditions. It extends to motives for remembering and the question of those on whose behalf one remembers. Precisely because acts of remembering are implicated in how people understand the past and make claims about their versions of the past, memory is an inescapably intersubjective act. As W. T. J. Mitchell insightfully suggests: "memory is an intersubjective phenomenon, a practice not only

of recollection of a past *by* a subject, but of recollection for another subject." Memory is a means of "passing on," of sharing a social past that may have been obscured, in order to activate its potential for reshaping a future and for other subjects. Thus, acts of personal remembering are fundamentally social and collective. (20–21)

Issues of intersubjectivity remind us that a life narrative cannot be limited to the story of a self detached from personal, historical, and cultural contingencies.[13] The relational component of autobiography, a topic of increasing critical scrutiny, reveals how acts of self-inscription necessarily acknowledge, more or less implicitly, the role of others in the life and in the literary engagement with that life. Eakin even proposes a typology of the relational autobiography he defines as "the story of a relational model of identity, developed collaboratively with others, often family members" (*How Our Lives* 68–69).[14] In ethnic writing, where the existence of the community distinctly shapes processes of identification, this relationality frequently extends beyond specific individuals or family, and beyond the limits of the text itself, to negotiate a relationship with a reader. Here, memory itself becomes "intersubjective and dialogical, a function of personal identifications, and social commitments. While it may be uniquely ours it is also objectified, a matter of public convention and shared rituals. The recovery of the past through personal testimony can have a political dimension depending on what is remembered and what is forgotten. The right to establish validity, authenticity or truth is never the storyteller's alone" (Cosslett, Lury, and Summerfield 5). The Asian North American writer's position within a developing discourse of memory and self-inscription multiplies the spheres of these operations: one writes not just *for* and *from* him- or herself but to engage a larger communal project.

In the context of Asian North American life writing, the appeal of the Childhood intersects with particular reader expectations and investments. In significant ways, Childhoods "solicit an active reader who will participate dynamically in the politics of the Childhood either by being represented by the autobiography or being confronted into witnessing what occurs within it" (Kate Douglas 229). Yet, I would argue further that negotiating a childhood memoir becomes more than a passive act of witnessing because it requires a dynamic engagement with community building and social mobilization. Even when the texts privilege nostalgic perspectives, there are clear invitations to transcend sentiment and engage in social action. To be an autobiographer of childhood at this particular moment has become a highly significant cultural gesture. In this sense, we can also argue that readers shape Childhoods because of their role in interpreting and inscribing meanings upon these texts (228).[15]

We need to explore the plural nature of memory in the context of ethnic life writing. The collective nature of memory has been analyzed by many critics, and we cannot deny the powerful force that collective memory has on contemporary Asian North American life writing. Memory allows our consciousness to link concepts and experiences, such that "we 'remember' not only things that have actually happened to us personally, but also, and perhaps even more importantly, we 'remember' events, language, actions, attitudes, and values that are aspects of our membership in groups" (Singh, Skerrett, and Hogan 17). Collective memory is our passport to membership in a group and, in *Childhoods*, personal memories may be harnessed to represent community stories. As such, through crucially located generic choice and narrative structure, these memoirs transcend the individual to speak *of* and *for* a wider community. These autobiographies should therefore be read as active interventions on existing historical or cultural records as they reinscribe official versions or provide supplementary material for cultural construction. They function also as palimpsestic and intersecting "systems of remembering," which Smith and Watson argue are both personal—manifested in dreams, photographs, family stories—or public—contained in documents, historical events, collective rituals (20).

Importantly, the existence of a multiplicity of these texts facilitates what Whitlock calls "connected reading," a strategy vital to the process of creating cultural memory (203). By eschewing the entire truth within a single text and "making links between and across various narratives, tropes, sites, figures, movements," readers participate in a process of "supplementation rather than completion, for complexity rather than closure, for the making of truth rather than its revelation" (203–204).[16] This plural and palimpsestic approach privileges association as a creative reading strategy that configures a wider scope for the enactment of historicized subjectivity. It also evidences a reciprocal process: as a text or a group of texts empowers a community, the community also conspires to validate the authors and produce more texts.

The question remains of how *Childhoods* create or endorse communities and engage the racialized nature of Asian North America. I propose that the texts negotiate cultural memory in significant ways.[17] I define cultural memory as Bal, Crewe, and Spitzer do, referring to memory "as a cultural phenomenon as well as an individual or social one" (ix), stressing the extent to which processes of remembering depend on social, cultural, and temporal locations and rely on a sharing of those memories. As they suggest, "the memorial presence of the past takes many forms and serves many purposes, ranging from conscious recall to unreflected reemergence, from nostalgic longing for what is lost to polemical use of the past to reshape the present" (ix). This is the form of narrativization these Asian North American *Childhoods* enact. By using stories of a "real" past, they reshape perspectives of those past events in order to understand the present. Or, to continue to expand the historical paradigm, these texts invite us to reexamine our perspectives on uncritical narratives of history. Further, by appropriating an established form, they dialogue with literary history, expanding ways of self-representation. As Marita Sturken explains, "cultural memory represents the stories that are told outside official historical discourse, where individual memories are shared, often with political intent, to act as counter-memories to history" (31), suggesting that this process is always in flux.

Cultural memory, as negotiated in Asian North American life writing texts, is closely linked to collective memory, "those broader patterns through which culture may shape the parameters, structure, and even the content of our sense of history" (Frisch 34), even as it highlights the fragmentation of historical processes.[18] This formulation accommodates the dynamic character of memory, which is "activity occurring in the present, in which the past is continually modified and redescribed even as it continues to shape the future" (Bal, Crewe, and Spitzer ix). The writing of individual autobiographies blends to create collective remembrance and facilitate its continuity. What we consider collective memory in this discussion, then, arises from the dynamics of independence and interdependence of a series of texts that support the exchange of information, memories, perceptions, and designs among individuals who compose the group. Collective memory in this context "is a matrix of interwoven individual memories" (Winter and Sivan 28), narratively enacted to create a dynamic community that uses these texts to empower their history and cultural location in society. Further, as James Wertsch suggests, this "usable past" is empowering and can be harnessed for diverse purposes in the present (31). From a formal perspective, the realization of collective memory promotes continued participation as it encourages the writing of more texts. Jay Winter and Emmanuel Sivan describe this as the structural dimension of collective remembering, "an interpretative code which endows individual memories with meaning according to the *living tradition* of remembrance of that specific group" (28, italics in original). The strength of the autobiographical tradition in Asian North American writing attests to the link between this form of remembering and the generic choice that endorses and sustains it.

Interestingly, Samuel Hynes suggests that collective memory is "vicarious memory" that evokes a shared myth—understood as the dramatized story that has evolved to contain the meanings of historical events—rather than a shared experience (207). Autobiographies of childhood, read collectively, play a pivotal role in the construction of this kind of cultural memory because of the way they validate each other and expand the meanings of similar experience. The collective memory endorsed in this case by the Childhoods we read is not grounded primarily in direct experience; instead it is "textually mediated"

(Wertsch 5) and enhanced by the collective reading process. Thus we return to the connection between the form used by the writers and their cultural purposes: these Asian North American Childhoods signify by the genre they embody which, by reason of its history and particular characteristics, enables it to function culturally.

The approach I endorse in this project that reads Asian North American autobiographies of childhood in terms of the subversion of traditional modes of autobiographical self-inscription and self-authentication gestures significantly toward an understanding of the problem of a search for forms of self-representation. Bergland affirms that "what is at stake in ethnic autobiography is the possibility of ethnic groups telling their own stories, naming themselves —in short, presenting their own histories, identities, and representations of truth and memory" ("Representing Ethnicity" 77–78). These autobiographers nuance the representation of the American and Canadian subject through an appropriation of the genre of "real life," which demonstrates subjects in the act of creatively ordering their childhood experiences. These accounts of individual struggles with ethnic self-definition present recollections and personal experiences of the heritage culture, immigration and shifting national and ethnic affiliation, and complex processes of socialization as pivotal elements of self-formation and self-representation. These autobiographies deploy ambivalent historical and cultural locations to speak effectively to their readers and make them participate actively in the processes of creation of collective cultural memory. Indeed, we know that reading transforms the reader as much as writing serves the writer: the larger context of historical and cultural reimagining shapes the autobiographical act, as part of a process of transformation. These texts present subjects actively negotiating their own histories, part of a creative adaptation and manipulation of a dynamic network of concepts that transforms them into artists of their own lives and protagonists of America and Canada's narratives of their history.

Chapter 2

● The Asian Childhood

Writing Beginnings

A significant number of Childhoods written by Asian North American writers focus primarily on experiences in Asia, with accounts of a pre-American life as the central experience of the text. For writers who identify explicitly as Asian *American* or Asian *Canadian,* the foregrounding of the non–North American experience provides a valuable perspective from which to read autobiographies that resonate in the context of the cultural memory of the community. These childhood accounts, importantly, offer the reading public access to versions of the history of Asian countries that correspond to private stories, unofficial records, microhistories. We cannot underestimate the discursive potential of these texts, considering the increased complexity of the autobiographical act, particularly by writers who make identification with specific ethnic groups and history a subtext of their personal narratives. Janet Varner Gunn explains that autobiography has shifted from being conceived as "the private act of self-writing" to become "the cultural act of the self reading" (8), implying that autobiographical discourse negotiates more than merely the notion of an authentic "I" to engage the subject's location in the world through an active interpretation of experiences in particular "worldly" contexts (23). The strategy involves an intentional positioning of oneself in history, geography, and culture. Ien Ang takes this point further when she posits autobiography as "a more or less deliberate, rhetorical construction of a 'self' for *public,* not private purposes: the displayed self is a strategically fabricated performance, one which stages a *useful* identity, an identity which can be put to work" (3, italics in original). Working within specific epistemic contexts, Asian North American writers consciously negotiate these boundaries, making the representation of location and chronology a vital subtext of their autobiographical performances.

When the autobiographical account focuses on a pre–North American experience, the author might conceivably be deploying two simultaneous operations. First, a didactic project—the reader accompanies the writer as his or her self-as-child learns about heritage culture and experiences historical events. This strategy gives the mainstream American or Canadian public access to events in Asia and validates the experiences of the families and communities of many Asian North Americans. By providing narratives of experiences that many immigrants have silenced for diverse reasons, these Childhoods nourish the community's process of cultural memory and serve as an avenue to healing. Marita Sturken affirms that remembrances of events of national importance moves "between the realms of cultural memory and history," where a tension emerges between history and countermemory, as these life writers negotiate different levels of private and public discourse (31). Yet, she cautions that "cultural images of historical events, both documentary and docudrama, biographical and fictional, have the capacity to usurp and replace the personal memories of those who participated in those events and lives. In fact, it is questionable whether one can ever speak of a personal memory of historical and biographical events that is distinguishable from the cultural narrativization of those events, or that one ever could. This is testimony to the way that memory works both individually and culturally" (32). This critical perspective highlights the serious work that these texts conduct within community contexts, while stressing the danger of substituting vicarious recollections for personal memory, or eliding the frontiers of personal and cultural memory.

Second, we may consider the way in which childhood reminiscences often provide emblems for later experiences, offer multiple layers of meaning, and serve many roles (Gullestad 26). These Asian North American Childhoods may be read as their writers' specific manner of explaining a current situation or dealing with a present that may, in some ways, mirror the conflict of the past. Though the texts focus fundamentally on a childhood in Asia, we can nonetheless argue that these accounts say as much about the authors' present position within a diasporic community as the actual events of the past. Also, as James Olney notes, just as the representation of the past depends crucially upon the sensibility that recalls it, "so too the sensibility that recalls it is vitally dependent on the past" (57). These versions of childhoods in Asia articulate how the past weighs on the present, and how trajectories that involve palimpsestic rebeginnings may be deployed to promote cultural memory. Though elements of continuity may be traced from the representation of the child in the past to the writing adult, a recurring characteristic of these texts lies in the way the authors' childhoods are clearly perceived to have ended. Though this occurs generally in all Childhoods, in these Asian North American texts the recognition of a break between one temporal point and another is enhanced by a spatial movement, as I will explain in more detail later.

The Childhood can be read as an independent artifact because it is temporally and spatially divorced from the present. The writer recollects him- or herself living through an entire experience and can thus trace patterns or uncover hidden meanings that may, in turn, give meaning to "the apparently patternless present" (Coe, *When the Grass* 77). So, for the Asian North American adult to revisit a childhood set in Asia implies examining the process that made him or her the adult in the present. These chronicles of childhood present experiences in ways that allow the writers and readers to work toward a positive reconstruction of the past in the present, rather than as negative evocations of the circumstances that provoked abandonment of that first home. Indeed, Bahktin's notion of the chronotope—the intersection of time and space from which the subject speaks (84)—promotes a gratifying reading of Childhoods set in Asia. Bergland argues that a chronotopic reading of ethnic autobiographies lead us to understand "the relationship between culture and consciousness of the ethnic subject by looking at the temporal and spatial arenas the autobiographical subject occupied" ("Representing Ethnicity" 80).

Liz Stanley offers another multidisciplinary perspective as she harnesses Mary Louise Pratt's notion of the "contact zone" to elucidate some of the strategies that transcultural autobiographies enact.[1] Stanley deploys Pratt's term in relation to that which took place within particular historical moments (such as colonization or war, for example), "and that of the claims made now about 'this moment,' who composed it, and what they were like, where they were and why, what happened, why, and what it all meant" (6). She therefore repositions the contact zone not as "the literal borderland of colonial frontiers, but instead as a figurative space in which things are done and time is undone" (10). This assertion is highly suggestive in the context of Asian North American autobiographical performances of childhoods in Asia, where a revisiting of the past becomes a reconstruction of that past for a reading community. The "contact" established brings together people previously separated by both geography and time, creating an arena that promotes spatial and temporal co-presences. Asian North Americans, specifically, include populations also separated by a history that caused that detachment. By writing the text, authors rework the notion of the contact zone, defined as a "time zone including 'now' as well as 'then' points up the inevitable privileging of 'now', the point from which we apprehend" history; writing authorizes "the return of the excised 'I' the author; and it also places this figure in a landscape with other figures" (27). This idea acknowledges the existence of an epistemic community within which topics, methods, ideas, and discourses circulate and where these texts resound culturally.

The Childhoods analyzed in this and following two chapters present a range of experiences in Asia that cover the late-nineteenth and entire twentieth centuries, allowing us to examine the ways in which autobiographies by ethnic writers have been written and received at different moments in North American literary history. The earliest known texts, Yan Phou Lee's *When I Was a Boy in China* and Ilhan New's *When I Was a Boy in Korea* respond to a specific interest in American cultural politics in the late-nineteenth and early-twentieth centuries, where interest in other lands led to the soliciting and publication of several ostensibly autobiographical (hence, "authentic") accounts of childhood experiences. The authors were charged with articulating a cultural, rather than purely personal, experience, which would serve to introduce mainstream American readers to other cultures.

Younghill Kang's *The Grass Roof*, published in 1931, draws from the trend of introducing Americans to Asia, where writers positioned themselves as "ambassadors of goodwill" to explain the East to the West in positive, and often simplistic, terms.[2] Later texts negotiated Asian culture, historical contexts, and political issues in more complex manners, and configured Asian American autobiographies of childhood epistemologically and phenomenologically.

Childhoods by Da Chen, Ved Mehta, Hilary Tham, and Sudha Koul offer a variety of experiences and perspectives of what we could consider daily life in diverse countries: in *Colors of the Mountain*, Chen narrates his conflicted experiences as the intelligent son of a landowning family in Communist China; Mehta's *Vedi* and *The Ledge between the Streams* focus on the life of a blind boy in India; Tham's blend of prose and poetry in *Lane with No Name* evokes a complicated childhood in Malaysia; and Koul's *The Tiger Ladies* marks a nostalgic recollection of life in a remote area of India.

War in Asian countries figures predominantly, giving the accounts a political disposition unusual in Euro-American Childhoods. Coe points out that, though children are not usually aware of politics, the exception is found when the political history of a country is so consistently tragic that it penetrates, as it were, into the communal subconscious—in which case it acquires the status of myth ("Childhood in the Shadows" 8). Though American children have not experienced a war in their own land since the Civil War, the histories of many children who become Americans certainly feature the dramatic experience of war, a significant prism for the ways they negotiate the arrival and adaptation to the new country. The Japanese colonization of China and Korea permeates the experiences of Kazuko Kuramoto, Richard Kim, Sook Nyul Choi, and Yoko Kawashima Watkins, for example, and analyzing their texts together offers complementary perspectives of the experience and recollection of colonization. The Communist takeover of Cambodia lies at the heart of Loung Ung and Chanrithy Him's narratives, giving parallel views of trajectories of forced dislocation and immigration.

Most of these texts conclude with immigration, a point in the narrative structure that replicates the lived truncation of a first history. This strategy dialogues in interesting ways with Coe's idea that a "sense of completeness" is thematically ("the conclusion clearly envisaged from the first sentence") and structurally ("that the work itself, as a literary artifact, comes to a full close at the point at which the adventure of childhood is felt to have reached its termination") central to the genre (*When the Grass* 77).[3] By ending the story with the anticipation of a voyage or recounting only sparing details of life in the United States, these autobiographers of childhood do function archetypically, according to Coe's definition.[4]

But precisely because Asian American writers' consciousness of present position is so crucial to the shape of their texts, the rupture at this point becomes more significant. In most cases, life in the United States is described only briefly, if at all. The itinerary of adaptation, the gap between the experience of the child who leaves the Asian country and the writer in the act of writing is not satisfactorily filled. The writers choose to leave the reader with the moment of dislocation, stressing the juncture of transitivity, and choose not to recount the process of adaptation. Concluding the narrative at this point illustrates discursively a point of rebeginning, a gap between a familiar world, where one belongs, and a state of liminality. It might also subversively indicate a cyclical movement in the writer's life: those who may have suffered forms of rejection in their own country might be condemned to repeat the experience. Importantly, and in opposition to Coe's prescriptive view of the text concluding at a pivotal point of maturity, formulated in terms of temporality, these Asian American Childhoods stress the import of the subject's movement through *space.* Rather than the individuated and spatially localized subject of the Euro-American Childhood, which privileges qualities such as wholeness and resolution, these texts propose a renewed configuration of subjectivity, where children exist in a state of cultural simultaneity and multiplicity. For these subjects, poised on the verge of travel, resolution is deferred, perhaps indefinitely.

Cultural Ambassadors?

The two earliest known Asian American Childhoods appear to present a model of subjectivity that almost obliterates the individual to focus on cultural concerns, specifically the need to describe Asian culture to American society. Yan Phou Lee's *When I Was a Boy in China* and Ilhan New's *When I Was a Boy in Korea* are volumes in a series of twenty-one books called "Children of Other Lands Books," produced by the Lothrop, Lee, and Shephard Publishing Company in 1887 and 1928, respectively. The editors of the series envisioned the books to feature, as noted in the inside jacket of New's book, a person "who has *lived* the foreign child life described, and learned from subsequent experiences in this country how to tell it in a way attractive to American children—and in fact to Americans of any age." As such, there is a formulaic structure as well as a clear cultural and didactic element to the narratives, which may have, in interesting ways, limited what the writers would have said and the direction of their accounts.[5] The chapter titles of Lee's text outline the structure and the primary concerns of these texts: "The House and Household," "Chinese Cookery," "Games and Pastimes, "Schools and School Life," "Religions," "Chinese Holidays," and so on. New's autobiography begins with the boy's memory of begging his father for more roasted chestnuts, but then quickly departs from the personal to engage the market system, Korean education, clothing, language, holidays, and sports, among other topics. The text ends with the description of a wedding, which signals the end of boyhood.

Interestingly, both texts contain numerous photographs, but only the frontispiece depicts the authors themselves. The remaining photographs are archival prints of market scenes, candy vendors, a family, and so on. These texts evince a particularly fascinating manner of using the paradigms of the Childhood to address a specific reading public. At first, the work done by Lee and New seems rather straightforward as it complies with the publisher's aim to introduce the practices of foreign cultures to Americans. Yet recent criticism on these texts suggests that these autobiographers were enacting strategies that may have been more multilayered than they appeared at the time. New perspectives on these texts allow us to understand how the Asian American community of readers has developed and how scholarship that critically reexamines these early autobiographies unveils possible authorial intentions that may have eluded contemporary mainstream readers.

In general, Lee and New seem to belong clearly in Elaine Kim's category of "ambassadors of goodwill," writers conscious of their role in explaining the customs of their countries to American readers. By presenting these primarily anthropological accounts of boyhoods in Asian countries, the writers hoped to enkindle understanding toward their homelands and their people. The concern is therefore cultural and political, rather than personal (as evidenced by the photographs). The individuals, Lee and New, are found in their texts only obliquely and in no significant depth. There is little character development, no process of change, and only cursory descriptions of immigration and adaptation. Also, the lack of personal references suggests a collective rather than a personal voice. These narratives, commissioned within the tradition of autobiographies of childhood, offer interesting readings on early Asian American subject positionality and the nature of the American prerequisite for writing about Asians. In the late 1800s and early 1900s, Asian immigrant writers were of interest primarily because of what they could recount of their country of origin, rather than as subjects actively negotiating American society. For my purposes, therefore, these texts are valuable, not because of what they recount, but because of the cultural work they enact and the kind of criticism they have aroused, which gives us clear perspectives on the way cultural memory may be negotiated through reader reception of texts. Further, the fact that these texts are Childhoods attests to the advantages of this form of life writing in articulating cultural perspectives.

One problematic aspect, addressed in the criticism of Lee and New, as well as that of other early immigrant autobiographers such as Etsu Sugimoto and Lin Yutang, is the way these writers elide many of the issues concerning the thousands of Chinese and Japanese immigrant workers in the United States at the time. First, the writers have been criticized for not negotiating more overtly the predominant racism against Asians. This may be explained by the simple reason that Lee and New, writing for a specific book series, could not stray from the central theme and a fixed perspective. Amy Ling suggests that Lee may have also avoided mentioning any episodes of racism he may have experienced personally because he was addressing a predominantly White audience on whom he depended and "silence on sensitive issues was necessary." Yet, she argues, we need to read his silences and extract meaning from actions, irony, and indirection, which are certainly found in the text ("Yan Phou Lee" 275–276). Second, the socioeconomic gap between these writers (a minority) and the large number of laborers made the representation of Asians in the United States at the time problematic. We may argue, nonetheless, that these writers, by privileging the positive aspects of Chinese and Japanese culture, were struggling to make other Asians understood.

Floyd Cheung observes that critics today tend to believe that the "elite" status of these writers is a less authentic position "from which to experience and write about being Asian American at the turn of the twentieth century" (46). Cheung's essay reappraises Lee's literary response by examining the opportunities that his privileged socioeconomic position allowed him to exploit in terms of genre and subject. I agree with Cheung regarding the dangerous tendency in contemporary Asian American studies to highlight the working-class experience to the extent of often invalidating the equally vital experiences of those immigrants of higher social class, of scholars, or of those who managed to achieve economic advancement. In this regard, Ling also notes:

> Lee wrote of what he knew, and he cannot be faulted for the class into which he was born. In fact, his choice of verb explicitly acknowledges the role of fate, for as he put it: "I *happened* to be both into the higher middle condition of life" (20, emphasis added). Furthermore, writing in the late nineteenth century, he could hardly be expected to treat "American race politics" in terms entirely satisfying to a late-twentieth-century post-civil-rights feminist consciousness. Finally, we should consider it an unexpected bonus that a book entitled *When I Was a Boy in China* contains any impressions of the United States at all. ("Yan Phou Lee" 274)

These perspectives highlight the danger of reading past texts out of context.

Similarly, New was a highly successful businessman who worked in the United States and Korea and wrote his Childhood upon first returning to Korea in 1926. Critics have questioned his strategy, particularly what may be considered a problematic classification of the book as an autobiography when, in fact, autobiographical elements are virtually nonexistent. Seiwoong Oh points out that the editor of the book even felt the need to offer a brief biography of New in the preface because his actual life cannot be gleaned from the information within the text itself ("Ilhan New" 282). The dearth of personal information is explained by the editor as a manifestation of "characteristically Oriental modesty" (5), itself a stereotype. Kyhan Lee nonetheless posits that the notion of "I" for New remained consistent with the traditional view of the individual as part of a "collective whole," a perspective that explains the author's decentering of himself in the text. Lee explores the notion of the impersonal voice that New creates, noting that the text was actually written in Korea, which may have contributed to the particular shape of the narrative. The autobiography was not an accredited literary genre in Korea at that time and, further, New might have actually been taking advantage of the invitation to write an autobiography to "[authenticate] generalizations concerning culture and customs" unfamiliar to his American audience (67). New may thus have consciously spoken in a collective voice as part of the role of cultural ambassador and spokesperson for Korean immigrants, a role he seems to take on quite willingly.[6]

Recent criticism, informed by sophisticated theories on genre, style, and rhetoric have suggested that these texts may be more subversive than originally thought, and that the position of "ambassador of goodwill" was merely a disguise that permitted the writers to enact a more substantial agenda. In fact, Amy Ling invites us to rethink Elaine Kim's definition of Lee (and by extension, I suggest, of New). Rather than as an "ambassador of goodwill," she suggests that these writers function effectively within Gloria Anzaldua's theoretical frame of the borderlands, the frontier of the encounter of two cultures. Ling perceives Lee as an Asian American "frontier man and founding father, nearly a century before the term 'Asian American' was coined. Although some may consider [his book] more anthropology than literature, I find enough evidence of artistic crafting and rhetorical grace to consider it the founding text of Asian American literature. Not only is it chronologically the earliest, but it bespeaks Lee's frontier position." In the Childhood, Lee develops the notion of the frontier between childhood and adulthood as a reflection of the border between cultures, verifying a psychological state of encounter that is significant for many reasons, among them that he anticipates the themes and issues of future generations of Asians in America (Ling, "Yan Phou Lee" 274).[7]

Further, Cheung analyzes issues of authenticity and cultural authority in

Lee's text in the context of autoethnography as well as the significance of Lee's role in the debate against the Chinese Exclusion Act of 1882. Apart from his autobiography, published in 1887, Lee continued to write articles like his famous "The Chinese Must Stay" published in the *North American Review*. Cheung suggests that Lee's text is more multilayered than it appears and speaks of the writer's choice of "tactically advantageous" strategies, such as "positioning an essentialized Chinese identity against equally essentialized African-American and Japanese identities; employing a rhetoric of cross-cultural simile vis-à-vis Greek, Roman, and British cultures; and embedding a critique of mainstream U.S. civilization in his storytelling. As problematic as the first two of these tactics are to many critics, they demonstrate that Lee armed himself with the 'tourist guide' role not merely to 'titillate' but rather to do battle with the 'virulent sinophobia' of his day" (Cheung 47). Even Lee's ostensible reinforcement of the stereotype of Chinese docility becomes, in Cheung's perspective, a strategy for a more important goal: because of the complicated situation of the Chinese at the time, "Lee found it more expedient to accent the characteristics of essentialized Chinese identity that the American public would find least threatening and most self-serving, rather than to sue stridently for Chinese rights. Thus, he framed the Chinese as voluntarily coming to America and as culturally conditioned to follow rules. Lee sought to draw a contrast between stereotypical Chinese-American docility and stereotypical African-American rebelliousness" (48). The fact that the text is presented as an autobiography of childhood allows Lee to perform more than he appears to precisely because the genre permits easy (even "ingenuous") access to the "authentic" stories of the past country while enacting important cultural work of refocusing American perspectives on Asia and Asians.

These two readings of Lee's text point to insurgent possibilities of the genre of the Childhood from its earliest appropriations by Asian American writers. It also supports a vital point that I noted in the first chapter—the creation of a reader for these texts. In the early decades of the twentieth century, Americans were unable to grasp the potentially subversive agenda of these texts, or else preferred not to consider anything more than the exotica it purported to represent. In the late 1990s and early 2000s, essays such as Ling and Cheung's invited us to examine the intersection between these ostensibly transparent ethnographic documents and their authors' possible intention to position Asians in American culture and literature. Because the tradition of ethnic autobiography has created readers conscious of the connection between genre choice and political agendas, contemporary readings of these texts have become more multilayered.

We can speak of these texts as the "contact zone" defined by Stanley, where the frontier becomes a temporal one between past and present. The experiences of childhood read from a culturally and politically conscious present may illustrate in what ways the texts dialogue with changing American perspectives on Asians. The key point in this contact zone would be the notion of "authenticity," where the speaker of the present in one place becomes the authoritative voice of a culture in another place and a past time. The context of the writing of Lee and New's Childhoods demanded a performance of authenticity, which was precisely the books' selling point. Our interest in them now is more nuanced, weighted with our awareness of the slippery notion and possibly subversive nature of authenticity and our own renewed manners of reading past texts.

The complex work that Lee and New might conceivably have been doing is taken a step further by Younghill Kang's *The Grass Roof,* a longer text that engages in overt ways the history of Korea and contemporary American prejudices against particular Asians.[8] This text, which hovers between fiction and autobiography—Elaine Kim defines it as "autobiographical fiction" (*Asian American Literature* 33) and Seiwoong Oh calls it "quasi-fictional" autobiography ("Younghill Kang" 149)—along with its sequel, *East Goes West,* has established Kang as the "Father of Korean American Literature." This designation presupposes an important process. Kang was different from most Koreans in the United States at the time because he came as an immigrant to stay, not as a sojourner. Kim notes that Kang, like Carlos Bulosan, "took part in a personal transition from Korean to Korean American and from Filipino to Filipino American; they are representative of the genesis of Asian American literature. Moreover, the differences in interpretation of Asian American realities by Kang and Bulosan emblematize the diversity of perspectives in Asian American literature" (*Asian American Literature* 32–33). Even before the term "Asian American" existed, the vital itineraries that led to its formulation were already being enacted by Asian subjects who had negotiated the cultural and political realities of America as well as their positions as immigrants of color.[9]

Yet again, the creative use of the Childhood allows the author to negotiate important historical events in Korea that the mainstream American public did not know about. Kang presents himself as a true Korean, stressing his devotion to his country and his culture as part of a valuable heritage. His emphasis on the rural setting of his childhood as well as descriptions of several journeys allows him to depict in detail the beauty of the Korean countryside. He describes his playmates and dogs, their travesties and education. In particular, the account of his education as a poet allows him to discuss the amplitude of Korean culture and learning. In his recurring comparisons between Korean traditions with other Asian or Western practices, he generally emphasizes the superiority of Korean ways. Because the Korea he describes was at the time in the middle of a complicated tug-of-war between tradition and modernity, independence and colonization, Western influences and Eastern practices, the auto-biographical mode permits comprehensive access to this complicated mesh of circumstances.

Kang's text differs from the traditional Childhood in the way he breaks the autobiographical pact by giving his protagonist a different name: Chungpa Han. It is also difficult to ascertain the facts of Kang's life, although much of the information given in the text appears autobiographical. Formulated with an American public in mind, the author privileges metaphors that American read-ers can identify with and frames his descriptions using constant comparisons between the East and West, and between the different Asian national groups. A close reading thus reveals a deliberately constructed narrative that functions in interesting ways in its context. Though Kang begins with a disclaimer—"I am not writing this to make anybody educated, or to put down any Babbitry, or to spread any new sort of gospel. My one aim is to tell you the life, the human story of one man, made up with the stuff called love, hatred, smiles, and tears" (3)—one detects a very clear political and cultural purpose to his style. His description of his childhood adventures reads like *Huckleberry Finn*—repeated references to Mark Twain (for example, on occasion he notes the differences Twain establishes between a "common lie" and a "damned" one [193]), among others, illustrate the sources of his text and affirm that the work is willfully articulated to dialogue with an established American tradition while introduc-ing new themes and cultural perspectives. Most of the epigraphs that open the chapters are quotations from American or European writers such as Shake-speare (spelled "Shakspere"), Browning, Shelley, Poe, and Wordsworth. But he also includes numerous quotations from Korean, Chinese, and Japanese poetry within the text, which introduces Asian literature to American readers and heightens the aesthetic flavor of the narrative. I suggest that these references serve an interesting discursive purpose: by establishing a dialogue between his life story and the literary context of his American readers, Kang validates him-self as an educated and therefore authoritative speaker for the Korean people and of Korean history. He deliberately encourages this position by his constant comparisons between Western and Eastern practices; for example, the ways men are entertained by women: "a young Western man takes to a party the kind of girl who can give him a good time, and a young Eastern man finds a trained girl when he arrives" (137).

The tone of Kang's text explicitly acknowledges his implied reader through a didactic mode of writing, careful descriptions of customs and practices, and direct address. Describing the significance of the sixtieth birthday celebration for Koreans, for example, he writes, "According to the universal idea in the Orient, the age of sixty years is life at its very best. Before this a man is dis-tracted by the five lusts. Now you are all over with the five lusts: life should be suave, easy, luxurious" (113). Significantly, Kang demonstrates his awareness of American perspectives on Asians, humorously subverting the stereotypical notion that all Asians look alike. As he explains, "to a Westerner, all orientals looks very much the same, just as to an oriental, all Westerners look high-nosed and red-headed" (245). His manner of reversing the point of view leads Western readers to confront their own stereotypes and see themselves as subject to stereotyping. Yet Kang succumbs to his own prejudices in his ironic descriptions of Asians meant to illuminate the Western reader.

> The term "oriental flattery" comes from a typical Jap rather than from a typical Chinaman or a typical Korean; the Jap, too, you will notice, likes to be flattered in return. . . . The Jap has a great sense of form and outline, instinctively keeping to a school of standards and unhampered by any blundering originality. Hence he is very aesthetic. He is all for the *petite* perfection, and devotes his talents to the details. His art is much slighter in quality and quantity than Chinese or Korean and has a gossamer fragility. . . . A Jap is not at all rationalistic. He easily sees faults in others, and exaggerates them out of proportion, particularly when the interests of the nation are at stake. . . . Yes, among all the nations, the Japanese populace is the most unreasonable and excitable. As a mob, Japs are very sensitive, and each man would die for the whole. Mob-spirit makes them patriotic. A Chinaman is different. He is individually sensitive, but he never shows his sensitivity externally. . . . At heart, he is independent, vigorous, original. He does not have a double personality. . . . A Chinese is himself, yesterday, today, forever. (245–246)

These descriptions, professedly from a speaker who has had close contact with all the ethnic groups, provide readers "authoritative" perspectives, which nonetheless simply reiterate established prejudices.

The use of the child perspective occasions an artless presentation of changing cultural practices and political contexts. It also highlights the increasing influence of Western practices into Korean life. The author provides a seemingly naïve negotiation of the Asian view of the West, particularly through the presence of missionaries in Korea. Kang is rather critical of the missionaries and, on several occasions, notes their hypocrisy and lack of commitment. Though his attitude toward Westerners is generally negative, Kang writes positively about Western ideas, which involve mostly aspects of scientific knowledge. The increasing popularity of Western practices in Korea leads to the two central conflicts in the book: the collision between Eastern and Western values, forms of knowledge, and power; and the struggle that the protagonist undergoes between his individual ambitions and the value that his culture places on community. The second difficulty is actually a personification of the larger debate, as Chungpa's growing desire for the most progressive education clashes with his family's traditional practices. As he explains, "The old Confucian school receded to the past, in my mind. It seemed to me more and more useless, as a bull-fight or a game of contract bridge, since I began to learn the law of gravitation, and Boyle's law and all the other laws. The study of the lives of Lincoln and Napoleon, and the geography of the World kindled my enthusiasm" (183).

He justifies his choice to leave home at the age of eleven by declaring that he needs an education to fulfill his patriotic duty to liberate his country from the oppressive colonization of Japan because "Korea was being punished by her conservatism" (182). Kang is highly critical of Japan's strategies for dominance in Asia and repeatedly emphasizes the Japanese's cruelty in their treatment of Koreans. Descriptions of his Japanese schoolmates in Tokyo verge on the farcical: they discussed "sex and sports; nothing but sex and sports" and excelled at competitions to see how many raw eggs one could eat (243). Interestingly, his animosity is articulated in terms that resound with contemporary American prejudices, to the point of referring to the Japanese as "the Japs." He recounts with unrestrained emotion his grandmother's death after being beaten by a Japanese policeman, the suicides of many important Koreans in protest over Japan's annexation, the events surrounding the declaration of Korean Independence, and the tragic consequences. His increasing desperation about life in Korea leads him to make what he presents as his only choice: immigration. The narrative ends with Chungpa Han on a boat to America, dreaming of the possibilities of the new life ahead.

Contemporary reviews of Kang's book were unanimously positive, as were those of most Asian immigrants at the time who catered to American expectations about Asian cultures.[10] But more recent criticism reveals a complex rereading of the text. Though she admires Kang's writing, Elaine Kim argues that he was "completely unrepresentative of his people, yet became something of a spokesman for Koreans in America almost by default" (*Asian American Literature* 33). As with Lee and New, Kang's aristocratic status and attitudes alienated him from the numerous Korean laborers and sojourners in the United States. I argue that Kim censures Kang's text because she reads it as primarily his justification for leaving Korea. She criticizes his portrayal of a protagonist who considers his country lost, its culture antiquated and hopeless, and justifies leaving his mother country through rhetoric on the philosophy of individualism and creativity of the West, and because "he flees from Korea as one flees a cripple or a corpse" (35).[11] Her view on Kang's position may also be validated by the choice of the autobiographical form, which, as explained earlier, is the genre par excellence for speaking about the present moment. Kang's narrative of childhood, his description of the changing winds in his country and the difficult choices that opened up for him, make the reader participate in his multilayered struggle with issues of loyalty. Reading the text as a justification explains, in a way, the choice of the form. Nonetheless, though the ethical component may be pulled into the discussion, we must still read Kang's text as primarily an exercise in presenting Korea to Americans, in the tradition of early writing by Asian immigrants, and appreciate the rhetorical strategies that made the text accessible and popular. For this purpose, the choice of genre is significant.

Growing Up in Asia

There is a notable difference between Childhoods written before and after the 1960s, when the term "Asian American" was formulated and a more nuanced perception of the relationship of an Asian past to an American present began to circulate. These more recent texts often have clear political or cultural purposes and offer visions of the homeland that are more complex, sanctioning particular processes of cultural memory for the increasing number and variety of Asian immigrants in North America. Most importantly, perhaps, the authors no longer feel they need to serve as "ambassadors," and their texts negotiate more freely the idea of home, the past, and the present. These texts revisit the concept of home from a prism that contemplates the present and looks toward the future in significant ways.

As Jennifer Browdy de Hernandez suggests, the concept of home in autobiographies by postcolonial or diasporic subjects is "a contested site on which the cultural conflicts of the larger society are played out in microcosm; and autobiography is not just an exercise in recapturing the past, but a future oriented project that seeks to establish a secure home ground where the subject may reside without fear of displacement or humiliation" (21). Also, because the writers do not perceive an obligation to explain their homelands to American or Canadian readers, their texts often focus on more personal concerns. Rather than ethnocultural prisms, these autobiographies engage the culture of childhood itself, with its attendant worries about acceptance, peer relationships, definitions of normalcy, generation gaps, poverty, and the like. The Childhoods I discuss in this section center specifically on issues of disability, politics, transculturality, the role of mothers, and a nostalgic portrayal of an idealized place. The intentions of the writers, gleaned from the manner they write, is more reflexive than didactic, more inventive or nostalgic than that of serving as cultural guide.

Ved Mehta is almost certainly the most prolific and comprehensive Asian American autobiographer. His first book, *Face to Face: An Autobiography*, narrates his life from childhood until just before he leaves for England. Written at the age of twenty-three, the text signaled Mehta's imaginative insight and potential as a writer, as well as the topic that would govern his writing: his blindness.[12] This text became the nucleus of his "Continents of Exile" series, eleven volumes of biography and autobiography that chronicle his family's life, his experiences growing up in India, his education in the United States and England, and his subsequent career. The first two books in the series, *Daddyji* and *Mamaji*, describe his parents' lives before and during the early years of their marriage, presenting a vivid portrait of middle-class India and ending at the point of his blindness. His autobiographies of childhood are set immediately after these books: *Vedi* centers on the boy's experiences in the Dadar School for the Blind from the ages of five to nine, *The Ledge between the Streams* continues the account of his childhood from nine to fifteen, which includes the traumatic experience of the Partition of India and his family's escape out of Lahore. His next book, *Sound-Shadows of the New World,* recounts his first three years at the Arkansas School for the Blind and includes the story of how he engages issues of homesickness and cultural alienation and discovers his vocation as a journalist.[13]

John Slatin explains that *Face to Face* and Mehta's subsequent reengagements with his past, like other autobiographical narratives by blind persons, illustrate two contradictory desires: on the one hand, to justify the writer's belief that blindness makes him somehow unique (and validates the writing of an autobiography at the age of twenty-three); on the other hand, the desire to be perceived as a normal human being whose blindness is almost irrelevant (174). Thus, *Face to Face* outlines the *form* that Mehta's life writing project will take, which privileges a specific kind of consciousness of the world and a quest for a language that can embody it. Indeed, as John Stotesbury explains, for unsighted or partially sighted individuals, "a significant part of their personal quest for identity, autonomy, and independence has consisted to a heightened degree of the struggle for control of a language within which the metaphoric nature of sight has been completely assimilated and normalised" (134).

Vedi and *The Ledge between the Streams* narrate Mehta's growing frustration with his family and India itself, as both prove incapable of giving him back his sight or furnishing him with a space in which he can pursue his fierce ambition. His desperate search for an education that would permit him to function not only efficiently, but also creatively, like its analogue—the search for language—is complicated by his disability in a country where poor parents blinded their children in order to make them more effective beggars. This explains his need for immigration to the United States and justifies this choice.

The experience of blindness predominates *Vedi* and *The Ledge between the Streams* in different ways. Mehta, a professional writer, endows his Childhoods with very specific metaphors that link his personal trajectory with the wider mesh of political and social issues that marked his history. Though his blindness is the structural motif, his ambition to overcome that disability shapes the tone of the narrative.

In *Vedi*, the writer brings the reader into a world where sight is acknowledged but not possessed. The book is entirely without visual descriptions and Vedi narrates in a sprightly prose his experiences with fellow students and teachers, the smells and feel of the school, games, and learning. The first lines of *Vedi* chronicle his first memory, leaving for the Dadar School for the Blind at the age of five: "I remember the train whistle. It blew with a rush of steam. . . . 'You are a man now,' he said. This sentence of my father's was to become the beginning of my clear, conscious memory. In later years, I would recall it again and again, as if it were the injunction of my destiny" (3). The rest of the narrative recounts in engaging detail the boy's education at the school: he learns how to eat with a spoon, dress himself, make his bed, sew buttons, play with other children, read Braille, and speak English. This Childhood is a joyful account of a bright child's learning experience, made more fascinating because it does not involve sight. Vedi learns the shape of animals from the student-teacher Miss Mary, and from their finding a stray cat and a myna bird he is later given by a servant at home. In this sense, the Childhood privileges his process of learning, rather than cultural issues.

The Dadar School, an underfunded home for orphans, was clearly not the place to send an intelligent, imaginative middle-class child, but his parents did not know of other options and trusted the school's Christian foundations. In a world where all the other children were totally or partially blind, Vedi learns of other markers of difference, particularly language, religion, and class. He hears Marathi here for the first time and needs to learn it to communicate. As the only middle-class child with parents, he is given special treatment. He is aware, for example, that he is the only boy with shoes and numerous changes of clothes; his companions note that his hands are soft; he is the only one (at the beginning) who is never ill: "the other boys could not understand why I seemed so healthy: why they never heard me scratch my head, why I never coughed at night, why I never complained of a stomach ache—above all, why I never had a fever. The boys kept coming up and touching my forehead and exclaiming, 'He still doesn't have a fever!'" (34). He also acknowledges the hierarchy in the school: the partially sighted boys were "much in demand as a friend by the totally blind boys" (66). This small difference determined a person's position. "Some of us who were totally blind had been sighted once, but we could no longer remember what that was like. We thought of sighted people as awesome and powerful, always able to take a discarded shoe to someone who wasn't sighted" (197). But Vedi's social position separates him from the other boys in another way: he does not have to learn how to cane chairs or play musical instruments, so that he can avoid calluses and continue to read Braille. He is also the only one who has a home to go to for the Christmas holidays.

The landscape of childhood colors Mehta's autobiography: the touch and smell of his family, the sounds of the school, conversations with schoolmates, the adventure of learning. The Childhood focuses on friendships, authority, ghosts, early fears, the imagination that believes in magic. As time goes by, the boy at school begins to forget his home and Punjabi—"sometimes everything connected with home seemed so far away" (61)—as he immerses himself in his daily routine. The boys are typical children, capable of playing tricks. When the school headmaster, Mr. Ras Mohan, makes the boys tell him their dreams for a book he is writing about the perception of blind children, they know what he wants to hear and pretend to have visual elements in their dreams to claim the prize for their story, a sweet.

The narrative is also not without its dark side, in the form of the Sighted Master in charge of their dormitory. A particular episode involved Jaisingh, a deaf, blind, and retarded boy who "Mr. Ras Mohun [called] the Dadar School's Helen Keller. We didn't know who Helen Keller was, but we imagined that she was an American Jaisingh" (196). Jaisingh and another retarded child, Ramesh, cry incessantly at night and the Sighted Master often silenced them by beating them with a shoe. One night, the crying is particularly intense and the boys hear the Sighted Master remove a wooden plank from one of the beds. The boys listen, terrified, as they hear the plank crash down and Jaisingh and Ramesh's wailing stops abruptly. The next day the two are gone, their beds stripped. Whether the Sighted Master actually killed them is never revealed. This story is one of many that fill the boys' world and feed their active imaginations. Mehta's account of his childhood perceptions reflects his creative imagination: how he imagines the chess board as his dormitory and the dreaded Sighted Master as the opponent; how he battles the Bathroom Ghost by calling on "Jesus, Mary, Joseph"; how he decides he wants to become a Muslim because of the delicious spicy food they eat.

Vedi returns home after four years at the school, partly because Mr. Ras Mohan admits they have nothing more to teach him and because of the increasing violence in Bombay. But the narrative actually closes with a telling epilogue that repositions both the role of the autobiographer and alerts us to the fundamental trauma of Mehta's childhood. Written forty years after the events of the Childhood, Mehta writes about a visit to the old school only to learn that most of his friends died of consumption at an early age. He finds his best friend, Deoji, now a teacher for the blind, but the meeting only confirms to him their "differences." His description of the school is colored with the anxiety that arises when idealized memories of childhood are revisited with adult eyes: "the school and the entire building now housed only girls and women, with thin, shrinking, demented voices—it was as if the new residents were not only blind but also retarded. This made me wonder whether the school of my childhood had had the same atmosphere. The thought was depressing—the more so because I knew there was no way I could dispose of the question to my satisfaction, since the answer was a matter not of memory but of judgment and experience, which, as a boy, I could not have had" (255–256). This description can be read against the earlier narrative that, though it acknowledged the difficult conditions of the school, presented the perspective of an eager child. More significantly, his meeting with Rajas, one of the "success stories" of the school, who had married a school headmaster but was now a widow with three children, disturbs him profoundly. As he bids her farewell after an awkward conversation, she begins to whine and beg him for a Braille watch. He recoils and runs off, "her begging tone having stirred up an earlier memory and an old fear" (258). Through this episode, Mehta eloquently reveals what he has been fighting against all his life: pity. His struggle for an education is ultimately his struggle not to be like the beggars he hears his mother give alms to precisely because they are blind. His life writing exercise, and the forms it takes, signifies in this context of wanting to carve out a dignified place for himself.

Mehta's struggle continues in a more complicated way in *The Ledge between the Streams*. No longer at school and with a family that repeatedly moves house, he finds himself more and more relegated to a side role, his active mind losing momentum. This volume covers his life from the age of nine to fifteen and also deals with India's beginnings as an independent nation. Politics enter directly into family life, and history becomes a protagonist in Mehta's narration, as the developing configuration of Indian society shapes the way Vedi understands his world. Yet, in this book, as in the previous Childhood, Mehta's narrative consciousness focuses on the specific issues of identity that he wants to engage in particular moments.

Specifically, the titles of his books signal Mehta's changing perceptions of his place in the world. *Vedi* is simply about him as a boy still unable to comprehend the intricacies of society and culture, the history that would change his life. The title *The Ledge between the Streams* is based on an incident that occurred on a family excursion to Kashmir. Vedi wants to explore two streams that run side by side at the bottom of a deep gully and his father takes him there: "I squatted down on the narrow ledge between the streams and put a hand in each stream. The right stream felt glacial, and I could scarcely keep my hand in it. The left stream was thick and soupy, and felt almost tepid. I remember thinking that, in their way, the two streams were as different as Daddyji and Mamaji" (177–178). As they stand there, a sudden rainstorm unleashes a current of water and the family has to run to save their lives. Mehta makes this incident resound symbolically with the current family situation: the ledge, which seemed a safe place, reminds them of the perilous border between India and Pakistan; their narrow escape summarizes their forcible flight to the Hindu side of the border. But the ledge resounds on more levels than the political and also refers to the multiple liminal positions Mehta grows conscious of occupying. In the quotation, he literally notes the difference between his father, whom the children thought of as "educated, responsible, and compliant" and their overprotective mother, "uneducated, capricious, and stubborn" (66), who disagree in their approaches to their son's disability. But Mehta's attentiveness to his between-ness refers to other binaries as well, some of which were already negotiated in *Vedi*: blind and sighted, Muslim and Hindu, East and West, poor or wealthy, literate or illiterate, *satyagraha* and violence, India and America. Ultimately, he suggests that because he cannot find a space for himself in that treacherous middle ground, he must leave.

Vedi focuses on the boy's experience at school while *Ledge* centers on family life and describes numerous domestic scenes: kite playing with his cousins, listening to his sisters talk about clothes, repairing a bicycle and learning to ride it, exploring a village, talking with servants, taking trips with his father, learning music. But the boy chafes at the lack of intellectual stimulation. His father tried to encourage him "to look to music for solace . . . [but] in [his] view nothing could take the place of studying—of reading and writing and taking examinations, of learning English, of progressing from standard to standard like [his] sisters and [his] big brother and [his] cousins. [He] had the helpless feeling of falling behind" (214).

Mehta's descriptions of his family, which include happy events like his sister's wedding, peaceful interludes, and exciting games with his cousins, reveals an incongruity: his family's loving attention actually limits him from growing intellectually and socially. His mother and sisters' overprotection restrains his curiosity, and the refrain of his text is that he was *doing nothing*. Mehta continues to reject his blindness: "I also gave up screaming for silence, because screaming only drew attention to my blindness, which I wanted to forget and to make others forget" (72). At the same time, he grows aware of being able to function more and more effectively because of what he calls "facial vision," "an ability that the blind develop to sense objects and terrain by the feel of the air and by differences in sound. . . . Without knowing it, during the kite chases I was learning how to get around—by sensing the currents of air and by listening to the patter of feet on a roof, to the scrapes of shoes along a wall, to the rattle of a drainpipe as boys clambered down it" (17–18).[14] Only his father's faith in Vedi's intelligence gives him confidence. As he walks with his father down a gully, he notes, "But Daddyji walked in a relaxed, self-confident way, his little finger steady and straight. Because I *thought* I wouldn't stumble, I *didn't* stumble, and his movements and also the erosion and indentation of the steps told me when to step down" (176, italics mine). In this manner, the boy learns that his own self-confidence can open doors to the world.

In *Ledge,* Mehta describes the events that led to the Partition of India and how the family was obliged to leave their home in Lahore for Bombay. The historical circumstances also increase his desire to leave India. The final section of the narrative recounts his relentless efforts to get admitted into an American school for the blind. When the Arkansas School for the Blind accepts him, the family prepares for his trip with illusion and dread. Before he leaves, his father arranges a meeting with Prime Minister Nehru, who asks the boy, "Why Arkansas?" The boy replies with the deeply embarrassing truth: "that's the only place that would have me" (520). Interestingly, the book ends with no foreshadowing, except in the proclamation of his uncle who says to him, "I don't know when we'll meet again. . . . People who go to America nowadays never come back" (521). As with *Vedi,* Mehta ends this narrative with another beginning: his departure for the United States and the promise of a new life. Mehta's two Childhoods, read together, offer a coherent portrait of an intelligent child's struggle for an education, enacted in a context where the intellectual formation of blind children was virtually nonexistent. Mehta's representation of Indian history is focused from a family's experience, and the Childhood skillfully blends a personal story with the history of a country, allowing the genre to function on diverse levels.

Hilary Tham's Childhood, *Lane with No Name,* differs from the others in this section because of her unique narrative strategy, which blends diverse forms of knowledge and creative expression, pictures, and drawings. Moreover, she composes her text from stories, poems, photographs, and illustrations, making her Childhood a story cycle rather than a linear narrative.[15] This structure reflects Tham's awareness of the process of memory as nonlinear, associative, nontemporal, fragmented, and incomplete, making structure and content mutually reinforcing. Through the organization of the discrete narratives, she controls a series of fundamental memories, defining their significance for her own formation, not necessarily obeying the dictates of causality.

She often explores the same theme through different genres: Tham sets a story and poem on the same subject together. In this manner, she interiorizes experience and articulates it in two ways: through a realistic prose and a more poetic symbolism. This occurs, for example, with the poem "Moving Up," which immediately precedes the story "Lane with No Name"—both of which narrate her mother's buying of a house without her father's knowledge or support; the epigraph that opens the chapter "Family Labels" is a fragment of a previously published poem that symbolically introduces the theme of the story;

the chapter "Chinese Marriage," where she deals with her father's oppressive behavior toward her mother ends with a poem titled "Father," which depicts her disenchantment with the man she had innocently adored as a child.

Tham's blend of genres suggests a renewed terrain of self-expression, an exploration of the creative possibilities of the Childhood. As she crosses generic frontiers, she also expands the ways one creatively negotiates the past. By inscribing the same experience in both poetry and prose, Tham presents a dynamic manner of writing the evolving self, a literal metaphor for the task of negotiating identity. Her stories and poems, sustained reflections through different mediums, signify on the levels of both discourse and story. Her story of self-awareness and development is performed through her evolving art. By subverting traditional signifying strategies, the text reconfigures cultural and generic interpretation.

Tham's narrative relates specific customs and practices in Malaysia—she casually assumes the role of cultural ambassador and explains in detail customs such as marriage, naming traditions, birth and death ceremonies, superstitions, family structures, and attitudes. Though she consciously engages her Malaysian-Chinese childhood as an ethnographic gesture by an immigrant to the United States, her cultural explanations are secondary to two concerns: first, her growing awareness of the social structure oppressive to women (in particular, her mother) that made her a feminist; second, how her growing appreciation for the nuances of languages led to her development as a poet.[16]

In this Childhood, Tham explores her adult creative, ideological, cultural, and religious positioning from the very beginning. Interestingly, she notes that her immigration and the birth of her daughters in the United States prompted her to look back on her childhood: "I had not written about my Malaysian-Chinese heritage while I was in Malaysia, mainly because I had no occasion to think about it. Everyone knew what I knew; there was no reason to articulate the obvious. It was after I came to America and looked homeward with the eyes of the exile that I gained the perspective and the desire to write about growing up in Malaysia, the myths and gods my mother gave me, the effect my family and upbringing had on my character" (198). Susanna Egan's discussion of how geographies of the mind function to use space as a "pliable imaginative structure" applies in interesting ways to Tham's text. She writes, "Geographical centers are parallel rather than sequential. These writers destabilize boundaries fixed between places that are home, holding presence and absence in continuous and creative tension. For the autobiographer, several worlds coexist in this dialogic relationship dependent only on focus for full recognition" (123). Tham's engagement with the idiosyncrasies of multicultural Malaysia—the British notion of "Divide and Rule" that pragmatically separated the three ethnic groups living in the country and alienated the Malays from the experience of the Chinese and Indians—points to the palimpsestic cultural perceptions created by history and political interests, which she became aware of only after marrying an American, leaving her country, and converting to Judaism. Returning to Malaysia through memory, Tham's text suggests, is not a simple process because of the country's synchronic blend of cultural scenarios that coexist but do not always interpenetrate.

Tham's Childhood narratively displays this network of family connections, interracial, interreligious, and interclass contact. Zhou Xiaojing suggests that for Tham, "the experience of border-crossing is at once alienating and liberating; the interstices between different cultures have become an enabling cognitive and critical space for her to reexamine her received beliefs and reinvent herself" (366). Writing this text allows Tham to negotiate the complex social and cultural stratifications she ignored when she was living there. In the United States, she asked herself questions that did not occur to her as a child or young adult, and she began to pay attention to the political processes that separated her from those of her own country: "because the races were kept apart, we remained unknown, alien to each other; unfounded rumors and political lies became legends and took on a vicious subterranean life in our minds. When we met, our prejudices formed a distorting glass wall between us. Racist perceptions strip away the freedom to be what you want to be; they reduce you to the lowest common denominator of your group; you have to struggle to recall that you are more than what the other sees" (181). The book's longest chapter, "Bare Feet & Broken Glass," speaks of the complicated race relations among the groups and includes a series of line drawings of the Malaysian countryside, the National Mosque, and a market scene, among others. The only photograph is one of Tham as a college student sitting beside three friends, each identified with his or her name followed by a parenthetical reference to cultural affiliation, confirming the importance of this information in their social world.

The multiple voices and stories that Tham draws into the text—those of her parents, brothers, and sisters—illustrate the complex mesh of family relationships in Malaysia. In her "Finding Your Voice" essay, she explains how the "Asian tradition of self is as a social construct-identity defined by relationship, embedded in the interpersonal relationships of family and clan. In the Chinese tradition, a person's identity is in the person's place in the extended family" (para. 2). Her mother's story, in particular, forged Tham's feminist position. When, at the age of thirteen, her mother begins to confide in her, Tham understands how her mother—though surrounded by neighbors, relatives, and children—was "essentially alone," charged with the task of "saving face" for the family (*Lane with No Name* 119). Learning the truth about her parents' marriage is devastating: "I felt betrayed by both my parents. My father in betraying my mother had betrayed me. I felt honored by my mother's telling me adult secrets.

Yet the feeling was tinged with resentment. I felt burdened, weighed down, legs trembling like a colt carrying an overfed man. Looking back, I can name the thing I subconsciously grasped at the time. She made me grow up before I was ready" (119).

In relation to this nascent awareness, Tham's Childhood clearly evokes the process that made her a poet: the Cantonese nursery rhymes, stories, and proverbs her mother raised her on taught her the power of rhyme and images. To her, these proverbs were "like bouillon cubes: they are always compact, evocative word pictures that pack a lot of meaning and punch." Growing up with "a language that was terse, concentrated, and full of rhymes and images, it was natural for me to think in metaphors and to turn to the reading and writing of poetry" (44). Tham's insight into the subservient role her mother occupied in a patriarchal family and social structure inspired her feminist perspective and led her to write in order to examine "the shapes and shadows beneath the surfaces people present to the world" (115).

Recalling the death of her younger sister when she was six, Tham remembers the "fierce joy" she experienced when she began to write poetry: it "came from the feeling that I was defying death's eraser; I was leaving signs that I had lived, hoping someone coming along later would find my work, like signposts in a foggy night, helpful and comforting if lost" (85–86). One of the first transgressions she commits in her writing involves the Chinese obsession with saving face, the "unspoken contract with each other to keep doors tightly closed on family skeletons. The idea of writing my memoirs goes against the grain of my upbringing. Though I had breached the taboo with my poems, prose feels like a greater violation." She thus notes the liberating quality of her immigration, with its ideology of being anything you want to be if you work at it, which allowed her to write about "the real faces behind the preserved faces of my life, my family, and my people" (3). Also very significantly, her mother's insistence on the children's English education allowed Tham not only to learn perspectives counter to traditional Chinese ideas, but also gave her a language that granted her the "freedom to walk into non-Chinese worlds from which I would bring back ideas and a language with which I could invent myself" (133).

Malaysia's cultural mix also opened up the doors to Western perspectives for Tham. At school, she was exposed to alternative possibilities of womanhood, as the Irish nuns seemed infused with vitality and an openness toward experience that the generally work-worn and unhappy women in her home and neighborhood lacked. There, along with other girls, she could exercise a freedom of choice denied at home. She uses the metaphor of the Kelang River to describe the divide she perceived between her position and possibilities: at home, she was "a cog in a fixed social structure"; in school, the girls were "given permission to play, to have friends, to have fun," something that they had been programmed not to do. She began to see and comprehend nuances in a world that did not have to be "all browns and white" but could include "color, music, change" (131).

In the chapter "The Joyful Vanguards," Tham describes how she absorbed ideas antithetical to traditional Chinese culture through the mostly American songs they sang with the group—songs like "If You're Happy and You Know It," "Danny Boy," and "Yankee Doodle" made them entertain ideas of freedom of expression, loyalty and friendship, acceptance of justice, hope, and the right to struggle (133). Tham's Childhood therefore successfully performs on various levels—aesthetic, thematic, and generic—her process of maturity, her awareness of the place and time of childhood, and her artistic itinerary. As an example of a Childhood set in Asia, this text nonetheless engages in more sophisticated ways than the earlier texts the palimpsestic cultural and historical realities of Malaysia.

Tham's privileging of her mother in her recollection of her childhood and the role of her mother's life in her evolving perception of gender issues resonates significantly with other Asian American autobiographies that foreground the mother. The complex discourse of mother and daughter relationships, as well as the imaginative inscription of a lost homeland, occupies a prominent place in Asian American writing. Emblematic life writing exercises such as Kingston's The Woman Warrior and Sara Suleri's Meatless Days revolve around ambivalent relationships with the mother or mother figure, as well as other female members of the family. Lane with No Name and Sudha Koul's The Tiger Ladies negotiate the implications of specific maternal discourse (or the lack thereof) in the process of remembering childhood because the mother directs, modifies, and influences the daughters' responses to both individual and cultural demands. These texts highlight questions of identification with and differentiation from the mother, emphasizing a need for understanding and bonding between mothers and daughters as a fundamental step toward self-awareness. Often, the texts imply the need for daughters to take on and continue maternal stories, transforming them literally and metaphorically with their own lives and experiences. In both these texts, the connection with the mother extends to a specific ethnic affiliation—Chinese for Tham, Kashmiri for Koul—leading to a heightened sense of loss when the mother and the country are left behind.

In Lane with No Name, Tham's decision to become a feminist and challenge taboos through autobiography grows from her awareness of her mother's oppression. Koul's The Tiger Ladies, set in Kashmir, also privileges the matrilineal in its representation of a specific place. The author's description of her childhood evokes an Edenic time marked by traditional stories and legends, a warm family life, and deep roots in her surroundings, a time and place idealized perhaps because it no longer exists. "In any event," she explains, "the valley cradles us in her beauty and love songs, and does not leave us with much time or desire to hate anything. Visitors to the valley call us lazy, and the Western-educated among us call themselves the Lotus-Eaters, but we live in heaven" (33). Koul's prose is highly poetic and evocative, her style deliberately nostalgic, her words carefully chosen to provide the reader with the experience of the moment.

In this world, women had a central role based on the worship of the mother-goddess Durga, often depicted astride a tiger. Koul's title, *The Tiger Ladies,* makes explicit reference to the pivotal presence of this manner of strong women who kept the family together and whole, very often through the stories they told. The three section titles stress matrilineal positioning—"Grandmothers," "Mothers," "Daughters"—and Koul projects her nostalgic account of life as the daughter of a wealthy Kashmiri Brahmin family in the context of relationships with other women. Koul evokes this "universe of joint and extended families" (13) set in the valley of Kashmir, "which sits like an infant in the lap of the Himalayas," by describing in detail numerous customs, traditions, and manners of life. She discusses in detail the role of the pashmina in women's society; the way the winter, which lasts half a year, shapes their lives; birth, marriage, and death ceremonies; the traditions related to food; the generally respectful interaction between the Hindus and Muslims in that region. The nostalgia that tints Koul's Childhood is heightened by the date of her story—she begins her account with her mother's pregnancy precisely in 1947, when the Partition of India brings strife to the peaceful valley.

Koul enacts an interesting narrative strategy. In the opening section, she narrates in the first person plural events that she did not experience personally: the Pakistani raids on Kashmir, in search for Hindus, which makes the family realize that their lives have changed. Most important, after centuries of peaceful coexistence, her family must now accept that "to outsiders we are not Kashmiris but Hindus. There is no question of Kashmiris betraying other Kashmiris to some wild mountain people just because we are Hindus and they are Muslims. Our language and culture has bound us Kashmiris so strongly together that all other people, regardless of religion, are strangers to us. If someone does not understand our language, our stories, our songs, and our food, they are foreigners to us" (28).

Her appropriation of the stories of events before her birth and the use of the plural signals her identification not only with a particular family but with a group in a place, a collective voice. For Koul, perhaps more than for the other writers in this section, the loss of a place is much more than the result of a diaspora—it implies the relentless working of history which, in the case of India, divided more than it linked. In a manner similar to Tham's, Koul grows aware of an eclectic cultural perspective: studying at a school run by Irish nuns, she receives a very British education, which she nonetheless manages to accept without question, adapting new forms of knowledge to her own cultural milieu.

Her narrative tries to reconnect the stories of the land through personal recollection embedded in family life: she recounts the events of each season, suggesting a mythical passage of time, and uses the milestone events of life—births, marriage, death—to highlight diverse practices. To stress the umbilical connection with the land, she uses maternal imagery to describe the final destruction of the life of her childhood in the valley: "there are mothers and there are mothers. My mother cannot sleep at night because of an unwed girl and an overcrowded attic. . . . Mother Kashmir watches her children draw blood and degrade the valley with betrayal and putrefaction. We have lost our innocence, and there is a lot to hide from each other now. We are engulfed by an incomprehensible darkness, and we grope in the eclipse, looking for answers" (142).

In the final section, "Daughters," Koul describes her professional life and her immigration to the United States, where she raised children who grow up as Americans, intrigued by what they consider their parents' quaint Indian customs. The use of matrilineal imagery on several levels continues here when, describing her life in the United States, she comments, "As I watch [my daughter] eat I can see my mother and grandmother on either side of her and we smile at each other with contentment. My daughter is one of us" (179). The need for connection structures Koul's text, because the world of Kashmir she leaves behind effectively ceases to exist except in memory. Using the memories of her childhood, she recreates not only a past personal history but also the traumatic loss of a place. Blending the images of a land destroyed by war with stories of the women in her family transforms her text into a crucial intervention in the writing of the Childhood because the text itself preserves the past.

Complementary Memories of Asian History

The next two texts I discuss in detail reveal contrasting childhood experiences framed by the same historical events. The Childhoods by Kazuko Kuramoto, *Manchurian Legacy: Memoirs of a Japanese Colonist,* and Richard Kim, *Lost Names: Scenes from a Korean Boyhood,* offer opposing viewpoints of the Japanese annexation of China and Korea. Kuramoto identifies with the imperial Japanese and Kim suffers from the oppression wrought by colonization. Read together, these Childhoods present a multilayered portrayal of Asian history in the mid-twentieth century. Promoting the perspectives of the ones who were, at least for a time, on the side of the perpetrators of crimes or colonization, as well as those who endured persecution and domination, gives more complex versions of history, which takes into account not only the experience of history, but also the narrative strategies used to come to terms with the past. In the process of creating cultural or collective memory, these texts, Jay Winter and Emmanuel Sivan suggest, contribute to "collective remembrance . . . a set of acts which . . . may draw from professional history, but . . . do not depend on it" (8). The liberatory possibilities of a literary genre and figurative language complicate the relationship of autobiographical writing to official historical discourses. These memoirs oblige the contemporary reader to mediate alternative visions of events and make more responsible judgments on the unwitting players in these events. These life writing exercises elide historical oversimplifications and acknowledge layers of personal experience behind the public events. By presenting a human face to "public" events—such as the Japanese occupation—approaches to this history become more comprehensive and personal.

These Childhoods present binary experiences: here, the history of Japanese imperialism is narrated from what can be considered "insider" perspectives, that of a Japanese girl living in colonized Manchuria and that of a Korean boy living in colonial Korea. Postcolonial theory that centers on autobiography has engaged some of the specificities of this intersection between a historicized sense of self and the narration of those childhood experiences from the perspective of adulthood, usually from a location separate from the place of colonization. Gillian Whitlock has written extensively on this topic and argues that

> recollections of a colonial childhood are likely to incorporate (sometimes imperfectly) two dimensions of selfhood. Firstly, a retrospective understanding of the self as formed by a historicized world, in historical time, a world where difference and desire are taken into account. This is an understanding which usually escapes the child herself. . . . Secondly, the familiar post-Romantic idea of the child as an emblem of the self that remains deep within the individual recurs, and so the autobiographic narration of the childhood becomes a "complex way of revealing and giving meaning to the self." How a childhood in postcolonial spaces can be connected to the subjectivity and identity of the adult writer is open to question. . . . The translation of the sweet places of childhood into history and the present is fraught with difficulty for many autobiographers. (182)

Whitlock suggests that the use of the experience of childhood for particular types of memories (in this case, those marked by complex political situations) creates a tension between "history and myth, between colonized spaces and sweet places, [yet] tells us less about childhood subjectivity than the use of the idea of childhood in remembrances of things past in autobiography" and how these relate to the present (182). When the history of a place involves a process of cultural impositions and occupations, setting becomes a vital element in the construction of the child subject and the adult writer's recollection of that past self. Because these texts were produced decades after the fact, when cultural studies and questions of political identity had become quite sophisticated, authors often take into account these renewed ideas as they write about the past. Although Kuramoto does not try to justify her role in the Japanese colonization, she does admit that she accepted the political configuration she had been born into. One cannot avoid considering her another victim of her country's imperial ambitions and an innocent tool used to propagate a racist ideology against other Asians.

Kazuko Kuramoto's *Manchurian Legacy: Memoirs of a Japanese Colonist* imaginatively reconstructs spaces whose historical status changed according to political circumstances. Within these shifting spaces, she was obliged to renegotiate her growing sense of selfhood and cultural identity.[17] Her eventual immigration to the United States requires, thus, another paradigm shift in concepts of occupation on the level of permanence and possession. The subtitle of the Childhood signals a striking identification: she acknowledges her role in Japan's imperial policy, yet subtly distances herself from the political fact through the manner in which her name is written on the book cover. The book cover design is symbolic: a family picture dated 1931 of a couple and four children, the youngest of which, a girl who looks like she's about to cry, has the name "Kazuko Kuramoto" framing her face. This design immediately identifies the author as that young child, underlining the irony of the label she attaches to herself. Yet this label is apt: Kuramoto's Childhood narrates her painful itinerary of self-examination of racial and cultural prejudice and the consequences of imperialist oppression. The fact that she was born into a colonist family becomes the defining feature of her life in Dairen, the Manchuria port city in which she grew up, and the reason for ostracism when she and her family arrive as "returnees" to their homeland, Japan.

Kuramoto describes in detail her comfortable position as the daughter of a respected Japanese government official who supported the legitimacy of Japan's colonial occupation of Manchuria. Growing up separated from the Koreans and Chinese, she could not perceive that the Japanese were not welcome in Manchuria or that the system that nourished her was based on a policy of prejudice and oppression. "I was born in Dairen in 1927," she recounts, "at the peak of Japanese expansion in Asia. As a member of the third generation of my family in Dairen, I was born into a society of Japanese supremacy and grew up believing in Japan's 'divine' mission to save Asia from the 'evil' hands of Western imperialism. . . . Dairen was a rapidly expanding, tax-free commercial port city, the largest of its kind in the East, representing the international power of Imperial Japan. I was a product of this almighty Japanese imperialism" (x).[18]

Kuramoto's quest for an identity is complicated by her position as a "colonist." Rooted at first in a land that is not hers by heritage, she refers to another location as home, a place that will later actively reject her precisely because of her participation in its failed imperialist policy. This ironic turn of history produces a writing subject who negotiates shifting grounds of belonging and identification. In her memoir, Kuramoto focuses on the lives of family and friends, a strategy that achieves several objectives: it allows her to portray the colonists also as victims of imperial ambition they may not have totally supported and it presents the unofficial stories of the colonization of Manchuria.

The central narrative of *Manchurian Legacy* begins in 1944, when Kazuko is seventeen, about to finish her studies, though she intersperses memories of her childhood years into the chronicle of her growing awareness of the unjust system she had been born into. Though the text technically moves beyond her childhood, I read it as a Childhood from a psychological perspective: Kuramoto's late teen years mark, more than just a normal transition from childhood to adulthood, a more complicated psychological passage from one world view to another, which includes the devastating realization that her world was based on an oppressive imperialist system. This autobiography marks an important moment of change from an innocent idealized childhood to an adulthood marked by the destruction of the paradigms that framed the past. In that sense, we can consider this text a Childhood, though the actual age of the protagonist is that of a teenager and young adult. Interestingly, the discrete incidents of her childhood stress the idealized and almost unreal nature of that period, such as Kuramoto's memory of evening playtime with her father or the Chinese merchants who would come with their wares to their house.

Kuramoto explores the depth of her oblivion to the real situation in Manchuria. In one notable incident, she sings the only Chinese song she knows— the national anthem of Manchuria—to two Chinese friends and becomes confused and indignant when they get upset. Her astonishment at their reaction —why they didn't feel as patriotic hearing the Manchurian anthem as she did hearing the Japanese one?—makes her reconsider her position and recall her cousin's explanation that what really existed between Japan and Manchuria "was not brotherhood but mere military coercion" (38). Her naïve romance with patriotism, the idea of "self-sacrifice, total dedication, honor, and the possibility of the ultimate heroic death . . . touched the root of [her] romantic nature" (5). At one point, during a conversation with her cousin about the situation of Manchuria and Korea, she passionately defends Dairen as her home and Japan as her ethnic identity because of blood. He responds, "It means only that you think you love Japan, because you've been taught to love Japan, or because the adults around you talk of Japan with such reverence and attachment. And you think you believe in Japan because you've been taught to believe in Japan. You see, Kaz-chan, you are only what you've been taught to be" (25). This perspective shocks her, but opens her eyes to the contradictions her family lived. She realizes that her father is himself "frightened" by "blind faith in military propaganda . . . innocent acceptance of Japanese supremacy" (35). Though she admits that he was "one of the proudest and most faithful Japanese men [she] knew," she perceives "the complexity that [his] generation lived through and died with: a combined sense of guilt and pride" (35). Kuramoto's description of the gap between her developing consciousness of what was really happening in the Pacific war and her emotional need to believe that, for example, the Kamikaze were "the promises of tomorrow's victory" (35) reveals the contradictions of history within an individual who needs to locate a place for herself.

As soon as Japan declares unconditional surrender, things change quickly: the Chinese raid their home in Furanten and the family, along with all the other Japanese, are forced to return to Dairen, where they are no longer welcome. Crucial incidents make Kazuko aware of how her position in the world has changed. When her Japanese professor of Chinese informs her that they have lost the right to live in Dairen, her world shatters: *"I was born here. I am a native of Dairen,"* she whispers in agony (73). When they finally return to Japan, they are referred to as *hiki-age-sha* (the repatriates), "as if [they] were of another race, not 'real' Japanese" (118); she realizes they do not share Japan's history of suffering during the war and the bombs at Hiroshima and Nagasaki, just as the mainland Japanese ignore the colonialist's horror stories in Manchuria. Kazuko's growing sense of alienation leads her to take a drastic step: live with an American and eventually marry him. Her consciousness of the impossibility of belonging in Japan makes her conclude that a more radical relocation is necessary: "I knew I was a misfit in Japan. I had known it since my first step on Japanese soil in Sasebo. . . . I did not want to turn back and conform to a culture in which I knew I would not belong. I had no choice but to go ahead with this one direction open to me. Marry John. And get out of this whole mess and disappear into the land of freedom called America" (146). The decision is wrong from the start, but Kazuko uses it to obtain a passport to the United States and her notion of freedom, which includes renouncing, as soon as she obtains an American passport, her Japanese citizenship.

The author highlights her Childhood's didactic purpose. She writes that she felt the need to tell her story when, working with teenagers in the United States, she recalled her own childhood and became aware of two things: first, that many mainstream Americans and Asian Americans did not know what had happened in the Pacific during and after World War II and second, that she realized that there were actually two streams in the Japanese diaspora of the late-nineteenth and early-twentieth centuries, the move from Japan to the United States and Canada and those who went to Manchuria, like her grandparents. Significantly, she recalls, "while those who came to America suffered prejudice and injustice, those who went to Manchuria practiced prejudice and injustice against the native Chinese in Manchuria. The price for this injustice was high, and many paid for it later with their lives. The irony of all of this struck me. I had a story to tell the American public" (xi). Kuramoto's Childhood does not make a bid for pity, but strives to promote understanding by recounting her own confusion and misguided attempts at finding a place for herself in a third place: not Manchuria nor Japan, but the United States. She uses the memoir to think through her story and come to terms with a past composed of palimpsestic layers of belonging and location.

Of the writers considered in this study, Richard Kim was probably the most well known before writing his memoir.[19] Lost Names was actually solicited from Kim by Praeger, who planned a series of books on different countries, much in the same way that Lothrop, Lee, & Shepard, Co. had began publishing the "When I Was a Boy in" series a century before. Kim's idea was to introduce Korean culture through family life, but recalling his experiences soon gave the text an unexpected turn, transforming a cultural text into a personal one. The publishing house allowed him to write what he needed, and the text is an outstanding literary document that negotiates crucial transitions of boyhood and nationhood.[20]

Lost Names is episodic, written in the form of a short story cycle—independent but interdependent short stories—similar to Hilary Tham's Lane with No Name. This form allows Kim to select and narrate those memories that most directly reveal specific ideas. The first story, focalized through his mother, narrates the young family's escape into Manchuria, when Kim is only a year old. The story of the perilous crossing of the frozen Tuman River to Manchuria, where Kim's parents will work as teachers at a Christian school, symbolizes the family's resistance to adversity. In a sense, the story may be read as a valedictory to his brave mother, whose pride and determination helped to get them across into safety, after his father had been interrogated by the Japanese Military Police who were suspicious of their leaving Korea.

The second story, "Homecoming," begins with Kim's account of starting school back in Korea, after several years in Manchuria. The title is ironic: although they return because their grandfather needs their help with the household and orchard, the "home" they return to is not actually theirs—Korea was then being systematically stripped of its identity. When, on the first day of school, the teacher asks him to sing a song, he sings "Oh, Danny Boy," which he remembers from the farewell party hosted by the children of the missionaries in Manchuria. He then understands his liminal position: "and here I am, uprooted once again and transplanted into what was once ours but is no longer —an alien land that is not an alien land—finding myself cut off from my friends, forlorn, bewildered, and melancholy" (37). In this story, he also comes face to face with Japanese prejudice against Koreans, as well as the difficult association of the Japanese, Chinese, and Koreans. Most of the stories pivot around Kim's family life—the close relationships between his parents and grandparents, the Christian faith that gives them hope and fellowship, the blend of indulgence and irritation an older brother feels toward his little sister—as this contradicts with the increasing tension that the Japanese in Korea feel as the war comes to its dramatic close.

The eponymous story divides the narrative in two parts—the fourth of the seven stories, it marks a breaking point. Kim tells of arriving at school where the teacher insists on their having "new" names. The boy leaves in confusion to register: "my new name, my old name, my true name, my not-true name?" (99). His father takes him to the registry, along with others who proceed as though in mourning with black armbands around their sleeves. "We are a disgrace to our family," his grandfather says. "We bring disgrace and humiliation to your name. How can you forgive us!" (111). This event is clearly imprinted on Kim's memory. His father chooses the name Iwamoto, meaning "Rock-Foundation" (105), which the Japanese officials admire because of its reference to the mountains behind their house, but which the father selects because of its Biblical reference to the rock upon which the church is built. The father tells the son, "Remember it. Don't ever forget this day" (106). The son inscribes this memory: "today, I lost my name. Today, we all lost our names. February 11, 1940" (115).

The last three stories describe the growing desperation of the Japanese as they struggle to maintain control of the country—collecting rubber balls, having schoolboys build airstrips for Kamikaze planes that never come. The final story, "In the Making of History—Together," narrates the emperor's broadcast announcing Japan's surrender. The boy's grandfather pulls out a hidden Korean flag and flies it for the first time in thirty-six years; the people of the town, led by Kim's father, peacefully take over the police station and proclaim their liberation. The story is charged with emotion, as the people take control of their own destiny at last, and Kim's father can tell his son, "It is your world now" (195).[21]

Kim's perspective and positioning leads Robert Goar to note the essential humanism in all three of the writer's novels (The Martyred, The Innocent, and Lost Names). "There is a rich vein of humanism," Goar notes, "based on the author's belief in man's ability to overcome despair in himself and to heal the despair in others, to confront suffering and fear with courage and hope, to live under oppression courageously but without hatred for one's oppressor, and to refrain from violence against the oppressor when he has been defeated" (450). In this regard, for example, the relationships between the Japanese and Koreans, as well as between patriotic Koreans and those who supported the Japanese are presented in a nuanced manner. Montye Fuse argues that "the unifying theme of the memoir is the uncompromising resistance of Koreans to complete Japanese domination. . . . Korean resistance, especially Kim's own personal struggles and those of his family, serves as a backbone for the text and challenges the reader's expectations that childhood remembrances should consist of more pleasant stuff" (161). The complicated acceptance of the realities of colonization and the choices the Koreans made for their own survival lie at the bottom of much of the conflict, narrated from the point of view of a young boy. The question of the Koreans' pride in their country, culture, and ancestry lies behind their frustration at not having been able to resist colonization. The three generations that experienced colonization all lived it differently, and the two older ones look to the youngest one with shame and hope. As Kim's father tell the boy: "I am ashamed to look in your eyes. . . . Someday, your generation will have to forgive us" (*Lost Names* 110).[22] There is no real anti-Japanese sentiment in *Lost Names;* we feel a stronger sense of frustration on the part of the Koreans, perhaps for their perceived failure in resisting colonization or combating oppression.

Kim's engagement with the issue of language in the book reveals an important aspect of childhood memories of war. As he narrates the consequences of the Japanese occupation of Korea, he stresses the imposition of the Japanese language, specifically the replacement of Korean names with Japanese ones. Notably, Kim does not print a single Korean word in the narrative—no proper names are used (persons are identified by their roles, such as "teacher," "father," "grandmother," "store owner" or on occasion, by nicknames like "Pumpkin" or "Chopstick"), nor familial terms of endearment, nor words for food, which are described rather than identified—to textually illustrate the loss of a language. He therefore enacts the consequences of language prohibition and demonstrates how the process of subjectivity involves a negotiation with language. This narrative strategy effectively underlines the loss that the Koreans experienced under colonization, and how empty a text (by extension, a world) becomes when the specificities of language are erased.

The texts analyzed in this chapter offer multiple versions of life in Asia, negotiating the intersection of ethnicity, political positioning, and children's culture in ways that allow readers to appreciate historical contingencies and personal choices. They also give the Asian American community stories that acquire life in the context of American publishing. Their role as promoters of cultural understanding and collective memory, as well as critical interventions in the development of the genre of life writing should not be underestimated. In the next chapter, I will continue to read narratives set in Asia, but within the specific context of cultural revolutions and Communist invasions, texts which provide a distinct approach to history and to the forging of cultural and collective memory.

Chapter 3

● **Cultural Revolutions and Takeovers**

War as Structure

$\downarrow$

Specific events in Asian history of the twentieth century have acquired important visibility in the American collective consciousness, such as the Cultural Revolution in China, the Vietnam War, and the Khmer Rouge takeover of Cambodia. Understandably, the number of biographical, autobiographical, and fictional texts and movies on these events has heightened their prominence in the American scene, leading us, once more, to appreciate the cultural work they enact in the process of raising awareness of history and inviting comprehension toward the persons who have become dislocated as a direct result of that history. In the context of autobiographical writing, books on these experiences invite us to reconsider the unique cultural effect that numerous texts on the same subject might produce.

Reading Autobiographies Collectively

John Downton Hazlett's *My Generation: Collective Autobiography and Identity Politics* proposes a useful reading of texts that focus on experiences considered collective, a phenomenon he calls "generational autobiography." Although he centers on American generational autobiographies, a concern tangential to my study of the Asian North American Childhood, his theoretical formulation is helpful. Hazlett explains that these texts—which emphasize a sense of kinship with one's generational group over other forms of affiliation such as gender or race—demonstrate that autobiography's traditional individualism does not invalidate a collective conception of the self (4). When a cultural position or a political experience structures a life writing exercise to the extent that the personal story is fundamentally determined by that frame, we can speak of a particular kind of autobiography, one that tests the limits of the representation of individuality and collectivity. Hazlett deploys José Ortega y Gasset's ideas on generations to support the validity of these assumptions. Ortega suggests that the concept of a generation is partially determined by the length of the stages of the average life cycle: childhood (1–15), youth (15–30), initiation (30–45), dominance (45–60), and old age (60–75); each of these stages represents a generation. Importantly, Ortega notes that each of these generations is marked by a "vital sensibility," a partial result of a shared historical experience possible only among contemporaries (qtd. in Hazlett 11).

The Childhoods in this chapter negotiate those paradigms—read together, they represent important generational experiences, stressing the collective nature of autobiography. For obvious reasons, the collective aspect of Asian North American texts supports the cultural work of creating a reader, as they validate historical experiences that created the current communities. In any case, the experience of presenting and/or reading life writing texts collectively has been a generalized practice in ethnic studies. Anthologies such as Wesley Brown and Amy Ling's *Visions of America: Personal Narratives from the Promised Land,* Vickie Nam's *Yell-Oh Girls: Emerging Voices Explore Culture, Identity, and Growing Up Asian American,* or Luisa Igloria's *Not Home, But Here: Writing from the Filipino Diaspora,* among others, unite texts on specific experiences or from similar perspectives. These volumes stress the individual within the collective, making important cultural statements by articulating a plurality of perspectives on a unified theme. A recent anthology of short transcultural memoirs of childhood titled *Unrooted Childhoods: Memoirs of Growing Up Global,* edited by Faith Eidse and Nina Sichel, proposes another viewpoint that connects with my project, as the editors collect narratives on the theme of travel and displacement in memoirs of childhood.

The proliferation of collected autobiographical writing attests to an interest in textually linking experiences. This makes readers conscious of the shifting boundaries between the individual and the collective, focusing attention on how personal narratives elucidate particular shared histories. Jeremy Popkin also suggests that reading anthologies of autobiographies by academics illuminates social and intellectual history, making the autobiography resonate on multiple levels. Citing various authors, he notes how consciousness of autobiography as a social act in dialogue with other individuals or the experience of a generation or social group nuances the production and reception of these texts (781). Though Popkin explores anthologies of autobiographical projects, with its attendant issues of editorial ideology, selection, and contextualization, and therefore a strategy that does not relate to the texts I examine in this chapter, I believe his work clarifies the cultural implications of the existence of groups of autobiographies that are most often read together, either by design or due to specific personal or cultural interests.[1]

The four Childhoods discussed in this chapter reveal contrasting or complementary experiences framed by the same historical events. They may be read as generational or collective autobiographies because they share a timeframe and have as the governing structure of the account specific political situations. The first two, Rae Yang's *Spider Eaters: A Memoir* and Da Chen's *Colors of the Mountain,* are set during China's Cultural Revolution but recount the events from opposite perspectives: Yang becomes a Red Guard and participates actively in promoting the Revolution while Chen is a victim of the ostracism that Yang and her colleagues practiced. These contrasting perspectives on the same event, as with the Childhoods by Kuramoto and Kim, stress the individual experience within collective history. The contradictory character of these memoirs offers plural perspectives of childhoods during a time of extraordinary political, social, and cultural upheaval.

Next, the Childhoods by Loung Ung and Chanrithy Him, *First They Killed My Father* and *When Broken Glass Floats,* respectively, offer complementary accounts of the Khmer Rouge takeover of Cambodia. I suggest that a collective reading of these texts operate a renewed strategy in the formation of cultural memory—the shared character of these narratives multiplies the effect of the experience within the community. The individual narrators/protagonists of the texts come to represent the group, precisely because their experiences complement each other so significantly.

Cultural Revolutions and Child Revolutionaries

The Cultural Revolution has produced a body of work that gives us access to the experience of what we might call a "collective self," an entity composed of individuals who experienced the same events at a certain age in a certain place. In a sense, these texts have made the Cultural Revolution the defining experience of modern Chinese history for Americans and Asian Americans, in a manner similar to the way the Holocaust may be considered the defining experience of modern Jewish history. The number of texts on the Cultural Revolution has converted it into a structural myth in life writing. This emphasizes the shared nature of the experience as a crucial element to the forging of a particular worldview and narrative choice. Interestingly, in a context where persons were forced to write autobiographical "confessions" in order to "repent" for their transgressions against the government, the proliferation of autobiographical narratives written from a position of freedom of speech subverts the earlier exercise in superlative ways. Though these writers are now "free" to write what they want and present their life stories in multiple ways, the dehumanizing nature of the Cultural Revolution required them to engage the Revolution itself as a structuring component. The autobiographers who write within this context commit to the act of self-narrating as a strategy for selfhood because the previous autobiographical writing served to erase, rather than promote, individual subjectivity.

Yet, I argue that more than with other childhood memoirs, life writing about the Cultural Revolution and the Communist invasion of Cambodia—my concerns in this chapter—needs to highlight the place of the individual within the collective. Though the quantity of texts on these experiences invites us to read the history collectively, we must not elide the most important point in autobiographical writing: the centrality of the person, made more urgent in these cases by the previously imposed obliteration of the individual in favor of the collective. Autobiographies by subjects who experienced Communist revolutions and takeovers appropriate the form precisely to reclaim the subjectivity they were denied and in order to exercise the authority to write their own histories.

The Cultural Revolution structures numerous autobiographical and fictional texts, including Nien Cheng's emblematic *Life and Death in Shanghai*, Liu Binyan's *A Higher Kind of Loyalty*, Jung Chang's *Wild Swans: Three Daughters of China*, and Anchee Min's *Red Azalea: Life and Love in China*. Among the Childhoods that center on this experience are Liang Heng and Judith Shapiro's *Son of the Revolution*, Jaia Sun-Childers and Douglas Childers' *The White-Haired Girl: Bittersweet Adventures of a Little Red Soldier*, Yang's *Spider Eaters*, Chen's *Colors of the Mountain*, and Ji-Li Jiang's *Red Scarf Girl: A Memoir of the Cultural Revolution*.[2] Reading diverse versions of this experience shows how similar historical events affected persons of different social class, location, and education. Sun-Childers and Yang experienced the Cultural Revolution, in a sense, from the inside. As members of upper-class educated families living in large cities, they threw themselves into Mao's cause, renouncing their families, working in labor camps and pig farms. They had a strong sense of a mission to fulfill, which made their eventual disillusionment more tragic.

Yang's text, in particular, engages her trajectory in complex ways. This Childhood records Yang's life from her early years as the daughter of Chinese diplomats in Switzerland, to her girlhood at an elite middle school in Beijing, to her adolescent experience as a Red Guard and later as a worker on a pig farm in the remote northern wilderness. Her parents, Communist Intellectuals, were denounced by the anti-Rightist campaigns of the 1950s. During the Cultural Revolution of the 1960s, she traveled as a Red Guard, proudly spreading Revolutionary doctrine and denouncing adults that she considered counterrevolutionary. She describes the first violent months of the Cultural Revolution as the most horrifying and exhilarating of her life, as she espoused Mao's doctrine that teachers should learn from their students and parents listen to their children: at this time, she realizes with glee, "heaven and earth were turned upside down" (118). With a teenager's absolute certainty in her own legitimacy, she and her fellow revolutionaries punished members of their families, their teachers, their political leaders, and anyone who seemed to counter Mao's vision. The beginning of the Cultural Revolution gave her "a feeling of superiority and confidence . . . never experienced before" (118). The extraordinary characteristic of this memoir is that Yang does not portray herself as a passive victim of the Cultural Revolution; she acknowledges her role as perpetrator and oppressor, a warrior willing to destroy in the name of the revolution. Though she now recognizes the atrocities she committed during that period, she honestly recounts how, with her companions, she raided houses, brutally interrogated, beat up, and even killed one of the men they were punishing.

The violent nature of Yang's account is balanced by the loving remembrance of her family and the persons who nurtured her: her grandmother, for example, who dies as a result of political persecution, and her nanny, from whom she learned Chinese myths, legends, and folklore. Yang acknowledges her connection to a lineage that she struggles to deny during her revolutionary stage, even as it continues to draw her back to the basis of her selfhood. Because of this, her narrative voice hovers between two binaries: her political commitment to the Maoist revolution and her position as a daughter and granddaughter who needs to belong to a family. She blends these personal and political contentions through her recollections of diverse events, positioned in the text in parallel ways. Yang's memoir is loaded with the questions she retrospectively asks herself, giving the narrative an important interrogatory tone. Her narrative juxtaposes italicized segments meant to show her thoughts and feelings at the time the events were unfolding, in contrast to her understanding of the events in hindsight, emphasizing the difference between the focalizing child and the narrating adult.

She describes in ironic detail her process of self-conviction when, for example, a teacher encourages the students to participate in a campaign called "Exposing the Third Layer of Thoughts," defined as "the most dangerous . . . like a cancer hidden inside you" that will proliferate if kept a secret (97). This campaign leads her, at the age of fourteen, to her first "thought struggle," significantly the first time she inscribes her inner thoughts: *what should I do? Should I write them down and hand the report to the political teacher or should I hide them from him? If I hide them, am I hiding something from the Party? But if I am honest, I will incriminate myself. It is a foolish thing to do!"* (98, italics in original). But her dedication to the Revolution wins at this point, capturing her imagination, her dreams, and her future. In the chapter "Semi-Transparent Nights," for example, she describes how she renamed herself Red Army and tried to transform herself into the first revolutionary generation by walking the entire route of the Long March. As Kate Gilbert explains, "She is able to make the reader feel the child's passionate need to use her body recklessly to create an authentic 'political' self. She is also able, through the ironic reflection that creates the underlying structure of the whole book, to show us the hollowness of the political and cultural milieu that made emulation and self-immolation, rather than innovation, the only authentic political self toward which she could aspire" (1).

Yang perceives binaries through conflicting events that invalidate the distinction between victim and victimizer, aristocrat and peasant, Communist and counterrevolutionary. Her growing confusion even leads her, at one point, to contemplate suicide. The issue of women's positions disturbs her: even in the ostensibly egalitarian Communist Party, she notes how women were regarded as *jiashu* (stinking dependent), so that they had no right to the same wages as men. Her actions during her period as a Red Guard may be read as her revenge on those who imposed what she considered unjust formality or undeserving hierarchy.

The specific achievement of this Childhood lies in the manner in which Yang describes the lure of the political for an idealistic girl and her slow fall into the truth. The author honestly portrays how Chairman Mao's emotional demands for revolutionary fervor structured her life, leaving her to reconstruct an entire system of beliefs when she finally arrives at absolute disillusionment. Yang proceeds from thinking that she loved Chairman Mao more than her parents to a gradual recognition that the Cultural Revolution was a tremendous waste and unprecedented human tragedy because the true class struggle in China was being waged by corrupt bureaucrats against the Chinese people, who used the idealism of youth to propagate their personal aims. "We were deceived and used by a bunch of dishonest politicians," she states, recognizing that the revolutionary slogans were "empty talk and hateful lies" (217–218). Eventually, leaving the pig farm she was working at, she travels back to Beijing, is reunited with her parents, studies English, and obtains a scholarship to the University of Massachusetts.

Yang makes Chinese history the backdrop to her personal story; by writing the Childhood, she personalizes public history and defends her version's authenticity. She also gives readers an intimate account of the experiences of thousands of young people in the rural areas, particularly in the great northern wilderness, which widens perspectives on the experience of the Cultural Revolution. Gilbert defines the Childhood as a political memoir because Yang aims to "show how the passions of the political realm and the specific incidents of Chinese history have shaped her life" (1).

But Yang's strategy makes her text more than merely a political memoir. Her choice of the genre of the Childhood makes her dialogue with an existing tradition and process. As she moves between past and present, her fantasy life and harsh reality, nightmares and decisions, she conveys the richness of Chinese history and culture, as well as her own confusion when faced with the imperative to destroy the Four Olds that represent the past. The book's title gestures toward her commitment: the term "spider eater," coined by Lu Xun (1881–1936), refers to those unknown ancestral heroes who, having tried eating something poisonous (in her case, the Cultural Revolution), have left us a record of their actions as a warning. She admits, in the end, "I and my peers are the one who ate spiders. Long before we did, my parents and their peers had eaten spiders too. The spiders tasted bad. They were poisonous. Nevertheless, in my case, they became a bitter medicine. . . . The spiders I ate made my head cooler and my eyes brighter. Because of them, I cherish freedom and value human dignity. I have become more tolerant of different opinions. Lies, big and small, cannot easily hypnotize me" (284–285). Yang's Childhood attempts to recreate what she inadvertently destroyed: the narrative becomes an artifact that substitutes the stories of many that were lost.

Chen's narrative counters Yang's in many ways. His perspective is that of the victim, the village boy who, because his family had been landowners, found himself facing a dead end: he was mistreated in school and not permitted to continue his education beyond a certain point. Born in 1962, the Year of the Great Starvation, Da Chen says that this coincidence left "a permanent flaw in my character: I was always hungry" (3). His hunger refers to not only a craving for food, but also for a more spiritual nourishment that comes from education and culture, precisely the elements the Cultural Revolution denied people like Chen. The author succinctly describes his family's situation in the first chapter: his father is fired from his teaching job and sent to a labor camp and they are stripped of their property. One year, they eat moldy yams three times a day for four months and their grandfather spends weeks detained in a commune jail, waiting for public humiliation meetings. The family is targeted by those who resented their former privileges, and Da finds himself at a loss. When his repeated efforts to get to school are frustrated, he feels "defeated, poor, and pathetic" (13), impotent against the system that seems to enjoy working against his family.

In the context of increasing oppression against his family, education becomes for Da "the key to a bright future. I knew if I could somehow stay in school, I would do well. There was hope" (22). When the regime announces that the children of "landlords, capitalists, rich farmers and the leftists" would no longer be allowed to go to school, his determination to continue and succeed increases (21). Chen's Childhood centers on this struggle: his efforts to acquire an education against the dictates of the authorities. He sees his older brothers and sisters forced to leave school to work on farms and doubles his determination to remain in school. But the schoolteacher ignores him and his repeated efforts to win the teacher's attention only result in being told to write out a confession for anti-Party actions. Chen's account of the options offered to him would be ludicrous if they did not echo what other texts on the Cultural Revolution describe.

Eventually, the boy has no choice but to leave school, at which point he finds himself enrolled in an alternative educational system with some older boys who take to him as a sort of pet. These boys are themselves alienated from society and they teach Da how to smoke and drink and live by his wits, engaging in contraband. The description of this group of friends is humorous, their fellowship similar to those of gangs of outlaws from Westerns. Da, having been rejected by the little Red Guards, finds acceptance from those also alienated—illustrating ironic levels of separation from the norm. Ultimately, the boy manages to get the education he seeks so avidly: "I shone, despite their efforts to snuff me out" (42).[3] Against the odds, and after numerous setbacks, he achieves an education, learning also to play the violin and speak English. When Mao dies in 1976, the educational system begins to function again and Da gets a chance to return to school and apply for a place at the university, which he and his brother win.[4]

Chen's *Colors of the Mountain* is remarkably well constructed on many levels. Firstly, the cover of the book makes explicit statements about the act of autobiography. The most prominent feature on the cover is the Chinese character "*zao*," which means "to make, invent, manufacture, or fabricate." This character bears no relation to the title of the text, but alludes to its theme—a boy who remakes himself out of incredible adversity—and also refers directly to the act of creating the text itself, or to the subject of the text "inventing" or "creating" himself in the act of writing. Moreover, the sound character that means "to tell, report, or inform," again a direct allusion to the act of recounting a life, stresses the narrative element of the autobiographical act.[5] The children on the cover of the book are reading a text, signaling both the protagonist's desire for an education and the text as a manufactured product.[6]

Secondly, where Yang's text is poetic and complex, Chen's is informal, straightforward, and humorous. He maintains narrative tension without falling into cheap pathos. Finally, Chen's autobiography acknowledges his American implied reader in many ways. The struggle to possess English becomes crucial to Da precisely because it signifies a passport to a better life and, although the narrative is set entirely in Communist China, English represents the American dream of success. Though his attempts to learn English are pivotal in fulfilling his dream, in the text itself, Chen takes his mastery of the language a step beyond the believable. Chen's prose is loaded with American slang, making the reading informal, occasionally anachronistic, and surprising, as when he calls his parents Mom and Dad, speaks of his teacher Mr. Sun as a man who had "a sunny personality and was an outdoors kind of a guy" (15), decides with friends that "we better get our fat asses out of here quickly, before the cops bother us" (84), or refers to himself as a "born-again good guy" (253). This strategy, unfortunately, draws too much attention to itself, making the reader conscious of the writer's attempt to connect with a specific public. Yet, this reveals how important it is for many of these writers to identify with their readers and the community that will receive the text.

Yang and Chen's Childhoods exhibit the two binary positions that marked the Chinese Cultural Revolution from the perspective of victims of bureaucratic machinations for power. In important ways, as with the following texts, these stories highlight the surprising resilience of children who overcome war and the destruction of families. The existence of their autobiographies demonstrates a creative way of dealing with that trauma of childhood, as a gesture toward healing and to connect with a community that shares this history. By articulating strategies for survival—personal resolution and textual inscription—these writers give themselves another chance to begin again.

Invasions

Though the experience of war in Asia figured prominently in the Childhoods discussed earlier, two narratives in particular position their child narrators in the middle of extremely traumatic wartime experiences. In Ung's *First They Killed My Father* and Him's *When Broken Glass Floats*, personal accounts of the Communist takeover of Cambodia provide the story's structure.[7] Here, the historical events order the plot, such that the children are, in singular ways, acted upon rather than deciding actors in their own stories. More than in other narratives, where family decisions direct the children's lives, in these stories of war, control is wrested from families and the fate of the children falls into the hands of whoever controls the political scene at the moment. In the midst of the destruction caused by the wars that Ung and Him experience, their autobiographies of childhood may be read as their attempt to control, if not the past, then the narrativization of the past. When the past has been so exceptionally shattering—both Childhoods highlight the loss of family members, the separation of the nuclear and extended family, the experience of being refugees and of forced immigration—the need to control the past by writing it becomes more imperative.

Ung and Him's works dialogue significantly with the numerous texts about Cambodia that have been produced in recent years. There are intertextual references to other narratives about Cambodia in both texts, and both authors acknowledge their personal investment in aiding Cambodians in the United States. The most notable case is that of the 1984 film *The Killing Fields* based on the life of Cambodian journalist Dith Pran, who later coedited a collected volume titled *Children of Cambodia's Killing Fields: Memoirs by Survivors*. Him recounts in the preface to her Childhood how viewing the film was a cathartic experience—"For the first time in years, I had allowed myself to feel the pain of the past that was buried in my soul" (17)—that allowed her to creatively rethink her own experience and come to terms with it. Indeed, Haing Ngor, the actor who portrayed Pran, has himself cowritten an autobiography of his experience titled *Survival in the Killing Fields*. The influx of refugees from Cambodia and the efforts to help them adjust make the existence and reception of these texts important.

In their Childhoods, Ung and Him describe the prewar situation nostalgically as an ideal time in a happy place. As Coe notes, "The vision of paradise lost, then, only becomes truly powerful as a motivation when it is given life and intensity by some other force, when it is something more positive than mere regret or homesickness for the unattainable—in fact, when it is felt as the source of something supremely valuable or significant in the present" (*When the Grass* 62). Both Ung and Him highlight the memory of warm family ties, recall comfortable economic situations, and describe themselves as contented children. This orderly existence then contrasts more dramatically with the swift loss of family and home, the disruption of the harmony that had previously governed their lives. In addition, because both Ung and Him have left their countries and, indeed, the homeland they recall no longer exists, their Childhoods function as powerful documents that recapture that past and make it present. These texts serve as important tools for the development of cultural memory and as a way of unveiling the cruelties to persons—and children in particular—during the Communist takeover of Cambodia.

Both these texts must be analyzed in the context of what has been called "literature of trauma" by critics such as Leigh Gilmore and Kalí Tal.[8] Gilmore notes that the defining moment in autobiographical writing in the 1990s has been trauma—a deeply distressing experience that radically alters a person's perceptions on the world—resulting in a shift away from the autobiographies of "elder statesmen" toward "young" lives and alternative histories ("Limit-Cases" 128). Tal explains, "Trauma is enacted in a liminal state, outside of the bounds of 'normal' human experience, and the subject is radically ungrounded. Accurate representation of trauma can never be achieved without recreating the event since, by its very definition, trauma lies beyond the bounds of 'normal' conception. Textual representations—literary, visual, oral—are mediated by language and do not have the impact of the traumatic experience" (15).[9] Moreover, she continues, literature of trauma "holds at its center the reconstruction and recuperation of the traumatic experience, but it is also actively engaged in an ongoing dialogue with the writings and representations of non-traumatized authors" and is written from "the need to tell and retell the story of the traumatic experience, to make it 'real' both to the victim and to the community. Such writing serves both as validation and cathartic vehicle for the traumatized author" (17). This contextualization of literature of trauma expands the paradigms of Asian North American writing by highlighting the intersection of diverse perspectives from which we read specific texts. In these Childhoods by Ung and Him, therefore, the tension between nostalgic memory of an ideal period of childhood and the traumatic memory of the events that obliterated that childhood support the development of collective memory for the diasporic Cambodian community.

The plots of Ung and Him's Childhoods are identical: both begin describing their family lives—idealized representations shadowed by the threat of ominous change. Also, both writers include a map of Cambodia and chart a family tree, attesting to their connection with a country and their location in a family. A historical-didactic intent may be perceived as these maps help readers situate the story and, importantly, the forced successive relocations of the characters. The authors also include specific details about the historical circumstances of the war, with dates and details.

Ung's account is strictly chronological: her chapter titles include dates—month and years and even one specific day, "April 17, 1975"—which firmly fixes the narrative in historical time. Five years pass between the beginning of the Childhood in April 1975 to the end in February 1980; an undated epilogue summarizes several years of Ung's life in the United States. The first two chapters locate Ung as one of the younger daughters of a high-ranking government official in Phnom Penh, living a comfortable middle-class life. The author uses the child perspective to dramatize the absolute normality of her life at the age of five: her parents—"Ma is known for her beauty, Pa is loved for his generous heart" (4)—are charmingly idealized; she knows she is a pretty child, although her mother is often frustrated at her inquisitive, tomboyish ways; her father has told her that her name, Loung, translates into "dragon" in a Chinese dialect, an animal that is "powerful and wise and can often see into the future" (10); her six brothers and sisters. Things change for Ung in a day: "yesterday I was playing hopscotch with my friends. Today we are running from soldiers with guns" (27). The phrase she uses on several occasions to describe the Communists comes from her father—they are "destroyers of things" (18, 27), referring first to the soldiers' use of old tires for sandals, but later to their systematic annihilation of an entire community, society, way of life. Most importantly, Ung's childhood itself is annihilated. She then narrates in detail how the family is forced to leave the city and their situation, as well as that of millions of others, grows progressively worse—they live for a time in a small village with an uncle and his family until they are forced to leave and wander from village to village at the Khmer Rouge's whim for months. Each relocation lowers their status: from city dwellers to peasants, from well-fed educated people to emaciated victims of the Angkar's complicated rules, from slave laborers to child soldiers.

Ung's story narrates her rapid loss of innocence as she becomes aware of what the family needs to do to survive. At the age of five, she learns that "from now on I have to watch out for myself. Not only am I never to talk to anyone about our former lives, but I'm never to trust anyone either. . . . I am beginning to know what loneliness feels like, silent and alone and suspecting that everyone wants to hurt me" (47). One of the recurring tropes in the memoir is hunger—her descriptions of food, her longing for food, and the desperation that leads her to steal some uncooked rice from the family's secret hoard. These sections of the Childhood are among the most heart-wrenching of any of the autobiographies analyzed in this book: Ung's dramatization of the dwindling portions at mealtimes and her attempts to make the rice soup last attest to the vividness of that pain. In addition, she describes how the family slowly starves to death—"Hunger, always there is hunger" (81)—after eating everything edible, rotten leaves, rats, roots, turtles, grasshoppers.

The title of Ung's book, *First They Killed My Father,* is not really accurate. After narrating the family's downslide, she begins in the twelfth chapter, "Keav, August 1976," to narrate the true horror of the experience: the progressive deaths of family members. Her oldest sister, Keav, succumbs to food poisoning while at a work camp and dies first; their father is then taken away by soldiers and killed. At this point, the changes in the child become more manifest. Though her mother continues to hope that their father lives, Ung's heart hardens and she rejects this option. "To hope is to let pieces of myself die," she convinces herself. "To hope is to grieve his absence and acknowledge the emptiness of my soul without him." The child begins to hate for the first time, focusing her rage on Pol Pot for making her "hate so deeply" (108) and on the gods who do not bring her father back. At one point, her mother understands that she needs to send the children away in order to keep them alive—"if we stay together, we will die together" (121). Their mother keeps the youngest, Geak, who has stopped growing from malnutrition. Three children—twelve-year-old Kim, ten-year-old Chou, and seven-year-old Loung—leave for a work camp, where they claim to be orphans and choose new names to protect their family. The anger their mother provokes in order to force them to leave allows them to survive the inevitable: Ma and Geak are taken from the village and shot. Loung later goes to another camp to learn to be a soldier, where she also trains as a dancer, works in the rice fields, and is taught to shoot. Training as a soldier develops her hatred, and her imaginary world becomes increasingly marked by violence.

The invasion of Vietnam changes the situation radically and Ung reunites with her brother and sister as they make their way to a displaced people's camp where they find their two oldest brothers. The descriptions of returning to a semblance of normal life is filled with sensory images that illustrate vividly the deprivations of the earlier life. Ung's first colored clothes after years of wearing standard black Khmer pants is emblematic of the change: "[my aunt] puts me in a shirt and pants the color of a blue sky. The clothes shimmer as they touch my skin softly, making me feel nice and light—transformed!" (212).

Eventually, her oldest brother, Meng, decides to immigrate to Vietnam, escape to a refugee camp in Thailand, and later the United States, with his wife. They take Loung with them, leaving the other siblings in the care of their uncle. In the final chapter, Meng and his wife prepare Loung for the trip they will take and the story ends with the family boarding the plane with the child carrying with her the memory of her father.

The epilogue, framed by the chronicle of Ung's first journey back to Cambodia as an adult, narrates her attempts to immerse herself in American life even as she was haunted by nightmares of the war. Her obsession was to "make myself a normal American girl. I played soccer. I joined the cheerleading squad. . . . I'd hoped being Americanized would erase my memories of the war" (235–236). She even stopped writing to her sister Chou in an attempt to separate herself from that history.

The traumatic character of her experience may be divided into two categories. On the one hand, the real physical deprivation and early experience of death—of her family members and of countless others who died of malnutrition or were assassinated. On the other hand, and perhaps more significantly, she is traumatized by her early experience of hatred, mistrust, and the violence she recognizes herself capable of. Immersion in American culture—a different climate, language, culture—allows her to separate herself from what she had witnessed and the violent feelings associated with these experiences. But only through reconnection with that history, she eventually learns, can she overcome it. Her Childhood thus becomes a healing strategy. Her work with the Campaign for a Landmine-Free World is also liberatory: "as I tell people about genocide, I get the opportunity to redeem myself. I've had a chance to do something that's worth my being alive. It's empowering; it feels right. The more I tell people, the less the nightmares haunt me. The more people listen to me, the less I hate" (237). Returning to Cambodia becomes a final healing measure—revisiting the scene of her trauma and reuniting with her family allows her story to end.[10]

Him's narrative begins with a premonition of war when she is only three years old—her mother calling the children to see a comet one night: "*Mak* lifted me up and I saw the heavenly body with a starlike nucleus and a long, luminous tail. Its radiance was intensified by the dark sky and the surrounding stars. We were all in awe, crowded near our mother, leaning against the railing" (30). But this experience of beauty is offset by her mother's remembering a folk superstition: "when the tail of the comet pointed to a particular place, Cambodia would be drawn into war with that country" (30). Less than a year later, in 1969, the United States and South Vietnam invaded Cambodia to try and halt the Viet Cong, but only succeeded in driving the Viet Cong deeper into Cambodia. This Childhood opens seven years before Ung's and encompasses more time—from the time Him is three to her immigration to the United States at the age of sixteen. After this first episode of attack, the family settles into a peaceful life again—though two children die of illness due to lack of medical attention during the war, Him's mother bears two more sons and it appears that they have entered a period of normalcy. But this hiatus ends forever in 1975. Him also notes the date "April 17, 1975" as a crucial turning point in her life. She records two specific memories on the bombings that day: "I am nine years old. Never have I seen so much death" (60). She then describes the ghastly sight of the heap of dead soldiers, with swarms of flies gorging on the wounds. She notes then her awareness that things will no longer be the same: "tonight is a night of togetherness, the last wisp of freedom" (64).

The family's experiences after that first night echo Ung's: the flight to the countryside hounded by the Khmer Rouge, and subsequent relocations to worse places; the shedding of colorful clothes for regulation black pants and shirts; the obsession with hunger; children succumbing to malnutrition and illnesses like edema and malaria; forced labor; the haunting presence of death. Him's father is taken away for "orientation," forced to dig his own grave and killed with a hoe. Feelings of anger unnatural for a child invade Him: "along with sorrow come the companion feelings of frustration and anger. . . . I rage at the Khmer Rouge" (89–90). Her mother, weakened by starvation, malaria, and dysentery, is thrown into a well to die. Him watches four of her siblings succumb to illness and deals with the worsening situation by challenging herself emotionally—"*It can't be any worse. This is enough. They can do no more,*" words that were "a dare and a comfort" (106)—only to find that life could be limited even more to less food, less family, less freedom. The family eventually manages to leave the country, sponsored by an uncle in Oregon.

Him's narrative strategy is more richly multilayered than Ung's for several reasons. She manages to convey a stronger sense of Cambodian culture and of historical narrative. Importantly, she consistently notes the separation or juxtaposition between the public and the private, and how these might function independently or interdependently. She sets her recollections against official versions of the events by quoting from newspaper articles of the period as epigraphs for several of the chapters. This historiographical gesture makes personal memory of events in Cambodia resound against the impersonal reporting in American newspapers and journals such as *The New York Times* and *The Economist*. By juxtaposing simultaneous accounts, Him unites the personal with the collective and reminds readers that behind detached news reports about millions lie individual children's stories. This collation demonstrates the tension that exists between the versions of history that we receive and accept. There is textual evidence of her intention of preserving in the narrative not only her own story, but a country's history.

Him's Childhood focuses in detail on the nature of Cambodian cultural practices, again placing the human drama against a larger backdrop of a tradition being systematically annihilated. She emphasizes the links between language and culture, illustrating how Cambodian life—people and ways of living—was destroyed. She uses Cambodian terms more consistently than Ung does and manages to reproduce a strong cultural sense. For instance, Him uses the term *"Angka Leu"* (italicized) where Ung employs "Angkar," the more accepted English transliteration. This strategy allows the reader to grasp the emotional import of the Khmer Rouge's abolition of family and cultural connections for a people for whom family and tradition were paramount.[11] She includes the Cambodian terms for fruits and vegetables, quotes proverbs, and retells myths. She also inscribes Cambodian script, the English script equivalent, and a translation as though to preserve the tradition and pass it on to readers. In fact, the title of the Childhood, *When Broken Glass Floats,* comes from a Cambodian proverb about the nature of evil. Under the rule of the Khmer Rouge, the "broken glass" floated and only began to sink when they lost power. This poetic image becomes a balm that offers hope for the narrator.

Him conveys her childhood comprehension of the changes wrought by the Khmer Rouge through her perception of language. After explaining the importance of the respectful names and the development of family nicknames, she describes the first time she hears the word "comrade" and grasps its implications: "and these young soldiers, younger than the couple they're ordering about, don't use the proper courtesies in addressing elders, don't call them 'aunt' or 'uncle.' The way they speak to the couple suggests they consider themselves their equal. That's not the way we greet our elders, especially in a time of crisis. The lack of respect shocks me. Authority is reversed. Guns now mean more than age and wisdom" (67). This intelligent negotiation of the child's perspective focusing on a small issue—the use of respectful address—illustrates Him's process of understanding the changes in the country. This lack of respect symbolizes an escalating sense of violence, epitomized in a small detail that shocks a child because it destroys one of the systems that ordered her existence. Indeed, she notes that though the Khmer Rouge obliges them to change forms of address, she defends the meaning behind the tradition: "they may take our language from our family in public, but they can't take away the family itself, the bond that binds us. Our private words are our own" (101). This affirmation privileges the personal over the public and denotes a crucial scheme for psychological survival.

These childhood memoirs of surviving the Khmer Rouge highlight their narrators' resilience in the face of traumatic experiences and educate the American public on the history of thousands of immigrants who fled that war. Further, these autobiographies connect significantly with the particular causes their authors promote, reminding us how these texts function culturally and politically. In the case of Loung Ung, her autobiography of childhood significantly supports her work as National Spokesperson for the Campaign for a Landmine-Free World, a program of the Vietnam Veterans of America Foundation (VVAF).[12] Chanrithy Him is also actively involved in work related to the effects of war: since 1989 she has worked as a researcher on the Khmer Adolescent Project, studying post-traumatic stress disorder (PTSD) in Cambodian youth. She explains her dedication to this project—and the purpose behind the writing of her Childhood—in the following terms: "as a survivor, I want to be worthy of the suffering that I endured as a child. I don't want to let that pain count for nothing, nor do I want others to endure it. This may be our greatest test: to recognize the weight of war on children. . . . I also like to think that telling my story and assisting the PTSD studies are my way of avenging the Khmer Rouge" (20–21).

In his discussion on the structure of the genre, Coe notes that we frequently encounter Childhoods that have a double ending: "a clear-cut climax at the age of twelve or thirteen, followed by a long, dull, unspeakably painful period of adolescence; and then the gradual buildup to a second, more definitive climax some six or seven years after the first" (*When the Grass* 77). For the writers analyzed in this chapter, there exists the possibility of reading another ending of their stories in the production of the Childhood itself, particularly in the narratives where trauma figures as a defining experience. The healing potential of autobiographical acts is well known, but these texts suggest that the authors have chosen a literary path toward more than just personal recuperation. By engaging traumatic experiences and making readers aware of the silenced histories behind immigration, they promote intercultural understanding and support collective memory. Indeed, as Teri Shaffer Yamada points out, Ung and Him exemplify a path "from passive to active Cambodianness," enabling them to develop "an agency that involves a praxis of social change" (159).

Though the relationship between autobiography and collective history is complex, we can certainly argue that personal trajectories mirror group experiences, while accepting that collective identities are not necessarily the sum of individual experiences. Nonetheless, in the context of Asian North American writing and community formation, these texts support the preservation of cultural memory and also resonate with humanitarian issues, political interventions, and personal understanding of how history is created through stories remembered.

Chapter 4

● **The Liminal Childhood**

Biraciality as Narrative Position

While Childhoods by Asian subjects set primarily outside North America offer multilayered perspectives on issues of racial and cultural negotiations, texts narrated by biracial children complicate our views on the inscription of Asian experiences in both Asia and North America. The specific concern of this chapter, biracial autobiographies of childhood, evidence particular processes of liminality articulated through an established literary genre, which leads to a rethinking of racial and cultural affiliations. The manner in which Norman Reyes in *Child of Two Worlds,* Heinz Insu Fenkl in *Memories of My Ghost Brother,* Kien Nguyen in *The Unwanted,* and Michael David Kwan in *Things That Must Not Be Forgotten* negotiate their biraciality proposes a doubled strategy: first, the writers articulate a hybrid position that is increasingly common in Asian North American society but that has not yet received the creative and critical attention it merits; second, the reader must attend to questions of the intersection of genre and theme.

The question of biraciality for Asian North American writers acquires heightened prominence in the context of contemporary theories on race.[1] Issues of indeterminacy, location, identification, and affiliation direct the self-representation of persons who negotiate processes of racial ambivalence that exhausts the supposed fixity and impermeability of racial boundaries. Though we now understand "race" as a social or rhetorical model, rather than a biological determinate, the socially constructed status of "race" is complicated by the awareness of biraciality and the complex fictional and autobiographical engagements with this issue.[2] Importantly, as Jonathan Brennan claims, "an exploration of the world of mixed race identity both reinforces these essential categories of race and also provides one of the best opportunities to see the limitations and absurdity of racial categories" (7). Because race has traditionally been articulated in absolute (White/non-White) terms in North America, narratives dealing with the subject of mixed race characters oblige us to reexamine the discourse of race and its categories. Werner Sollors favors the need to acknowledge the "largely unrecognized scope of interracial literature" and by reviewing "some of its systemic qualities (the recurrences in various texts) as well as some of its historical unfoldings and transformations (represented in a few selected moments of revision, change, and rupture)" (29).

Eurasians have featured significantly in Anglo-American literature for more than a century, albeit in stereotypical terms that posited an uncomplicated binary between the "White" and the "Oriental." Moreover, as Elaine Kim affirms, "given the assumed biological incompatibility of the races, the dilemma of the Eurasian in Anglo-American literature is unresolvable. He must either accept life as it is, with its injustices and inequalities, or he must die" (*Asian American Literature* 9). The in-between position and tragic fate of the mixed race character molded generations of thinking about intermarriage and assimilation. Significantly, Helena Grice asserts, even Eurasian writing consistently highlights the failure to signify as either wholly Caucasian or Asian in negative terms because the biracial subject in question "defines herself as a non-member of either racial group, rather than as a member of both" (*Negotiating Identities* 142). Only when more contemporary biracial writers themselves began to examine their critical locations did we begin to acquire a wider perspective on the possibilities of representing this position.

The earliest Asian North American writing strove to convey a balanced perspective on biraciality. Edith Maud Eaton (Sui Sin Far) and her sister Winnifred Eaton (Onoto Watanna) deliberately created biracial characters in their stories and novels, providing uneven but fascinating portrayals. Indeed, the Eaton sisters both chose Asian pseudonyms in what Amy Ling suggests was a move to promote authenticity for writing careers based on ethnic themes (*Between Worlds* 21).[3] Contemporary criticism is unraveling the significance of their writing within specific cultural contexts, leading to further studies that analyze the forms through which biraciality may be performed. But this perspective evolved slowly: early autobiographical writing by biracial subjects unconsciously echoed the stereotypical binary imposed by Anglo-American criticism.

Paul Spickard observes that multiracial people of Asian descent in North America today take diverse approaches to ethnic identity, rarely identifying solely with one racial or ethnic category and adopting what Amy Iwasaki Mass calls "situational ethnicity." "They feel mainly White or Black or Latino (according to their mix)," Spickard asserts, "when among the White or Black or Latino relatives and friends, and act mainly Asian when among Asians" (50).[4] Recent autobiographies by biracial subjects provide discriminating visions of the individual's sense of positioning, accommodating this renewed fluidity.[5] In general, the question of a radical choice between one race or another no longer exists, and many of these texts contend that being mixed race is existentially real, imaginatively possible, and creative.

In the case of Claire Hsu Accomando's *Love and Rutabaga,* other concerns, specifically survival in World War II France, are more urgent than questions of racial positioning. Accomando, the daughter of a Chinese father and a French mother, writes about her four years in a rural French village. Her narrative opens in June 1941, with her father's departure from France to China after he had lost his job at the League of Nations in Switzerland, where Claire was born. The girl, her pregnant mother, and younger brother then move to Rahon to live with her maternal grandparents until the family can be reunited. This Childhood recounts the family's wartime experience and celebrates the heroic adults who not only fought for the cause of the resistance in France but also managed to spare the children the worst of the horror. Accomando rarely speaks of her biraciality, except in passing references to taunts by other children. She does refer to her family's Chinese connection—her maternal grandfather had spent years in China, spoke Mandarin, and they continued to possess many Chinese keepsakes—although her father is represented mostly as an absent person rather than a racialized presence.

In the texts I discuss in this chapter, the authors explore the shifting meanings of biraciality. As they narrate their childhood years, the evolving cultural, historical, and social climates of the countries they live in significantly modify local or "official" perspectives on race and mixed race children. This changing character of racial categorizations also illustrates evolving ideas on the acceptance of biraciality in North America.[6]

Recent literary criticism acknowledges the emergence of a critical vocabulary that privileges mixed race realities in the growing canon of ethnic life writing. Françoise Lionnet's perspective on *métissage* encourages negotiations with concepts in flux. *Métissage* becomes a password to articulating "new visions of ourselves, new concepts that will allow us to think *otherwise,* to bypass the ancient symmetries and dichotomies that have governed the ground and the very condition of possibility of thought, of 'clarity,' in all Western philosophy. *Métissage* is such a concept and a practice: it is the site of undecidability and indeterminacy, where solidarity becomes the fundamental principle of political action against hegemonic languages" (6). Incorporating this term into our critical vocabulary permits us to consider new realities, to reimagine previously unquestioned forms of affiliation. From the perspective of autobiographical writing, Lionnet claims that *métissage* as "aesthetic concept" merges biology and history, anthropology and philosophy, linguistics and literature (8).

Carmit Delman's *Burnt Bread and Chutney* embodies Lionnet's concept of *métissage* in superlative ways. Delman's mother, a member of the Bene Israel community in India, immigrated to Israel as a young adult, where she met her future husband, an American Jew.[7] The family settled in Ohio, though they spent time in a kibbutz in Israel when Delman was a child. The family identifies principally as Jewish, though they casually accept their Indian roots and the blend of Asian customs and foodways into their daily life. India is most clearly represented through Nana-bai, the maternal grandmother, with her Indian English lilt, idiosyncrasies, and traditional perspectives. Growing up surrounded by the American Jewish community and Nana-bai, Delman and her siblings are painfully conscious of their multiple differences: "maybe if we had connected deeply to the general Indian community, our family identity might have been more straightforward, a clear-cut piece of American immigration. But we were Jewish also and general Indian culture was another sphere entirely" (58). Indeed, she looks with envy on those immigrants of unambiguous identification with a heritage culture. To the mostly Ashkenazi Jews of their community, they didn't "look" Jewish and upon explaining that they were a mix of Indian and Eastern European Jew, "people automatically identified us by the brownness and what made us nonwhite. . . . We, Ashkenazi Jews, are the pure originals. You, Indian Jews, are mixed products" (151). Though she rediscovers India by enrolling in anthropology classes in college, she continues to be aware that she is mostly a spectator to their festivals and celebrations.

Delman uses food imagery to convey her indeterminate position. Her description of a Shabbat meal at a Jewish friend's house reveals to her the extent of their difference: "the table before us was full of things I had heard of but never tasted before. Here was Luchshen kugel. Tzimes. Cholent. . . . For me, a traditional Shabbat meal had always been elaborate Indian dishes. And I was used to the thick fire of their chili powder and chutney. So the heavy pastiness of this new food took me by surprise" (64). Ultimately, a McDonald's Happy Meal provides the tranquility the children seek: "this food was not kosher or spicy. But it came with bendy straws and toys and ketchup bags on the side. And that was enough" (66). Eating the "right" food (the right brand of cola and chips), as well as dressing the "right" way (store-bought matching clothes, rather than hand-me-downs), becomes an obsession for Delman, who longs to fit in. Food, which also strongly reminds her of Nana-bai's story, the frame of her narrative, later allows her to function creatively and crossculturally. The memoir's title gestures toward the use of food imagery in the process of understanding the role of women, cultural differences, and the meaning of religion.

This Indian Jewish Childhood challenges even working definitions of what falls into the grouping "Asian American Childhood" because Delman's amalgamation of racial, ethnic, and cultural affiliations defies easy categorizations. The difficulty in classification gestures toward the real nature of mixed race writing, which invalidates many existing categories and requires us to invent new ones. In Delman's case, Judaism is the primary cultural factor she negotiates, though she admits that one cannot separate the strands that make her family Jewish and Indian at the same time. The Bene Israel's palimpsestic history of successive diasporas exceeds definition, even within North America's complex ethnic consciousness.

Jonathan Brennan's *Mixed Race Literature* explores the multiple implications of literary engagements with race and posits that attempts at defining the communities that surround mixed race writers, as well as the particular affiliations they profess, complicate the manner in which they deploy the social construction of race and attend to its ramifications and meanings in their writing (6). In the context of American literature, for example, Brennan signals that reference to the role of "mixed race texts within previously defined categories of literary inquiry and as part of a wider body of mixed race literature will define a new way to inform our understanding of the development of American literature, to complicate it in ways that interrogate our notions of race, gender, and cultural formation. The examination of the construction of identity in mixed race autobiographies should shed new light on identity formation and representation in existing fields of American autobiography" (48).

The indeterminate position of the biracial writer becomes the site for the negotiation and performance of identity. Brennan notes that for the mixed race writer, "identity exists in a state of liminality, a site where a mixed race narrator negotiates and transforms identity, yet often the communities in which the writer negotiates attempt to overwrite multiple identities, to maintain limitations on both form and content" (49). I argue that the writers in question transform biraciality into a literary strategy by enacting a revisionist agenda: by subverting the prescribed model for the Euro-American Childhood, they carve a space for themselves in the American generic scene. Here lies the crucial point. By offering accounts of biracial negotiations set in Asia, these writers enact narratives that themselves question American or Canadian literatures' articulation of race and racial indeterminacy. If we consider the positions of the two protagonists of the story—the child focalizer and the adult writer—and reflect upon how they engage the issue of biraciality from different locations, we can gain insight on the possibilities of diverse forms of self-articulation. Presenting the story of the biracial child in an Asian past from the perspective of an adult writer in a North American present offers a formally creative and thematically enriching syncretism.

The texts analyzed in this chapter have several features in common that allow us to examine similarities and differences in the representation of biraciality, as well as individual processes of identification.[8] All the autobiographical accounts are set in Asia, and all conclude with the boys' leaving for the United States or Canada. The children experience the crises or advantages of biraciality in Asia, rather than North America. This perspective widens approaches to biraciality and its representation, particularly from a North

American position. Because all the texts were actually written in North America for a primarily American or Canadian audience, we can argue that they articulate Western views of mixed race as much as Asian positions. For Reyes, Fenkl, and Nguyen, their one (White) American parent nuances the boys' perception of themselves in the Philippines, Korea, and Vietnam, respectively, as well as their notion of and access to the American Dream. Significantly, these texts also permit us to examine the combined effect of class and race in a manner alien to the social construction of the United States. Reyes' biraciality offers him privilege; for Fenkl and Nguyen, biraciality is a treacherous space between affiliations and influences the mode of their interaction with their peers. Kwan, the son of a wealthy and influential Chinese businessman and his Swiss second wife, experiences difficulties only with the onset of the Chinese Revolution; until that time, social class was more important to his self-perception than his biraciality. In different ways, the first three children demonstrate a distinctive ambivalence in their inscriptions of their homelands, perhaps because of the adult writers' consciousness of the transitional role of that place and the culture it nurtures. Particularly for Fenkl and Nguyen, the representation of familial, social, and communal life is modulated by the instability of that system in the narrator's life.

Further, because these books are autobiographies (and marketed clearly as such), and their speaking subjects authoritative, the adult authors explain twentieth-century Asian history, in particular, the Communist takeover in Vietnam and China, and the American occupation in the Philippines and Korea. World War II also figures significantly in the narratives. In all the texts, the experience of war in an Asian country becomes a catalyst in the protagonists' process of racial positioning. It requires them to critically negotiate their biraciality and enact a program of national and cultural refiguring and renewed affiliation. In the context of these sociopolitically charged events, the chronotopic location of the biracial subject articulates an even more complex process of subjectivity. The deployment of the Childhood thus signifies multiply, on racial, social, historical, and cultural domains. These Childhoods trace their protagonists' itineraries of national and ethnic affiliation by focusing on their processes of socialization in their birth countries. These texts allow us to explore a series of questions: what positions do these biracial subjects occupy in their societies and how do they articulate those spaces? What kind of processual discourse of selfhood or, more specifically, self-in-place, do they employ? How does biraciality as *theme* influence the *form* these Childhoods take?

Homi Bhabha has articulated the "in-between" as a "terrain for elaborating strategies of self-hood—singular or communal—that initiate new signs of identity," a position that resists fixity (37). These protagonists affirm their subjecthood characterized by racial indeterminacy as they make important choices on national affiliation. To begin the discussion on the texts, we will examine briefly the diverse manners race is viewed in different Asian countries in order to arrive at a more comprehensive understanding of the significance and changing meaning of race. In general, Asian countries tend to view the children of mixed race marriages negatively, as Yen Le Espiritu explains how, for example, "in a society such as Vietnam, which values racial purity, the Amerasians were treated as virtual outcasts from birth. But this rejection can also be traced to the racial and class origins of the Amerasian. Although all Amerasians were marked as different and inferior, black Amerasians (*my den*) encountered the most discrimination" (28). In Vietnam, as in the Philippines, Korea, and China, because of a specific intersection of historical and social forces, race and class have become intricately linked, particularly with regard to mixed race children. Espiritu notes that the "largely traumatic and dehumanizing experience" of Vietnamese Amerasians demonstrates the deplorable effects of the combination of class and race on the community positions on biracial people. Specifically, in Vietnam, the "presumed social and economic background of the Amerasian's parents also affected his or her status. In the eyes of most Vietnamese, every Amerasian in Vietnam was the child of a Vietnamese bar girl or prostitute and an American GI. Thus these biracial children also bore the stigma of immorality, illegitimacy, and the underclass" (28).

In Vietnam, a comparison of the experience of Eurasians—children of French and Vietnamese parents—and Amerasians illustrates how social class marks the true distinction among these children. Because marriage between French officials and Vietnamese women of prominent families was frequent during the French colonial period, the children of these marriages were accepted in both French and Vietnamese society. A similar pattern emerged in the Philippines during the time of Spanish colonial rule, where the *mestizos* (children of Filipinos and Spanish) "occupied positions of power and economic advantage over the rest of the 'unmixed' Filipino population" (Espiritu 29). Indeed, Reyes' account shows that this positive view of the mix between the Filipino and the Westerner continued to exist (and still does) in Philippine society after Spanish colonization, where the *mestizo*—now also a blend of American and Filipino—is privileged and considered of a higher social class (even if economically this might not be the case).

In Norman Reyes' view, the presence of American colonizers in the Philippines was a door to the future. His American mother, Grace, had met his father in the United States and moved back to Manila with him in the 1920s. The boy's biraciality was perceived by his parents as a blending of the best of their different worlds. When Pons Reyes sees his son for the first time, "he looked wonderingly at the baby's *café-au-lait* skin and dark brown hair and thought:

this is not an American and not an Asian. If that is me, then who have I become? Am I a foreigner in my own country?" (29). But this consideration of possible liminality is immediately canceled out by the anticipation of a new world order: "his family was *ambos mundos,* both worlds . . . neither Filipino nor American. . . . They would be a bilingual, even trilingual household. They would blend American progressive traits with Filipino supportive ways. . . . They would prepare their children to make their way in a new, American-inspired Philippines" (34). Pons' reaction was typical of upper-middle-class Filipinos of that time, who were generally supportive of the new regime and hopeful about the advantages of American colonization. Norman's biraciality and predicted biculturality is therefore articulated in fundamentally positive terms by his parents, who teach the boy to consider himself the fortunate recipient of the advantages of both cultures. Reyes concludes his idyllic description of his childhood with: "I simply had no concept of a monocultural life" (40). His forays outside his home introduce him (and the implied reader) to Filipino life and culture, an exuberantly eclectic blend of the Malay, Chinese, Spanish, and American influences in a process of discovery laden with cultural multiplicities.

Reyes plays a shifting role as his story's narrator: he is, simultaneously, an insider and outsider to his culture because he identifies as a *mestizo* in early-twentieth-century Philippines. Reyes' biraciality allows him access to both cultures, something denied to other Filipinos. As he notes of the mid-1930s, "While nation-building was evident everywhere, so was a wall of estrangement: the social line between Americans and Filipinos of Manila. While they rubbed elbows all day at work, they drew apart when the sun went down. Filipinos were not invited to be members of the American clubs. American social events from balls to picnics were Americans-only affairs" (10–11). American racial prejudice against Filipinos was rampant, particularly among the military. A popular limerick at the time in Manila criticized Commissioner William Howard Taft's benevolent welcoming of Filipinos into the American mainstream as "little brown brothers": "they say I've got brown brothers here / But still I draw the line. / They may be brothers to Big Bill Taft / But they ain't no brother of mine" (11). From his privileged position in middle-class Filipino American life, Reyes consciously performs the role of "cultural ambassador," who introduces the American public to the customs, traditions, and idiosyncrasies of the Philippines. But though his strategy echoes that of other writers, Reyes' choice of a specific autobiographical form lends added credibility as well as symbolism to his perspective, while it performs its didactic purpose.

Reyes' memories of his childhood center on his participation in local cultural events: a typical fiesta, a Filipino cockfight, the idyllic rural life, eating local food, learning about the history of the Chinese presence in the archipelago, and so on. Because as a hybrid subject he is not completely Filipino, a crucial part of his narrative involves his process of learning to "be" Filipino, an itinerary he shares with the reader. His description of his narrative as a "quest" (xiv), a "journey" (1), implicates the reader in that pilgrimage, as evidenced by the title of the first chapter, "Journey's Start." In this sense, Reyes is permitted to occupy multiple spaces as he develops the diverse facets of his identity.[9] This is how Reyes uses his biraciality as a narrative strategy—his own liminal position structures the text, which is to a large extent composed of discrete accounts of his cultural learning process.

The local terms that denote biracial subjects are suggestive in this context. The Spanish term *"mestizo"* has positive connotations, mostly springing from a problematic colonial mentality.[10] As Reyes notes, "'Mestizo' was not a label I wore lightly. The word had a negative flavor among some Filipinos, sometimes even the flavor of a taunt. The English versions of the word—'half breed' and 'half caste'—sounded explicitly negative, as did the word 'mongrel,' and I tried to pretend they did not exist. My mixed-race fellows and I often casually thought of ourselves as American, but we accepted the word *mestizo* as a realistic term for our racial identity and certainly a preferable word to 'half breed'" (205–206). Importantly, Reyes does have a choice because the privileged role of both the Spanish and later the Americans in Philippine society gave *mestizos* a certain entitlement. To be able to "casually" think about themselves as "Americans" already signals the social position that Reyes occupies, one considered a step above other Filipinos. Whichever name the *mestizos* preferred or chose, they would still be referring to a subject considered by the average Filipino to be socially and economically superior to that of the "unmixed" Filipino.

Reyes' ostensibly clear perception of the differences between the two ethnic influences on his life is belied by his inability to see the facile differences he establishes and the way he mimics stereotypical forms of representing biraciality. He restates the binary of East and West, and uses the symbols that had been popular in earlier writing. Notably, for instance, he sees himself as a bridge: on his paternal side, he belongs to "the last of three generations whose lives formed a bridge from 19th-century Spanish colony to 20th-century American outpost" (2). Though his outlook is fundamentally positive—"my life has been enriched by the blessings and burdens of having two simultaneous cultures" (5)—like Sui Sin Far, he notes the loneliness felt by the bicultural person who is not completely at home in either place he inhabits. He sees himself occupying a space different from either of his parents: "I was clearly someone in whom Filipino and American outlooks lived side by side and therefore someone with an apparently wider range of behavior than either a Filipino or an American" (132). He notes, on diverse occasions, how his parents look upon their biracial children as part of them, yet different. His father's reaction upon seeing him has already been described; his mother, Grace, who expected a black-haired baby, was comforted by her brown-haired son, "relieved that her own identity was not to be entirely submerged in this very alien land so very far from home" (28).

Reyes' cultural perception is solidly located in an important historical context: the new colonization of the Philippines by the Americans, with its attendant imaginative reinvention in the eyes of the natives. As he explains, "In the Philippines, wherever the Filipino and American cultures came face to face, it was not a matter of meeting and mingling. American culture always made the impression on Filipino culture and not vice versa" (147). Cultural loyalty to Spain (with emphasis on Catholicism, the Spanish language as the language of the educated, customs, and practices) was rapidly being replaced by the explosion of American movies, along with other "eye-popping wonders" such as ice cream, automobiles, and golf (9).[11] He watches early-twentieth-century Manila become more and more Americanized and describes the irresistible power of the movies and the promise of America that they offered, explaining the Filipino fascination with the country: the movies "were all windows on the same land of dreams, a fantasy place inhabited by white-skinned people who were free of small daily concerns, who did not perspire, whose clothes never wrinkled. A place where meadows were free of mud and excrement, where every town had streets and sidewalks that were paved and spotlessly clean, free of garbage and debris" (2). From the perspective of an adult in the United States, Reyes acknowledges the discursive implication of movies in the formation of pro-American sentiment prevalent in the Philippines at that time: "the most persistent and persuasive promoter of America's language and personal freedoms was the American movies that became such a part of Philippine life. They were the liveliest textbook, the largest classroom, the most sought-after teacher. No colonial master's legacy ever had such an ally. No colonial master's culture ever had such an advocate" (3–4).

Biraciality offers Reyes the privilege of social, cultural, and national choice. Allowed to occupy multiple spaces confidently, Reyes' itinerary of affiliation seems a happy and relatively uncomplicated one. Welcomed everywhere he goes, he participates as a member in both American and Filipino social and cultural events. Yet Reyes proposes a binary model of cultural duality, distinguishing behavioral traits that he identifies as "Filipino" and others as "American." These classifications are rather stereotypical and must be read in the context of the assimilationist practices prevalent at the time, which mandated a certain manner of viewing traditional Filipino qualities as opposed to American progressiveness. Specifically, Reyes speaks of times of "being Filipino," episodes away from his immediate family in rural areas or with "authentic" local people. He identifies particular forms of behavior or attitudes as one or the other and notes how he shifts from one to the other: "merry confusion" is Filipino, while a "penchant for orderly things," American (82); his American side strives for "self-improvement and professional success" while his Filipino side "yearned for the wonders of my unfettered, unconfined barefoot days when I was in love not just with life but with living, too" (235); he notes that "the essential difference between American and Filipino cultures is the difference between individualism and interdependence" (99). From his rural experiences, he acknowledges picking up "certain personal traits that would surface later in my life in times of 'being Filipino': speaking only when spoken to, unquestioning respect for elders, suffering inconveniences quietly, and pleasing other people" (56). Moreover,

> in the midst of so many Americanizing influences, something in me that I could not understand kept me always on the watch for such times—though they might be few and far between—when I would "be Filipino." This was perhaps because on such occasions life felt simpler than usual, gentler and kinder, with more laughter and fewer cares. . . . Times of "being Filipino" also included feelings of belonging, a feeling that people are more collective than individual. "Being American" felt like life was a matter of each of us being out on our own, while "being Filipino" felt like life is about supporting each other spiritually and materially. (76)

This quote exhibits an interesting ontological slippage: Reyes links "being" with "behaving," which may be partly explained by the position he chooses. Even as he narrates his barefoot rural adventures, the boy's imagination manages to transplant his fascination with Tom Sawyer onto local soil, converting his friend Pelagio into a Filipino Huckleberry Finn. This comparison demonstrates the kind of immersion in American literature that successfully transformed middle- and upper-class Filipinos into subjects proficient and comfortable with American cultural paradigms. On a discursive level, this reveals Reyes' awareness of his implied reader, mostly Americans unfamiliar with Filipino customs, for whom this kind of reference would ring significantly. Reyes, as mentioned earlier, does seem to take his role as cultural ambassador seriously, and uses the Childhood as his tool. He invites the readers to accompany him on his own journey of discovery of Filipino life and customs, making his search for identity itself an analysis of culture.

Ultimately, Reyes defines himself as a "child of two worlds" whose cultural positioning undergoes an important epiphany at the outbreak of World War II: "on the eve of war, my personal cross-cultural journey that had begun in my barefoot days seemed to be approaching a fork in the road; I was experiencing times when the Filipino and American sides of me were tugging in different directions" (234). Joining the army and fighting for both countries serve as a catalyst for his united sense of self. After narrating the fall of Bataan and Corrigedor, he notes,

> I also realized that I would no longer hear the inner question that had walked with me all through my boyhood and teen years: am I Filipino or American? The question was irrelevant now; the "or" between us had been replaced by an "and." . . . Furthermore, I realized that, for the duration, whenever the chips would be down, *how* I lived was going to be more meaningful than *who* I was. . . . I was free in the future to move back and forth between my two cultures as I needed or pleased, free even to add more cultures, not owned by any one but belonging to all. (285, italics in original)

Reyes' final "assertion of multiple identities does not entail a destruction of all identities, but an insistence of the right to claim one's true self" (Brennan 3). Through his Childhood, Reyes rationalizes the trajectory of his complexly acquired selfhood: he does not claim only one alliance because he has the battle scars to demand the right to both. When he eventually moves to the United States and marries an American, his journey seems have reached a satisfactory ending, one which endows him insider perspective and a sense of belonging to the two countries he identifies with.[12] But he nonetheless continues to fret about his liminal role in both places. Though he moves back to the Philippines with his family for a time, he eventually returns to the United States. In the end, in spite of his idealistic portrayal of Filipino family customs, it is these that will lead him to choose life in the United States, as the social pressure on *mestizos* "to live privileged and elitist lives" and that placed an inordinate regard for family connections makes him wish for a simpler life in the United States, "where [he] could be an ordinary working man and still have something" (289). For Reyes, therefore, the intersection of class with racial affiliations marks the choice he eventually makes to leave the Philippines.

The most narratologically complex text in this section, Fenkl's *Memories of My Ghost Brother,* performs the protagonist's process of memory through a doubled voice: the author intersperses sections in italics with plain text narrative to convey a childhood experience and his adult reading of that experience.[13] Because biraciality marks the child's growing perception of the world, the doubled voice also reflects shifting notions of his own identity. The author describes this strategy as "the world of my childhood over-written by the darker meanings of the world as I know it today" ("A Few Notes" para. 7). He therefore subverts the traditional chronological form of the Childhood, which privileges the child's perspective, by interjecting the adult's version or reflection on those events, teasing out the complex meanings and motivations the child was oblivious to, and locating the child narrator in the future.[14] The short italicized chapters, as Alicia Otano explains, provide a visible presence of the mature self who "fills in the gaps" to what the child narrator cannot articulate: "as another option to narration in the past tense, the use of these graphically-signalled short chapters remind the reader of the presence of a governing consciousness that filters and interprets the events experienced and narrated by the child. Reminiscent of interior monologues and poetic in their imagery, they serve to further emphasize the dual perspective necessary to come to terms with the meeting of diverse worlds in the transcultural subject" (44). Because of the existence of the dual narration in the text, focalization and narration split at some moments into two separate activities, a loaded strategy in the context of life writing. For example, the actual timeframe of Fenkl's narrative covers a short period—approximately six or seven years—of his life with his mother, who lives outside the American army base in Seoul, his ambivalent relationship with his father, and the family's return to the United States. Yet this narrative strategy expands the narrative time of the autobiography to include the perspective of the adult living in the United States.

The early part of the text shows a young boy immersed in the dynamic of his Korean family's life—his mother's struggles to make ends meet, his uncle, aunt and cousins, and distant father who must be attended to. The mythical world of Korean legends and fables is the intertext of Fenkl's childhood version of his life, and he inscribes many of the stories his uncle tells him, illustrating the development of his own creative imagination. Fenkl weaves Korean tales into his story: for instance, he describes his mother's daylong labor giving birth to him as a dream she has where a serpent beckons to tell her a secret; the airplane that will take them to the United States is "a giant white serpent with scaly wings of silver" (271). His perception of the death of a bird and the explanation he gives himself on his cousin's suicide also stem from his mythical cosmovision. He also feels comfortable in the liminal place between waking and dream, or in the early mornings, when he knows he might get a glimpse of the ghosts of the Japanese Colonel or his cousin Gannan, and he understands serenely the place of his "ghost brother" in his dreams. Visited by these specters, Fenkl enacts what Avery Gordon describes as haunting as "a very particular way of knowing what has happened or is happening. Being haunted draws us affectively, sometimes against our will and always a bit magically, into the structure of feeling of a reality we come to experience, not as cold knowledge, but as a transformative recognition" (8). As a "particular form of knowing," haunting implies a specific attitude toward the past that gives that past a power to be present and act on our consciousness (or unconsciousness) often independent of our choices or intentions. The child narrator becomes, in a sense, possessed by the lack of knowledge about that mysterious presence that haunts his mother and, consequently, him. Fenkl's doubled narrative supports this dual form of knowledge—the child intuits "haunted" knowledge while the adult's version of the story intervenes in this poetic process.

Identification with the "American" father (Fenkl's father is a German immigrant to the United States) complicates the boy's process of identity. His clumsy attempts to belong to his father's world illustrate both a child's need to identify with a father and a biracial child's struggle against his own liminality, personified in his parents. His attraction to the English language, for example, represents his entry into his father's world of privilege and possibility, so totally alien to the everyday Korean world of his mother.

> I believed I would learn something about my father's world at the American school. I believed there was something mysterious about the pale-skinned children with the yellow hair and the blue and green eyes, whose tongues were more suited than mine to their slippery English words. I believed there was something grand and magical about America because those who came back would march in rank, their arms interlinked over each other's shoulders, chanting, "Hey! Hey! Get out of my way! I just came back from the U! S! A!" I was thirsty to drink in the source of that mystery, but like the others who were like me, I would come away more parched than before. (92)

Though his emotional connection is to his mother's Korean world, he wants to please his father and achieve all that America promises. But English separates father and son: the father teaches the boy that the language learned at the American school provides education, while Korean represents ignorance and poverty. Thus the "home" language and the "White school's" language elucidates the binary oppositions the child must negotiate, which imply a series of beliefs, family relationships, manners, and behaviors.

One of the classic marks of biraciality, apart from the phenotype, is the personal name, what Boelhower has called "a paradigmatic virtual text" (*Autobiographical Transactions* 14). Linda Hutcheon refers to a process of "cryptoethnicity," when the nominal marker of ethnicity is blurred or "encrypted" (28).[15] A series of reasons justify this: marriage, international adoption, or as in Fenkl's case, biraciality, which gives him a first and last name that belie his mixed heritage. Though the boy and his father share a name, it becomes a "contested terrain of affiliation" (Otano 50). While his mother calls him "Insu," his German American father addresses him as "Heinz." When the father writes to his son from Vietnam, the letters *were always signed, 'Your Father, Heinz,' as if to remind me that he was my father and not some yellow-haired stranger"* (62). His father obliges him to identify with the culture and history of his own ethnic group, in this case German American, not with any other, including his mother's. But the child does not identify himself as "Heinz" until he begins to go to American school, where he is forbidden from using his Korean name, or speaking in Korean. He must then construct another identity, one demarcated by a word he can barely pronounce. "What's your name, young man? Answer me," the teacher asks. "'Heinz,' I said finally. It sounded strange to me, more like 'Ha-inju.' I had only said it a few times to myself, and from my mouth, it didn't sound the way it did when my father called me" (99).

The names Fenkl uses on different occasions correspond to the discrete spaces he occupies. As Daniel Nakashima explains, we read names as signifiers of membership in particular racial, ethnic, and/or cultural group, more than as simply signifiers of personal identity or family membership. When we read the name of a multiethnic person for racial or ethnic clues, "challenges arise both for the 'reader' and for the multiracial/multiethnic person being 'read.' The 'reader' might be confused by a name that does not 'match' with the person's physical appearance or mannerisms, whereas the multiracial person might feel that his or her name is not an accurate reflection of his/her race, ethnicity, and identity" (114). The text thus negotiates the boy's "shifting parental affiliation, inseparable from the cultural, since his mother *is* Korea and his father *is* the United States, offering an evolving vision of the possibilities for division and unity, adaptation and adjustment, separation and bonding" (Otano 50).

The boy's father recognizes his son's problems. The adult narrator acknowledges his father's dilemma about having a biracial child in Korea: "*when he saw me for the first time after my birth. . . . He had held his son and turned bright red from the shame of having a mixed-blood child—or was it simply that he did not know how to hold an infant? . . . Later he erupted at my mother for daring to let him be seen in public with a child presented to him by a Korean.*" Fenkl recalls one of his father's presents to him, Kipling's *Kim*, and explains, "*My father died believing I had read the book; believing I had made some decision about its contents, his message to me; believing I had forgotten or not cared enough to mention the remarkable coincidences, the ironic resonances*" (63). Fenkl's biraciality leads people to impose requirements on him, as Elaine Kim observes, and "challenges assumptions about the interchangeability of race and culture. Even though the boy has only lived in Korea and only speaks Korean, Insu's American father and his Korean uncle expect him to know certain Western things because Yankee blood flows in his veins" ("Myth, Memory, and Desire" 82). Father and son try, in parallel ways, to reach each other: the father in order to claim his son after having obliged his wife to give up her oldest child, and the son in order to identify with this man. Toward the end, Heinz understands the futility of this exercise, seeing that their differences and the lack of a shared history and ethnicity will always alienate them from each other. Hearing his father and another soldier sing together, the son understands what he cannot have.

> They must have sung this together a thousand times, I thought. They must work together, eat together, sleep in the same barracks, worry the same worries and fight the same fights to have their voices merge like this. I could not imagine my voice joining with my father's the way Jonesy's did. I could not imagine how I would even understand their secret language of knowing glances and inside jokes. That was something only yellow-haired soldiers could do. I would be forever tainted by a Koreanness that would make the words "gook" or "dink" sound strange coming from my lips, like the word "nigger" spoken by a Black GI to anyone but his brothers. (253–254)

The boy connects most meaningfully with other biracial children, all of them mocked by both Korean and American children. His neighbor Cholsu calls him a "mongrel dog" and insults him about the way the Americans have a "yellow smell" (86). At the Korean Sunday School, he hears the other children speaking about him: "'his father's an American soldier, I saw him. He's big and scary like a long-nose goblin. His hair's all yellow and he has fur on his arms.' No one would play with me during recess" (76). His friends, many of whom were offspring of liaisons between Korean women and American servicemen, were also condemned to a liminal existence—not accepted in traditional Korean society and excluded from American. Maria Root has noted that while there might be debate about whether being multiracial constitutes a specific cultural experience, "it clearly constitutes a phenomenological experience because of the meaning of race in this country [and in Asia]" (30). The dynamics among the children at the Korean American school reflect this complicated situation. Fenkl, for example, the legitimate child of married parents, occupies a more secure position than the other biracial children around the base.

The connection between race and privilege shapes Fenkl's understanding of his place in school and in contrast to other mixed race children. Maintaining their Korean identity at school becomes a creative challenge, as the children speak a form of Korean-English and discuss their uncertain futures. The chance to actually attend school is accepted casually by Fenkl, even as he sees how one of his neighborhood friends, yellow-haired Jani, cannot attend the school until his mother finds an American husband with the same yellow hair willing to claim paternity. In Fenkl's case, as with Nguyen as we will see later, a bond exists between children of mixed parentage particularly because of the extreme situations of war that they find themselves in. The social role of these children in the world in and around the army base is complicated: they are viewed as the immoral result of liaisons, yet simultaneously considered a *commodity* by desperate Korean women who seek a better life in the United States and wield them as sentimental bargaining tools with which to claim or keep a man. Fenkl's accounts of his friends James—a half-Black boy who drowned in a sewer creek behind his house when his mother was set to marry a White American—and Changmi—whose mother slept with a Black man to produce a half-Black child in order to keep her African American husband—illustrate the desperate situation of these Korean women and their children.

Fenkl's concern with the fate of these other children haunts the memoir. He recounts how Jani finally did get an American father and went to the United States, but then learns that his friend had died of leukemia. The most tragic story Fenkl remembers is James', who he writes "back to life" (211), noting the irony of the women negotiating their own futures through the color of their children's skin. His memory of James materializes through images of actually "seeing" his friend: "I see him looking back at me as his mother takes him home to Paekmajang, where he has no friends and the Korean children throw stones at him because he is part Black" (213). James' story illustrates the nuances of skin color even among the biracial children, who were not always conscious of these differences themselves: *"he did not seem to notice, any more than I, that his difference went further than simply being of mixed blood. To both of us, I think his Blackness was lost under the labels we heard –ainoko, chapjong, t'wigi– and that commonness obscured the fact that when people looked at us oddly, they looked at him more oddly than at me. Even a decade later, I could not look back and see that James's tragedy was in the fact that his father was Black"* (232). Later, he questions whether these women were truly guilty for what they had done to their children: *"bartering sons for their own welfare . . . I would learn that women— even seemingly devoted mothers—will traffic in children for the mythic promise of America. And they would all look back in regret from the shores of the Westward Land"* (232). The final revelation—that his own mother had given her oldest son up for adoption because his father had demanded it—leads him to understand the continual presence of ghosts in his life. Though the ghost of his brother Kuristo seems to be left behind in Korea as they board the plane, the memory of that haunting remains and clearly shadows the inscription of Fenkl's Childhood, making the issue of biraciality and multiple liminalities resonate beyond the text.

Kien Nguyen's Childhood focuses on the tragic and eventually liberating role his biraciality plays in his family. Root's observation that the complexity of a mixed race subject's itinerary of establishing "a racial and ethnic self in relationship to a nation that is structured around race—and a monoracial model driven by assumptions that racial purity exists and is desirable and somewhat necessary or sufficient for the retention of cultural heritage—can make the process difficult" (31) explains the complexity of Nguyen's position. Though Root refers to the situation in the United States, her assertion is equally valid in the context of Vietnam; the two countries Nguyen lived in are significantly structured around race, a paradigm that informed his childhood and his adulthood. Critical historical events unfold quickly in his story—the Communist takeover makes the family suspect and, eventually, destitute. He witnesses contradictory cultural and societal processes: the supposed liberators of the country endorse the destruction of traditional Vietnamese culture and traditions—even the all-important value of family—as his mother's own sister leads a campaign to isolate and humiliate them, culminating in hunger, desperation, and fear. In this sense, Nguyen's Childhood is the most tortuous and agonizing of the texts described in this chapter, as he describes his family's journey from security and affluence to near starvation, a frustrated attempt to escape by sea, and imprisonment. Recounted chronologically in a direct, unadorned style, the weight of the narrative lies in the complex psychic negotiations the protagonist engages.

Nguyen is fiercely devoted to his mother, yet she maintains a distance from her children that gives them feelings of inadequacy. Watching her at her mirror as a child, he comes to believe that she "was the rarest, most beautiful creature that ever walked the face of the earth" (7). Yet he learns that "her heart had no room for any relationship stronger than a detached friendship, and she admitted to [him] on several occasions that this deficiency was innate to her personality—except that, in her own words, it was not a deficiency but a successful adaptation to life. [She] was simply unable to trust anyone but herself" (15). Two more or less stable relationships with American men—a long liaison with a civil engineer and marriage to a soldier—gave her two biracial sons, Kien and Jimmy, and a small fortune that allowed her to buy a mansion and a partnership in a bank. Her awareness of Vietnamese ostracism of mixed race children and consciousness that these would point to her relationships with the enemy Americans makes her protect the boys. Though also subject to subsequent colonizations, the Vietnamese have long resisted interracial connections. As Robert McKelvey notes, there is a Vietnamese saying that "it is better to marry the village dog than a man from another village. This traditional Vietnamese prejudice against outsiders was even stronger for women who entered liaisons with foreigners, specially if they did not marry" ("Vietnamese Amerasians" para. 4). As Nguyen notes, "My mother also had the tall wall erected around the mansion, which not only shielded the house from outsiders' curiosity but also sealed us up, as if covering something shameful. We were meant never to be discovered" (23).

After the fall of Saigon, Nguyen and other Amerasians were ostracized not only for being "half-breeds" but because their mothers, having had affairs with foreigners, were viewed as having "collaborated" with the American enemy.[16]

Amerasians in Vietnam, estimated at thirty thousand in 1975, were singled out for humiliation with the use of words such as *con lai* (half-breed), *my lai* (American mix), or *my den* (Black American) (Brennan 12). The word "half-breed" reverberates in the text, a word defined to Jimmy by a cousin: "a half-breed is a bastard child, usually the result from when a woman has slept with a foreigner. Like you" (97). Nguyen deploys significant rhetorical implications of race when he admits, "There had not been a moment of happiness since the day I was taught the word *half-breed*" (281).[17] This institutionalized societal rejection led many women to abandon their children or face relocation and open discrimination, as well as earn another name, *bui doi* (dust of life), condemned to live on the fringes of Vietnamese society. Interestingly, Kien's earliest memory of awareness of difference is based on class, rather than on race. In his first memory, that of an elegant dinner party the night of his fifth birthday, he describes his family's opulent mansion and the difference between him and the children outside. He played with toys and wore sandals; the barefoot children watched him with fascination. "According to my mother," he notes, "those children were either too dirty, or I was too clean, for my association with them" (6).

The children repeatedly suffer the condemnation of "pure" Vietnamese, who link their illegitimacy with racial impurity. "And forgive your cousins," Nguyen's mother is forced to say to her nephews. "They are just bastard children" (114–115). This incident illustrates the rhetorical, rather than purely "biological" implications of race: Kien's mother was viewed as fortunate because of her relationship with Americans while they were in power. After the Americans left Vietnam, the same situation is viewed negatively, and she is forced to accuse herself of prostitution. Her sons' biraciality is read positively or negatively, depending on the historical moment, leading us to reconsider issues of class and social position. As Pelaud explains, the alienation that a mixed race person experiences arises, among other things, as "the result of the nation's readings of political affiliation" (122) that logically shifts with time and history. In the case of Vietnam and China, the rapid change transformed the cultural hostility toward mixed race persons into a political weapon.

Logically, the pressure leads Kien to reject himself. When their mother buckles under the tension of trying to protect her sons from the "rumors, stares, and judgments that our American features drew" he feels the stirring of an insidious self-rejection: "for the first time in my life, I was overwhelmed with self-hatred, for I realized that I was different and so was my brother, for whom I held a similar and intense dislike. I wanted to pull the fair hair out of my head, scratch off my pale skin, and peel the expensive sandals from my feet. I prayed for something to happen—anything at all, so that the shame would no longer haunt my mother's eyes" (44–45). The mixed race experience has a phenomenological angle of physical appearance that, in contexts such as Vietnam, affects identity in crucial ways. As Grice explains, in the racialized gaze, "which fails to acknowledge individual response/nuance, the subjectivity of the individual disappears. The face, the eyes and other physiognomic features visibly signify difference from a culturally normalised ethnic or racial minority; and through the gaze as spectacular act the 'minority' ethnic subject is objectified." Thus Kien and his brother are judged on the basis of the normative phenotype, a standpoint that causes anxiety in the boys because of the way that they, as ethnic subjects striving to blend into the only world they know, find their "self-identity produced by, and reflected back" by another (*Negotiating Identities* 134).

The photographs incorporated into the text or placed on the cover of the book signify discursively in this context. The role of photographs in transcultural autobiographical narratives requires detailed examination because, as Rosalia Baena states, "photographs of the authors' childhoods offer crucial insights into the relationship between the subjects' bodies and the various kinds of spaces they occupy. Above all, this relationship is most poignant when it comes to the representation and performance of race and the embracing spatial contexts of the images" (361). When a book cover features the child protagonist of the text, contact is established that mediates between the reader's perspective and the content of the book. In autobiography, the cover functions as part of Lejeune's autobiographical "pact," inviting the reader to receive the text as a truthful narrative, recounted precisely by the person on the cover. Nguyen's book contains only a cover shot of the boy, understood to be taken on his fifth birthday, who sits with his hands crossed in front of him, showing a Mickey Mouse watch. The boy's features are clearly biracial, and he looks at the camera with a melancholy gaze, directly interpellating the reader. The photograph conveys a sense of innocence because of the direct gaze, which contrasts with the harrowing experiences recounted of life after this photograph was taken. Patricia Holland argues that photographs like Nguyen's on his cover, as well as the collages in Fenkl and Kwan's texts, mediate between "personal memory and social history, between public myth and personal unconscious" (qtd. in Kate Douglas 72). Douglas asserts that when these "personal" photographs become "public" by their paratextual incorporation in an autobiographical text, they can be read "in terms of the public and private imagery of childhood that is circulating within culture" (72). The photographs on the cover of Fenkl, Nguyen, and Kwan's Childhoods are particularly important because they foreground a speaker whose features testify to indeterminate racial classification. The reader unconsciously seeks to identify the author, something more easily done in texts written by "pure" Asians.

The child's frustration at the insidious racialized gaze leads him to want to blend and strip himself of the markers of racial and class difference. At one point in the narrative, a caring and probably secretly subversive teacher, Miss San, tries to help Kien and Jimmy blend in. She instructs Kien to cut his tell-tale curly hair short for a school parade in order not to "cause some distraction among the spectators" (141). Later, she explains to them one of the most superlative contradictions of Communism to allow them to find their place and seek a sense of identity: "you should not be ashamed of your humble condition or of who you are. In fact, you should be proud. Look at it this way: you are no longer a capitalist. In the Communists' eyes you have achieved the lowest and most desired status—the class of the poor. Be pleased, Kien, for now you have nothing to lose but much to gain" (143).

An important part of the boys' processes of identity formation includes their itineraries of personal cultural affiliation and alliance. In this respect, these Childhoods set outside the United States differ notably from many Asian American protagonists' attempts to assimilate into mainstream (read "White") society or occupy a significant place in class hierarchy. Because Reyes, Fenkl, and Nguyen have one American parent, Americanization, in a sense, always exists as a possibility. Yet, significantly, all demonstrate strong loyalty to the culture of the land of their birth. Reyes' narrative repeatedly stresses the positive aspects of traditional Filipino life and customs. Fenkl is more comfortable in Korean culture, viewing his father's American base as a magical world alien to him. Biraciality disqualifies Nguyen from being truly Vietnamese and accepted by others—his own aunt and cousins maltreat him.[18] Though his mother tried to protect her children, their secret was written on their bodies, in the color of the boys' skin and hair. Vietnam, an "unforgiving society," obliges them to leave it—"Our only hope was to get out of Vietnam and move to a more accepting place" (23). Kien articulates the shift in position describing their return to their old house to ask their ex-maid for food: "I found myself playing the role of an outsider, looking in like one of the dirty children my mother had trained me to despise in the old days" (167). He sees himself from the outside and notes how their cousins observe them with "the same astonishment that they would show to a pair of rare Christmas ornaments" (99).[19] Yet this rejection initially offers them no options: Kien has no direct access to the United States, except his dream of eventually reuniting with his father, who never responds to his letters.

The boy studies English, a skill which will eventually help him leave the country. This strategy, which the desperate adolescent enacts in order to carve a psychological space for himself, may be read, according to Robert Elbaz, as "perhaps the most telling episode in these life stories. The child in these stories is the agent who must grapple with the violence of language if he is to survive in a world that is not his from the start." Nguyen's ability to master the language gives him a space from which he can then manipulate the events of history, and free himself and his family. In a sense, by learning English, he makes a choice for his future. Aware that he is not wanted in Vietnam, he "pays the price of the basic inner struggle between a language of the minority from which his or her identity is hewn and a language of the majority that makes material life and historical becoming possible" (Elbaz, "Language and the Self" 159). This skill will not only allow him to earn money working part-time, but also opens up the door to his departure.

Ultimately, the country's rejection of its biracial denizens allows him to leave. Kien's desire to emigrate enacts the revision of Coe's myth of childhood: the reality of the American Dream, which liberates him from a marginalized existence in the country of his birth. When he receives the letter with information about the Orderly Departure Program for Amerasians: "I relived my family's years of hardship, my wretched attempt to escape the country, the many painful paths I had walked since paradise lost" (281). This chance for a new beginning, realized precisely and ironically through that which had caused him to want to leave—his biraciality—becomes a cause of envy among the Vietnamese family and friends who had once scorned him. In the last days of his stay in Vietnam, Kien helps other young Amerasians fill out the necessary papers. He also witnesses the deceptions other Vietnamese practice to acquire the coveted papers—such as buying Amerasian children to pass them off as their own. Yet, the rupture of the narrative at the point of departure from Vietnam—typical of Childhoods—raises more questions than answers and attests to the suggestive possibilities of the genre: what is Nguyen's life in the United States like? Is he truly able to escape all forms of racism and marginalization? The answer may be found partially in Nguyen's extratextual story. The existence of this text serves as proof of a form of success.

Michael David Kwan, along with Richard Kim, Laurence Yep, and Yoshiko Uchida, writes his autobiography of childhood after a long career as a successful translator and writer. His Childhood was published the year before his death.[20] Kwan's narrative is a consciously developed work of doubled memory—his own and that of his father's. As he notes in the introduction, "This is a book of memories. China from the mid-1930s to the late 1940s was a tangle of contradictions. The joy and pain of those years shaped me into what I am" (ix). This text conveys a sense of a man trying to recover the lost years of his childhood as well as, or probably through, the life of his father. Two specific textual references to this—one at the very beginning, the other at the end of the memoir—attest to his concern. Kwan recalls having asked his father whether he would one day write a memoir: "[my father replied with] a resounding no. A man is born, strives to lead a decent, useful life, and dies. He saw nothing remarkable about that and preferred to leave the way he is remembered to those who knew him. He cast an uncommon ambience around my early years, when charm and elegance often existed a mere breath away from squalor and despair. Flashes of real beauty and grace sometimes came from unlikely sources, while pain and humiliation were inflicted by those from whom one could reasonably expect better. Therein lies my tale" (ix–x).

Kwan's perception of the China he lived in until the age of twelve is significantly shadowed by his father's life. Toward the end of the narrative, when political events escalate, and they realize that the father will be imprisoned, the boy watches him spend hours writing "Things that must not be forgotten" (155). This eponymous phrase suggests two possibilities. First, that the son's account of his own life is articulated through the father's chronicle, and indeed Kwan explains in the introduction how he used his father's journals as background material for the book. Second, that John Kwan's life is the mirror against which his son's process of self-identity develops.

As with Fenkl, Kwan's text is as much about the father as about the son. Because his mother never really had time for him before she runs away with a Swiss clockmaker, he is raised by his nanny, Shu Ma, and Zhang, the major-domo, until his father remarries an Englishwoman, Ellen. Shu Ma and Zhang are, for a significant part of the narrative, the central forces in the boy's life: they care for him, play with him, and generally take over the role of nurturing that his parents neglect. Significantly, in the early part of the narrative, he speaks of his parents as "they," stressing distance and lack of confidence. He speaks of his mother as "Marianne" and remembers that her "terrible joys and sudden rages frightened [him]. Her face has always been a blur, like a faded photograph, except for the vivid red mouth" (3). She married John Kwan when she was barely twenty, thinking she was entering a dream world of luxury and enjoyment, and was singularly ill-equipped to manage a household that included a full staff of maids, gardeners, and chauffeurs as well as two teenage sons from a previous marriage. Marianne also had to deal with both xenophobic Chinese society and the socially conscious expatriate society. Her life was lonely, her son notes: her husband's frequent work-related absences did not make it easier and she was not ready to have a child (4). His father, "the sort of man whose presence is felt even in a crowded room, always impeccably dressed and groomed, always preoccupied" (2), was forty-five when the boy was born and didn't seem to know how to deal with his young son. After his mother leaves, his father removes all traces of her from his home and spends more time away. When the boy is young, he suffers greatly from his father's emotional distance—the man doesn't know what to do with his son, treating him like a small adult. Kwan, in turn, strives to please his father, acting like a little man: "under my father's careful tutelage, I was groomed to enter society [at the age of four]. He showed me how to enter and leave a room, unhurriedly, head held high, shoulders squared, back straight. He taught me how to greet his guests, when to shake hands and when to bow and when to combine the two, modifying the bow to a slight inclination of the head. He taught me to answer the questions I would be asked. He turned it into a game that was challenging but fun" (11). When his father remarries, the child slowly becomes comfortable with his father and stepmother. Traumatized by the memory of his mother, he cannot deal with the "thought of kind, sweet, patient Ellen turning into another shrieking horror," as his mother had been (43). The harder she tries to win the boy over, the more he rejects her. Ellen feels the boy's rejection keenly, until a kindly doctor understands the nature of the boy's rejection of her—not of Ellen, but of the idea of another "mummy," a term the boy feared. An epiphany comes when he begins to call her "mother."

Kwan's chronologically structured memoir positions war as the central catalyst to family tragedy. The events of the 1930s and 1940s in China frame the narrative of the family's story, their social and economic position, the place of this biracial child in China. Personal family details are blended in with political observations and commentary to convey the critical connection they have in the boy's memory of his childhood. John Kwan is an administrator for the railroads until the Japanese invasion in 1938, when he takes a position as commissioner of finance in the pro-Japanese government and secretly works for the Resistance, even sheltering a wounded U.S. airman. After World War II, with the battle between Communists and Nationalists, he finds himself caught in the middle and falsely imprisoned for collaborating with the Japanese. This period of unbridled nationalist patriotism, where strong sentiment against the wealthy and mixed-race persons arose, was hard on the boy, who suffered abuse at school.

Inquisitive, intelligent, and articulate, he was a solitary child in a world peopled by adults. "I was precocious, silent but inquiring. . . . I seldom spoke, but when I did I spoke clearly and could switch from Chinese to English without effort, though my Chinese vocabulary was broader. I grew used to having my own way. I had no playmates, nor do I remember craving any. I watched and listened" (8). His solitude and need for the company of other children is palpable—his best friend for the first seven years of his life is, literally, his dog, Rex. Coe suggests that this solitude has become one of the characteristics that marks the writer of a Childhood, a person who was conscious of being "not necessarily lonely, but, in all essential ways, conscious of being alone" (*When the Grass* 51). Moreover, Coe continues, "the solitude of the child who, sooner or later, will grow into the adult describing his own solitude is perhaps the most universal of all characteristics of the Childhood. . . . And if this sense of overwhelming isolation prevails even among happy and integrated children, how much more is it accentuated by unhappiness—by family quarrels, lawsuits, or divorces—or simply by the consciousness of being alien, of being different, and so somehow wrong: of being Jewish, or Black, or Québécois" (52).

Kwan's biraciality marks him as "wrong"—even within his privileged world. He experiences the absurd cultural demarcations that the expatriate community drew and the false world they sustained in the person of his Aunt Hester Findlay-Wu, who ran an English household and was angered by the idea of her sister marrying a Chinese man in spite of having herself married a Eurasian. This attitude personifies the extent that the double standard existed and how it was maintained at all costs. But, because George Findlay-Wu looked White and could "pass" and they moved among the most important families in the foreign community, she "lived down or ignored everything his—and her own—hyphenated surname implied" (29). Kwan explains in detail the apparently incomprehensible classifications and stratifications of who was in and who was out: "regardless of how the Eurasian saw himself, however, both sides saw him as the result of moral degeneracy and, therefore, as a lesser human being. As a child I was blissfully unaware of the differences between one human being and another. I would learn the meaning of the expression 'half-caste' in all its variations soon enough" (20). The racial issues arise when the child steps out of his privileged and protected world.

A solitary child, Kwan becomes a keen observer of the world around him. Descriptions of his hours watching his Japanese neighbor and wife from his treehouse as they listened to classical music in the evening captures poetically his isolation. His friendships with his tutor, "Midder," the peasant Xiao Hu, and Maria, the Italian proprietor of an antique shop—themselves solitary adults—provide his only real company and emotional sustenance for long spells of his childhood. The tasks he engages with them—cricket-hunting and farming or gardening—allows him to be part of nature and the work of other people. One of his most cherished childhood memories, for example, is of eating roasted grasshoppers with Xiao Hu. With the peasant, who treats him kindly, he understands the nature of class difference when he begins to consider Hu a friend: "children know nothing of the invisible line separating one human being from another, but they feel it. Between Hu and me, the line came suddenly clear. I picked up my things and ran blindly for the house, the hot earth burning the soles of my feet" (42). As an altar boy, his fascination with church ritual is closely bound up with his desire to belong, to establish a place for himself.

Three important school experiences color his perception of his liminality. In this sense, the author follows another of Coe's paradigms on the development of the Childhood—foregrounding school in the child's development. The changing cultural situation in China in the 1930s led to Kwan's attending a series of schools that forced him to face his racial ambivalence. At the International School, his ambiguous racial features made him a misfit among other children: "with my shock of light brown hair and Chinese features, the other children, all Caucasians, regarded me as a curiosity, to be teased now and then. Most of the time they left me alone" (46). Though he "was not conscious of being the only non-caucasian at school . . . [he] felt an instinctual sense of *me* and *them,* so that bonding with the other children was always superficial" (94–95). When this school closes and he goes to Chinese school, the taunts escalate and the children call him a "foreigner" or a "stinking half-caste" (102).

> They joked about my hair, my nose, jeering and jabbing at me. The teachers monitoring the corridor averted their eyes. . . . The bird-like teacher reappeared and began a most curious lesson. In a strident voice she told the class, "Foreigners are evil. Especially the British, who poisoned our bodies with opium, and the Americans, who ruined our minds with their god and other silly ideas!" The class chorused, "Evil! Evil! Evil!" as she beat time with her willow switch. I found myself shouting with them in spite of myself, until the teacher's stick cracked down on my desk. There was instant silence. Her eyes narrowed, "What are you yelling about? . . . *Yang bi zhi,*" she spat, and "foreign nose" became my nickname. My formal education had begun. (103)

Like Nguyen, Kwan's attempts to fit in make him unconsciously reject his own racial heritage. Catholic school offered him another kind of experience. The rituals of Catholicism were powerfully attractive to the solitary boy, as the lives of the saints inspired him to emulate their stoicism, to make his "daily pain endurable" (127); the contradictions he observed between the teachings and the teachers gave him "a bleak appreciation of the unfathomable contradictions of this world" (127). Like Nguyen, he also cuts off his tell-tale brown hair to fend off insults, angrily asking his father why it was so wrong to want to be like the rest: "[my father] spoke in a low voice about being proud of one's heritage. Switching to English, he quoted from Shakespeare: 'This above all: to thine own self be true.' He added, 'You'll always be who you are,' and somehow made me feel that was a good thing" (153). Yet this early fascination with religion soon disappears and he becomes an agnostic and refuses to continue to serve Mass.

In 1946, during his father's imprisonment, when the family comprehends that there is no longer any place for them in China, they smuggle Kwan to Hong Kong, with only $100 and a scrap of paper with the address of his half-brother, Tim. Interestingly, Ellen had packed a small bag for him, which "contained only necessities, except for a cigar box holding a few treasures—Rex's red leather collar with a tiny bell attached; a few marbles [he] had won from Buzzy and Donald; the wrapper of a Hershey bar dropped from an airplane; a crystal that shone like gold which Xiao Hu had brought up from the bottom of the sea.

There were reminders of less happy times too—a pocket knife and badge from the Boy Scouts, and the Marine's badge Shao had given [him], which sent an arrow through [his] chest every time [he] looked at it" (220). Later, the boy adds a clod of earth that his father gives him to his treasures. The contents of the cigar box are, metaphorically, the contents of the book—the lost mementos that the writer reimagines in his narrative to guarantee their remembrance. The story ends with the boy's solitary departure—an ironically fitting conclusion to a solitary life—not knowing if he will ever see his parents again. An epilogue tells of the family's reunion two years later.

As narratives that rearticulate Coe's paradigms of the myth of childhood, these texts use the idea of America as the structuring frame for three of these biracial children's perspectives. Reyes, Fenkl, and Nguyen can and do claim America as a birthright—one paid for in blood: Reyes, for having fought as a soldier in the combined U.S./Philippine Army;[21] Fenkl, because of the ghosts he left behind; and Nguyen, for the rejection in Vietnam that his biraciality entailed. While Reyes' eventual relocation to the United States is largely a matter of personal preference and Fenkl's his father's decision to bring his family "home," Nguyen's journey enacts his only hope of finding peace and a place to call home. Only Kwan's narrative is free of references to a specific North American ideal, except in general terms of his father's admiration for Western ways and insistence on his son's proficiency in English. All these narratives, significantly, end with departure from Asia and do not offer a glimpse of what we imagine can be an equally painful process of adaptation to the new country. As opposed to life writing texts that actually narrate processes of immigrant adaptation to the United States, these texts limit the concept of America to something idealized, precisely because it is not experienced in reality.

These Childhoods, because of their protagonists' biraciality and their specific strategies of closure (really nonclosure), must be read differently from that of other immigrant autobiographies that also reference the immigrant's desire to become "American" and partake of the American Dream. The itinerary of North Americanization is negotiated in these texts in specific ways. First, it occurs as a process primarily in the narrators' imagination, and as a future endeavor; the actual social process enacted on American soil remains unnarrated. In a sense, their desire to "claim" America is markedly different from that of characters in texts set in the United States or Canada, who must also often deal with their resentment against North American racism. Thus, Nguyen's perspective on America as a land where his biraciality will not marginalize him is never contradicted in the text. Reyes' condensed account of his American life summarized his adaptation process succinctly: "there were not many adjustments for me to make in America" (288), an affirmation that, nonetheless, leaves room for doubt.

Second, in a sense, therefore, the strategy of (non)closure employed in these Childhoods gestures toward the need to read beyond the texts themselves, and critically reexamine American sociopolitical, historical, and cultural circumstances. Extratextually, the existence of published Childhoods attests to at least a measure of success for their authors. The processes of Americanization for Reyes, Fenkl, Nguyen, and Kwan are narrated by their *act of autobiographical inscription*—the emblem of Americanization par excellence—rather than learned about in detailed accounts in the texts. One can also reasonably assume that, having been educated in North America and acquiring advanced academic degrees (as we learn from published biographical information), these writers consider the discursive potential of their appropriation and rewriting of an established Euro-American form of life writing.[22] By having become empowered to write their own stories, Reyes, Fenkl, Nguyen, and Kwan transact individual forms of agency through their exercise in biracial self-representation in the North American context.

Chapter 5

● **Citizens or Denizens**

Inscribing the Tropes of Asian North Americanization

This study posits that autobiographies of childhood should be read as an imaginative restructuring of personal history that allows adult writers to explore past selves in the context of larger social, cultural, ethnic, and historical configurations. As described earlier, Childhoods explain the present time through a narrativization of the prisms of knowledge that the self-as-child did not possess. Further, that inscription relies on forms that are historically contingent, based on the time in which the writer was educated and from where he or she writes past time. As cultural critic Stuart Hall argues, discursive practices "always implicate" the positions from which we speak and therefore "though we speak, so to say, 'in our own name,' of ourselves and from our own experience, nevertheless who speaks, and the subject who is spoken of, are never identical, never in the same place" (222). The position of the adult writers who renegotiate their childhoods are thus explained by the specific account and vice versa; the narratives allow the writers to reexamine the past life, the trajectory that leads them to the positions they currently occupy. In all the Asian North American Childhoods considered in this study, the authors consciously identify with being American or Canadian; the texts I consider in this chapter focus particularly on the process of becoming American or Canadian, not only for the child him- or herself, but also in the context of the mainstream who posits the criteria of what it means to be and/or look North American. The three Childhoods I read in this chapter present early experiences of consciousness of North Americanization and processes of socialization: two of the texts, Jade Snow Wong's *Fifth Chinese Daughter* and Wayson Choy's *Paper Shadows: A Chinatown Childhood,* are set in San Francisco and Vancouver's Chinatown, respectively, and highlight the physical and psychological boundaries the children must cross. M. Elaine Mar's *Paper Daughter* is a Childhood immigration story of a girl's passage from Hong Kong to America as part of a process of transformation. The writers inscribe their experiences from the position of knowing their place in society, of having somehow successfully (in different degrees) become incorporated into society and having the opportunity to actually write about it.

The open-ended process of people identifying as denizens or citizens, according to William Boelhower, is articulated in the form of tropes or recurrent motifs that connect with canonical texts but that acquire new meaning in these autobiographical exercises. As he notes, "troping in ethnic autobiographies, in other words, can work both ways at once, as an apparent confirmation of already canonic texts and as an act of cultural and literary criticism" ("Making of Ethnic Autobiography" 128–129). This emphasizes the notion that tropes are not merely rhetorical strategies that transfer meaning from one word to another but strategies that carry meaning across texts. Troping, in a sense, results from negotiating the existing structures of narrative; the autobiographical self is generally constructed by appropriating structures of representation that already form part of literary tradition. When—as in the case of early ethnic writing such as Yan Phou Lee, Ilhan New, or Jade Snow Wong—the writers appear to base their frame of reference on existing American perspectives on Asians, we perceive the books as stereotypical. In relation to this argument, Patricia Chu posits that stories of "individual subject formation must fit, or at best challenge, recognized forms, which in turn are negotiated in relation to public accounts" (10). Moreover, the author's narrative of formation must be structured in a way compatible with official narratives and discourses such that "the author's capacity to write and publish a narrative of subject formation—that is, to position himself or herself in relation to the 'language' of his or her culture's narrative conventions—determines his or her survival as an 'author,' a subject known through words" (10–11). More contemporary writers, as discussed in this book, interpolate a wider range of ethnic writing and forms of inscribing experience. They have available to them a broader field of tropes with which to negotiate, based on other autobiographical representations as well as fictional texts.

Boelhower claims that the variations on ethnic autobiography nonetheless illustrate a single theme: "the hyphenated self's attempt to make it in America," narrativized through strategies of sign production that results from "the double dynamic of consent and descent" ("Making of Ethnic Autobiography" 133).[1] Strategies of consent, he argues, lead the immigrant/ethnic self to privilege professed cultural homogeneity where those of descent claim consistent cultural difference. Specific tropes have been used in Asian North American writing to illustrate processes of self-representation. Some of these are taken up in Childhoods and given new meaning as they are marshaled to illustrate crucial moments or metaphorical elements in the authors' processes of self-awareness. One of the most important tropes is the structure of the bildungsroman, particularly in the manner in which it socializes readers by inviting them to identify with the protagonists. In Asian North American Childhoods, this formula is complicated by the genre and by the difficult access to successful socialization.

Chu's study on assimilating subjects clarifies the complexity of the narrative of formation (fictional or otherwise) for ethnic authors who seek to both "establish their own and their character's Americanness and to create a narrative tradition that depicts and validates the Asian American experience on its own terms" (12). Because Asian North Americans have difficulty identifying simply as "American" or "Canadian" subjects—they are regarded as perpetual denizens rather than legitimate citizens—they need to appropriate and transform the narrative structures that forge this depiction. When authors reconstruct genre, they make their own experience part of mainstream discourse and write their differences into the structures that help define the "American" or "Canadian" childhood. Moreover, by using the genre of the Childhood, authors establish their legitimacy within the field of discursive representation by claiming ownership of the narrative articulations of that culture as well.

The act of narrating the defining events of the past becomes a strategy of reconstruction that converts the elements of the past—place, self, experience— into tropes that signify on multiple levels and resonate across texts. Boelhower notes, for example, the "black holes" as opposed to "the guiding stars in the American cultural firmament": "the Chinatowns, the Little Italys, the Hester Streets, the barrios, and the Afro-American neighborhoods that make up those extra-territorial cultural zones within the political boundaries of the nation. The guiding stars are not only the textbook ideals that make an ethos possible but also the rhetorical scaffolding that mainstream autobiographers use to give their narrative a form of closure" ("Making of Ethnic Autobiography" 129). Boelhower points to the use of specific ethnic locations as tropological markers, which resonates with Coe's argument that the North American child "appears fascinated over and over again, not by its own past-Self, but rather by that Self's relation to the Community: not the 'I,' but the community-framework in which it developed is essential" ("Childhood in the Shadows" 6). These Asian North American Childhoods also dialogue with Susan Stanford Friedman's questions regarding standardized attitudes toward life writing that emphasize "the individualistic concept of the autobiographical self," arguing that the self-consciousness of ethnic groups results in autobiographical forms that foreground the collective, stressing interdependent identification within a community (35). The family structure plays a pivotal role in most of these narratives, as does the community. *Fifth Chinese Daughter* and *Paper Shadows,* for example, foreground the role of the Chinatown community as part of the protagonist's itinerary of self-awareness.[2]

Significantly, by focusing on community, we see how these writers' positions and, more importantly, their creative strategies for agency arise from their negotiation with shifting ethnic affiliations. Rather than serving as simply a new alternative designation, however, Bhabha's "terrain" is the space, "unrepresentable in itself," in which racial self-articulation is disconnected from "primordial unity or fixity" (37). The protagonists of the texts each undergo highly individual itineraries of cultural denial and affiliation, represented by a pivotal "in-between" space. Boelhower describes these spaces as "extra-territorial cultural zones within the political boundaries of the nation" ("Making of Ethnic Autobiography" 129): literally, Chinatown for Wong and Choy and figuratively, the position they occupy as ethnic subjects. Negotiating these American spaces is part of the narrators' awareness of their positions and roles as ethnic subjects caught in American historical and social construction. These places also become alternative spaces for self-discovery and self-assertion and illuminate processes of subjectivity in the context of twentieth-century American history.

Language and food are two other crucial tropes that operate in these texts. Specifically, language becomes a contested site for identity formation as the presence of two languages in a child's life invariably creates an arena of conflict. Some texts deal with this issue through a superficial binary opposition between the child's desire to assimilate and the parents' attachment to the heritage culture. Nonetheless, a critically informed close reading might suggest that the nuances of such a problem are more subversive than they may seem. In most Childhoods set in North America, the question of language obsesses the child or parents, who fear that the acquisition of English will lead to the loss of the heritage language. The children grasp at English to belong in school and the neighborhood community. Many of the texts also suggest that the loss of the heritage language is a requisite to the process of North Americanization, something the children seek.

Though these tropes recur in many fictional and nonfictional accounts of Asian North American life, we must consider the *manner* in which the writers appropriate and use them. Because the tropes are readily identified in ethnic writing with processes of adaptation and/or assimilation, writers who are critically aware of the political nuances of stories about denizens or citizens often subvert the tropes to heighten meaning. Moreover, many writers incorporate new and unexpected tropes into their texts, challenging the paradigms of ethnic theories in which the parameters of ethnic immigrant success allow and encourage subjects to be "ethnic" only through certain tropes of ethnicity that are accepted in American culture, such as food and art (Su 22).

In particular, for example, we can read how the food tropes in Asian North American writing are, on the one hand, linked to the establishment of stereotypes and, on the other, how certain types of "less acceptable" foods have been used by Asian American writers as a literary trope to deconstruct the myth of the model minority (Sau-ling Wong, *Reading Asian American* 37–42). By reading the ways in which these writers use these tropes and in the case of Jade Snow Wong, how criticism has revised its opinion of her successively in the last four decades, we observe how these autobiographers intelligently read not only the manner in which mainstream culture requires formulations of ethnicity, but also write through and against imposed paradigms to heighten creativity and be more representative of the complexity of their experiences.

Finally, to signal an important paradigm of Coe's discussion of the Childhood, these texts posit complicated processes of socialization, which are enacted in alternative ways by these Asian North American subjects. Though the existence of the Childhood implies a certain form of favorable incorporation into society and participation in cultural production, the articulation of the situation of these subjects remains problematic on diverse levels. As I argued in the introduction, these Asian North American Childhoods recontextualize the forms and themes of traditional North American autobiography to propose alternative modes of being American through itineraries marked by separation and difference, rather than by integration. The lack of closure or the unsatisfying conclusions to many of these texts continue to suggest that the issue of self-identification within the mainstream or majority cultures remains open-ended.

Exoticizing Chinese-ness

After Yan Phou Lee and Ilhan New, autobiographers of childhood began to explore processes of North Americanization more critically. This development responds to an increasing awareness of the nuances of subjectivity as well as to the traditions that shaped autobiography in the United States and Canada. In the pluralistic American society, as Betty Bergland suggests, we must "recognize the multiply situated subject in autobiography, socially and historically shaped. In such a context ethnic autobiographies provide a meaningful site for exploring multiple subjectivities with implications for the larger culture" ("Postmodernism and the Autobiographical Subject" 134). In more contemporary texts, protagonists struggle with the alternatively divergent and intersecting markers of personal and cultural identity through the tropes that have marked the representation of ethnicity. As the narrator of *Fifth Chinese Daughter* notes: "she was now conscious that 'foreign' American ways were not only generally and vaguely different from their Chinese ways, but that they were specifically different, and the specific differences would involve a choice of action" (21). To an extent, Jade Snow Wong follows the pattern set by Lee and New, as she adopts what Sau-ling Wong denotes as the "stance of the cultural guide" found among Chinese-born and American-born autobiographers, many of whom are "conscious of their role as cultural interpreters who can obtain a measure of recognition from whites for the insider's insight they can offer" ("Autobiography as Guided Chinatown" 262, 264). Wong embraces her role as interpreter of the "life and heart of the Chinese people" in order to "contribute in bringing better understanding of the Chinese people, so that in the Western world they would be recognized for their achievements" (235). To transcend her liminal place between the sharply divided Chinese and American worlds of her childhood, she decides to serve as a reciprocal guide: she introduces her family to the customs of the American world and wields her insider familiarity with Chinese customs to win acceptance from mainstream Americans. The issue of acceptance by mainstream society recurs in the text, which narrates her childhood to early adulthood as a constant struggle to find a place in America. Wong's text is epistemologically very complex, as she often uncritically links opposing perspectives.[3]

Wong uses the Childhood to tell her story in a way that resounds in the American literary imagination. Nonetheless, she alters the central narratological device by shifting the first-person point of view to the third, subverting the heretofore unquestioned individualistic narrative perspective. The reasons— explicit and implied—for Wong's renegotiation of narrative perspective are interesting in two ways. First, she uses the third person to refer to herself, claiming that this stems from the "Chinese habit [where] the submergence of the individual is literally practiced. . . . Even written in English, an 'I' book by a Chinese would seem outrageously immodest to anyone raised in the spirit of Chinese propriety" (xiii). This choice has been analyzed in detail by feminist scholars, who regard this decision as the writer's acquiescence to the patriarchal system she claims to challenge. As Shirley Lim points out, "The fifth Chinese daughter, struggling in her schooling in the father's strict patriarchy, escapes and does not escape his narrow definitions. The third-person separation of autobiographical subject from narrative point of view subtly reinforces this 'distancing' or 'muting' of female subjectivity" ("Tradition of Chinese" 263).[4] Clearly, the Childhood may be read as the fight against a patriarchal system, where the narrator's rebellions are more often repressed than enacted, and "the objective author/narrator, describing the (auto)-biographical subject, represses the very subjectivity of the subject, objectifies it into a distant third-person protagonist" (258).

Though it appears that Wong manages to escape the rigidity of the system, she actually reinforces it.[5] Narratologically, her use of the third person also stresses the distance that she, as an adult writer, takes from her subject: herself as a child and as a developing subject positioning herself in the ethnic script of America. Here, Wong highlights a recurrent theme in ethnic Childhoods—

the conflict between the ways of the county of the parents and the child's America. When she informs her parents that she is going to a movie with a boy, the clash between her father's patriarchal stance and her American "unfilial theory" (128) climaxes: "'oh Mama! . . . This is America, not China. . . . Both of you should understand that I am growing up to be a woman in a society greatly different from the one you knew in China. . . . You must give me the freedom to find some answers for myself'" (129). But the father challenges her Americanized desire for individual freedom with a reminder of her heritage and her tenuous position as an outsider: "'your skin is yellow, your features are forever Chinese. . . . Do not try to force foreign ideas into my home'" (130). The Asian American child's need to identify with the American ethos of individual freedom—which includes the liberty to choose his or her cultural affiliation—becomes part of the itinerary of subjectivity.

Second, Wong positions herself clearly as a Chinese subject who gazes upon America as a land to be discovered, rather than as exclusively a Chinese person who explains her culture to Americans. The genre of the Childhood is once again a useful prism through which she elucidates for the reader the contradicting compulsions that direct her ambitions to be her own woman, even as she is buffeted on the one side by her family's strict adherence to tradition and, on the other, by America's racialized gaze. Wong clearly draws her liminal position: "no matter how critical she was of [her parents], she could not discard all they stood for and accept as a substitute the philosophy of the foreigners" (130). She consistently labels the Americans as "foreigners," producing an unexpected epistemological shift that reveals her ambivalence of point of view.

The notion that she and her family might consider the average American a "foreigner" when it is the Chinese who are classified by all as denizens forces a reevaluation of the positions from which belonging must be judged. Wong insists on carving a place for herself in that world, a decision that requires her to leave Chinatown—first for school, then to work—only to return in what she labels a "rediscovery" of the place where she was raised. As a young adult, she continues to experience, but does not critically negotiate, the subtle shifts in attitudes toward her. Owning a pottery business in Chinatown, she does not seem to mind that her only customers are Americans: the Chinese do not buy her products. Moreover, the Americans and Chinese watch her work through her window, marvel at the spectacle, speak and act in front of her as though she were deaf and dumb. Wong seems to actually *perform* her assertion of independence at the store window as she works at her pottery wheel. Yet this performance is disturbing: it highlights the independent ethnic female subject as an oddity to be observed through glass, as though she herself were a continent to be discovered, but which will remain unknown and unreachable. She thus occupies an even more indeterminate position: still a denizen in the eyes of Americans, she has now become also an outsider to the Chinese—though she alone seems unaware of this position, claiming that she has actually managed to achieve a balance.

Wong is conscious of the cultural role her text plays: "at a time when nothing had been published from a female Chinese American perspective," she explains, "I wrote with the purpose of creating better understanding of the Chinese culture on the part of Americans. That creed has been my guiding theme through the many turns of my life work" (vii). Her chapter titles illustrate the itinerary of explication that she embarks on: "Grandmother and Her World Back Home," "Lucky to Be Born a Chinese," "Learning to Be a Chinese Housewife," "Marriage Old and New Style," among others, focus on the cultural paradigms that shape the form of her autobiography. She describes how her self-as-child begins to learn proper Chinese behavior: "respect and order—these were the key words of life. It did not matter what were the thoughts of a little girl; she did not voice them" (2). She is not praised for achievements; when she tells her father that she has skipped a grade at school, he acknowledges that "that is as it should be" (19).

Inevitably, she contrasts these perspectives with those she begins to experience outside the home. Her account of the first hug she receives from an American lady was a "strange feeling," mostly because she was not accustomed to being embraced in consolation. "In fact," she notes, "when she was hurt either inside or outside, it was much better not to let Mama or Daddy know at all, because they might criticize her for getting into such a situation in the first place" (20). These early recollections clearly posit a Chinese form of behavior specifically highlighted to contrast with American ways. Most importantly, Jade Snow reveals how her independence is stifled, in clear contrast to the possibilities offered by an Americanized life: "at eleven, this daughter could hardly find a moment in her life which was not accounted for, and accounted for properly, by Mama or Daddy. She had not yet been allowed to visit any friend, of any age or sex, unaccompanied. She had never even gone to the playground, a block away from home, without a grown-up relative or friend in attendance" (65).

As Jade Snow begins to explore the outside world with increasing confidence in her own ability to make a place for herself, the problems with her family multiply. Wong's perspective on American customs is generally positive: she notes how in the American world people are more affectionate, and how creativity and independence are encouraged. This limited perspective, Elaine Kim observes, leads her to attribute all the negative aspects of her family or community to Chinese culture, rather than evaluate if these might be particular to her own family or conditioned by the social and economic restrictions that affected the Chinese American community in the early decades of the twentieth century (*Asian American Literature* 67).[6] Her admiration for American democracy leads her to disregard the contradictions of her own position as a domestic servant and unquestioningly accept that all of the kitchen workers at the Hall of Residence at Mills College are Chinese. The difficulty, she acknowledges, centers on her "desire for recognition as an individual" (91) in contrast to her family's perspective of her as a part of a group.

Yet the narrative is occasionally contradictory: even as Jade Snow emphasizes her father's strict dominance, she also notes that he encouraged her to master Chinese in order to go to China to continue studying after high school, believing that it was the place where a Chinese person could achieve further success. Jade Snow herself echoes this sentiment in her commencement speech: "but it seems to me that the most effective application that American-Chinese can make of their education would be in China, which needs all the Chinese talent she can muster" (135). The repeated discussions with her father make her see that she "was trapped in a mesh of tradition woven thousands of miles away by ancestors who had no knowledge that someday one generation of their progeny might be raised in another culture. Acknowledging that she owed her very being and much of her thinking to those ancestors and their tradition, she could not believe that this background was meant to hinder her further development either in America or China" (110).

Therefore, a central part of Wong's narrative of childhood focuses on her efforts to define herself as both American and Chinese, a strategy that appears unrealistic in her context and according to her perspective. Notably, for example, she explains how she changes her personality after being away at college: "Jade Snow no longer attempted to bring the new Western learning into her Oriental home. When she entered the Wong household, she slipped into her old pattern of withdrawal, and she performed her usual daughterly duties— shopping for Mama, household chores, writing business letters in English for Daddy—in the role of an obedient Chinese girl. But now she no longer felt stifled or dissatisfied, for she could return to another life in which she fitted as an individual" (168). This double life becomes her only outlet for negotiating conflicting forces.

Boelhower contends that "it was due to xenophobic pressure and the consequent need to allay spreading nativist fears that most immigrant/ethnic autobiographers sought to pass themselves off as Americans by didactically copying and promoting officially acceptable behavioral codes" ("Making of Ethnic Autobiography" 127). Wong not only adopts behavioral codes, but also arguably markets her Chinese-ness through the tropes that Americans welcome as acceptable ethnic manifestations, notably food. Wong vacillates between her deep appreciation of the worth of Chinese culture, her own struggle for American-style independence, and her unconscious appropriation of the stereotypes ascribed to the Chinese in America. Taking into account the demands of the reading public at the time, which was increasingly curious about Asia, Wong's text is illuminative. But her stereotypical renditions of habits or customs sound like an anthropologist's version of an exotic culture: she explains in detail things like cooking rice, wedding customs, festivals, and funerals. She notes uncritically that her acceptance in mainstream society is based specifically on her insider access to Chinese culture, her point of distinction that earns her high grades in essays. She also wins acceptance when she cooks an entire Chinese meal for the dean's guests. In a metaliterary gesture, she even includes detailed recipes for the dishes she made that evening: tomato beef and egg foo yung. Once again, Wong welcomes the gaze of mainstream America as she performs the role expected of her as an ethnic subject, doing the "ethnic" thing by preparing exotic food. Her naïve perspective on her own manner of influencing people's view of different cultures is articulated through her reflections after this meal: "Jade Snow ceased thinking of famous people as 'those' in a world apart. She had a glimpse of the truth, that the great people of any race are unpretentious, genuinely honest, and unpatronizing in their interest in other human beings" (173).

Boelhower sees the "ethnic feast" as "perhaps one of the best and most transparent literary topoi" for reading strategies of ethnic sign production (*Through a Glass Darkly* 113). This *Childhood* eagerly enlists that strategy, using images of food and the making of food to support, explain, validate, and promote Chinese culture. Sau-ling Wong says that the author takes the reader on "a verbal gastronomic tour" and notes that the autobiography is "openly solicitous in anticipating the white reader's curiosities" (*Reading Asian American* 63–64). This critic defines the narrator of *Fifth Chinese Daughter* as a "food pornographer," one who, according to Frank Chin, makes a living "by exploiting the 'exotic' aspects of one's ethnic foodways (qtd. in Sau-ling Wong, *Reading Asian American* 55). Moreover, by foregrounding her skill as a cook, Wong capitulates to her mainstream context's standards for acceptable Chinese behavior. Karen Su points out that to *The Big Aiiieeeee!* editors, Chin and Jefferey Paul Chan, "Wong was the epitome of the cookbook 'model minority' Christian who conformed to stereotypes of Asians held by the dominant culture: 1) being good cooks, 2) having a venerable high Asian culture, and 3) having been 'saved' by Christianity from the cruel aspects of Asian culture" (21). Her excellent meals prove to her friends that she is authentically Chinese; her difficulty with American meals suggests that she can never be "truly American." Therefore, because Wong's narrative conforms to the paradigm that allows her to be Chinese through acceptable tropes of ethnicity, we recognize that "Wong's relationship to Chinese ethnicity is assimilationist not because she identifies with Chinese culture *per se,* but that she identifies with it in the ways prescribed by American assimilation, opens up the possibility to affirm rather than to negate Asian ethnicity within the formation of Asian American identity" (22).

Wong pointedly draws attention to herself on several occasions, beginning in her childhood: she excels at school, demands independence, asserts her talents, christens a ship, cooks for admiring audiences, and works on her pottery by a glass window. This sense of a constant performance of both her Chineseness and American-ness supports her self-chosen position as a cultural bridge. We might argue that this self-proclaimed role as a cultural interpreter is "a calculated response to the opportunity for making a living in mainstream America, rather than one motivated simply by a desire to assimilate. She capitalizes on mainstream curiosity. Having embraced her newfound identity and mission as cultural interpreter, no longer is the author torn between two cultures, rather, she espouses the clear benefits of maintaining 'a balance between old ways and the new ways'" (Chun 63–64). In this sense, Wong's process of socialization is problematic. Su suggests that Wong, though apparently a successfully integrated member of society, remains very much an "exotic" figure, almost a symbol for her model minority status, performing her ethnicity in disturbing ways. Ironically, Wong herself appears to play into this role constructed for her by society and that she seems to accept uncritically. Nonetheless, the balance she posits, as the text demonstrates, cannot be attained, at least through the strategy that Wong espouses.

Chinese Cowboys and Secrets

Another important literary trope that Wong exploits, and which is also negotiated in Wayson Choy's *Paper Shadows* is the place known as Chinatown, a location that has acquired important resonances in the North American literary imaginary. Inscribing Chinatown is complex because of the multilayered meanings the site has acquired. For authors writing Childhoods, detailed depictions of the streets and cities that the children function in often limn their acute sense of marginalization from those specific places that, ironically, they know so well. Indeed, many narrators of their Childhoods undergo highly individual itineraries of cultural denial and affiliation, represented by a pivotal "in-between" space. These spaces correspond to Boelhower's definition of "extra-territorial cultural zones within the political boundaries of the nation" ("Making of Ethnic Autobiography" 129). Chinatown constantly reminds these children that they are considered Chinese, even as the context of the site—San Francisco for Wong and Vancouver for Choy—beckons to the children as, in a sense, their true place.

Childhoods such as *Fifth Chinese Daughter* and *Paper Shadows*, where Chinatown becomes a cultural space for the enactment of ethnicity, inflect the process through which place reconstitutes and transmits originary national culture. The word "Chinatown" itself is laden with sociohistoric connotations, and a realm of complex, dynamic valences lies beyond the name. To most of the Chinese population of any given large American or Canadian city, Chinatown connotes *habitation,* a permanent home, a locus of familiarity, security, and sustenance. To tourists seeking exciting but ultimately safe cultural encounters, however, Chinatown means *spectacle,* a diverting, exotic sideshow (Sau-ling Wong, "Ethnic Subject" 253). To move beyond the exotic and negotiate the dynamics of this cultural space involves rewriting the borders of the space to make readers rethink notions of uncritical classifications. Ultimately, these autobiographies invest multiple meanings into a sociospatially segregated Asian North American cultural space. More importantly, because of the location of Chinatown in the (Asian) North American imaginary, these texts produce a radical reframing of the role of location in multiethnic writing.

In theory, the Chinatown structure suggests home and family, yet these narratives use the authors' memory to disclose alternative approaches to Chinatown, signaling a critical junction in both Asian American subjectivity and the organizations of collectivity within the community. Wong and Choy reconceptualize the connection between place and subject, expanding the boundaries of this location of origin for many Chinese North Americans. They problematize the definition of "home" and suggest that leaving it is imperative. These engagements with Chinatown rearticulate the very notion of space, belonging, and heritage for Chinese Americans and Canadians, as Chinatown is represented as a seemingly static place that habitants must struggle to escape from, while at the same time it is marked by particular forms of travel and transitivity. This ambivalence is experienced by both children, though Wong's depiction is more circumspect, perhaps because of the stance she negotiated. Choy, on the other hand, writing at the end of the 1990s, uses a freer prose because he is not burdened by the need to "explain" Chinatown to readers. As his aunt explains to his mother: "Sonny lives in Canada, not just Chinatown" (241). Even as it leaves it, Choy himself acknowledges his permanent link to the place: "even as a *mo-no,* someone who would one day lose almost all his first language and live for more than two-thirds his life away from Vancouver's Chinatown, I would always be, and still am, as Grandfather said, *tong-yung*—Chinese. . . . I belonged" (137).

Elaine Kim notes that Wong's depiction of Chinatown is "exoticized" and presents only "a partial picture of community life." She argues that the efforts of some second-generation writers to win acceptance in American society leads them to present these incomplete perspectives in order to explain themselves to mainstream society, an orientation that "represents but a fraction of the concerns within the Chinese American community at large" (*Asian American Lit-*

erature 91).[7] In any case, because Wong portrays the child's perspective, at least in the early part of the narrative, some of these omissions might actually be explained by her own oblivion to the nuances of the Chinatown experience. Choy, on the contrary, does negotiate the subtleties of Chinatown culture in humorous—even ironic—ways. He offers a doubled perspective, complicating the stereotypical view of the trope of location. On the one hand, he describes the increasing influx of tourists who begin to enter Chinatown during the war.

> Up to the mid-1930s, Chinatown was an impoverished, undesirable place for tourists. The restaurants and tailor shops were mostly empty of visitors, who came either for the New Year's fireworks or as part of a trouble-making gang. Perhaps Hollywood movies initiated the changing attitudes towards Chinatown. Films featuring Anna May Wong and Charlie Chan made Chinatown seem exotic and less frightening than the Fu Manchu opium-addict world of the silent era. Chinatown was now seen as a friendly two-block exotic adventure, safe terrain in which to spend the extra wartime dollars pouring into West Coast port cities such as Vancouver.

On the other hand, he examines his own shifting identification with the cultural markers of both Chinatown and North American culture, specifically the opera and American Westerns. As tourists were discovering Chinatown, he explains, "I was discovering my own exotic landscape: East Hastings Street. To me, not anything in Chinatown could prove as interesting as what I now worshipped: *c-o-w-b-o-y-s*" (69). The instability of the word "exotic" is clearly articulated though the child's perspective, which Choy deftly manipulates.

Most of the narrative of Choy's memory is filled with the elements of children's culture that permeate most Childhoods: his close relationship with his mother, his playmates, entering kindergarten, the liberating experience of learning how to read, among others. This writer graphically portrays the traumas and world of childhood—his nightmares, his entry into school for the first time, thinking that it was a place for the dead, the imagination that allowed him to play by himself for hours. Nonetheless, because he is a Chinatown boy, his story reflects the cultural shifts that he must negotiate. Wayson is taught that "home" is always a village in old China—"where they still wanted you, even dead; where you belonged. For ever" (31)—even as he mumbles the words to "God Save the King" when they play the Chinese national anthem in Chinese school.

But Choy's Childhood is unique in an important way: the story grew from an enigma about his past. In the first chapter of *Paper Shadows,* he explains how at a radio interview after the publication of his novel *The Jade Peony* a woman called to tell him she had just seen his mother who, he insists, had died eighteen years earlier. This call produces a "shift" in the past (5): at the age of fifty-six, Wayson Choy learns he was adopted. Ironically, then, his novel about Chinatown secrets becomes the key to revealing the one secret of his life: "one single call had shifted all the pieces; I felt trapped between fact and fiction. This real-life drama beginning to unfold, this eerie echo of the life of one of my fictional characters, struck me as the ultimate irony. Suddenly, nothing of my family, of home, seemed solid and specific. Nothing in my past seemed to be what it had always been" (280).[8]

A sense of urgency pervades this Childhood: Choy revisits his history to understand how he could not have known the truth about his biological parents, sift through the memories of the past to see if there was something he could have or should have known. He then embarks on the narrative of his childhood, most of which is set from about the ages of four to nine, before the family leaves Vancouver's Chinatown to move to Ontario. Trying to repossess his biological, ethnic, and cultural identity, he conducts extensive research into Chinatown archives and museum and library records; he interviews old relatives for information about his birth and education; and he recreates his childhood to reexamine his past. Choy begins by confirming his family lineage to underline his sense of biological and cultural belonging. He explains that his grandfather came from Victoria to name him. The chosen name, Way Sun, literally means "to rehabilitate," and that it was "an epigram in Old China," a promise "to reform old ways through peaceful means" (16). This description becomes a plea for legitimacy: where, in all these details, is the fact of his adoption? Only one unexplained incident remains: he recalls being taken to see a woman who is ill and instructed to repeat the words "I'm fine. My name is Choy Way Sun and I'm a good boy" (13). The reader wonders if this might be his biological mother, as Choy himself seems to contemplate. But no definitive answers are given at this point, or later in the text.

The narrative, then, pivots around two axes: one, his astonishingly vivid memories of his childhood; and two, the present knowledge that things were not what they seemed. The account is laden with sensory detail, humor, and explicit descriptions of the manner in which this energetic, spoiled, very intelligent, and creative child encounters the world. In this sense, Choy's Childhood—superlatively the childhood of a writer—is a pleasure to read, as he unselfconsciously presents his childlike manner of apprehending the seeming contradictions of his Chinese Canadian world. In one of the few studies about Canadian Childhoods, Thomas Tausky posits that at some point "a Canadian child is reminded, gently or harshly, of a racial or regional inheritance that molds her being as much as any individual personality traits she may possess. The Canadian autobiographer always tells the story of tradition and the individual talent; moreover, the tradition is often that of another country, not of

Canada" (44). Choy manages to conciliate seemingly disparate traditions and forms. As Eva-Marie Kröller points out, "as a child, he is forever torn in several directions at once. Thus his fascination with Cantonese opera and its costumes is paralleled by an infatuation with cowboy movies; he loves opera dolls as much as he does Disney's Dopey, and he is as conversant in Chinese legends as he is in Andersen's fairy-tales" (179–180).

His memory of storytelling with his grandfather is particularly illustrative. As the child learns how to read and link the shifts between the Chinese language and English storybooks, he tells the story of *The Three Little Pigs* in the language he calls Chinglish: "I HUFF-foo! I PUFF-foo! I BLOW nay-gah *house* DOWN!" (161). The energy with which the child appropriates all these seeming contradictions, only to emerge smiling, nonetheless hides an incomplete history. Choy revisits these memories to find clues to the secret: the reader also seeks the clues. Thus, as Choy traces the trajectory of his cultural and biological identity through a creative rendering of his childhood, we understand the ways in which his ethnic identity as a Chinese Canadian intersects with his cultural identity in Vancouver's Chinatown in the mid-twentieth century, a site at which two cultures and two national histories constantly competed for domination and eventually created a transcultural dynamics especially in terms of language, religion, and culture.

The dynamics of this hybridity is illustrated by Choy's use of photographs that support the narrative of his fascination with the icons of Chinese and North American culture. The Childhood includes about thirty photographs, which range from reproductions of scroll portraits of his great-great-grandfather and his great-grandfather, to photographs of his family, friends, and many of himself—most often with his parents. These imply that Choy needs to locate himself narratively and pictorially in the context of a family. Yet photographs also signify importantly in the context of writing about issues of transculturality. Rosalia Baena argues that photographic discourse in autobiography enacts memory to limn narrative tension between body and location, making biopolitical statements about positions of multiethnicity (361). Using narratological theories that endorse the constitutive character of the photograph within autobiographical texts, she reads the photograph as a site of contested ethnicities for transcultural subjects. In particular, she analyzes the more emblematic photographs that Choy includes in his Childhood—pictures of himself dressed as a cowboy—arguing that the incorporation of these photographs signify discursively: "specifically, photographs of childhood tend to reveal how transcultural writers make use of the child figure to negotiate their past and present identities and create a metaphor of the ironic contrast between the body and location of the ethnic self, made more poignant because of the child's oblivion to the nuances of his or her cultural displacement. It is the adult autobiographer that chooses to offer discrete images in the attempt explore his or her past" (363).

Reading these photographs reveals Choy's particular process of cultural hybridity through one of his most persistent childhood dreams: wanting to be a cowboy. Yet, he narrates how his fascination with cowboy stories actually grew from his early introduction to Chinese opera where, because he could not understand what was going on, his mother fed him simplified versions of the plot, with happily-ever-after endings, unknowingly preparing him for the straightforward good-conquers-evil plots of American Westerns. Later, his "uncles," the Chinatown bachelor men, would take him to see the Westerns: "no one had to know much English to understand what was going on. Soon I refused to go to the Cantonese opera. Canyons and cactus and the bright stretches of the desert horizon captivated me, and made the table-and-chair landscape at the Cantonese opera laughable. The living dramas that had once stirred my imagination now seemed ridiculous" (82).

Choy effectively communicates the intense emotions that support his imagination and, as Baena points out, "the cowboy photographs become a site in which, and from which, the writer speculates on issues of cultural assimilation and possibilities. The image of an Asian child dressed as a cowboy is a powerful visual symbol of both the process and the struggle of assimilation towards the [Canadian] Dream. The costume of a North American heroic icon helps to mediate the otherwise painfully indeterminate position of a Chinese Canadian subject" (364). As Choy watches more films, his imagination becomes more galvanized by North American heroes—Robin Hood, Tarzan— and his rejection of the models of Chinese opera is completed. Subsequently, he also begins to feel aversion for his own racial identification, opting for the standards of goodness and beauty proposed by his Western heroes: "through the mostly cowboy movies, and the few cowboy-and-Indian ones, I began to wish I did not look like a Chinese boy. Good and Evil became crayon strokes: Good Guys were handsome, and Bad Guys ugly. . . . Like most Chinatown boys, I wanted to ride in the saddle and shoot away at the bad guys. I would be one of the Good Guys, of course—fair-haired, pale-skinned, grey-eyed, and tall in the saddle" (80–81). Though the photographs show the boy smiling with satisfaction at looking like his heroes because he can dress like them, the representation remains an illusion. The irony of the photographs lies in the child's fantasy of an impossible cultural amalgamation because a Chinese boy can never be a cowboy, except in his imagination.

Nonetheless, the child narrator holds to the impossibility of the dream of becoming a cowboy, painfully aware of the ironic connotations that this carries: "my English world . . . centred around the boyish images of Hollywood. Nothing Chinese could save me. . . . Soon, Chinatown began to fade, like a ghost. I was turning into a banana: yellow on the outside and white on the inside. Many nights, I dreamed I was sitting tall in the saddle, posed heroically on a rearing palomino, speaking English words I pronounced perfectly: my face flowing like moonlight, my eyes gunsmoke-grey, my cowboy hand waving a cowboy farewell—to silk, to jade, and, most of all, to boring arias" (84). Choy describes how he and his Chinatown friends gradually moved away from Chinese to English: "soon, English words and phrases became more interesting for me to speak. More and more, English vowels marked the rhythms and sounds [that] my Chinatown playmates and I responded to." His mother's simple logic— "You Chinese. You speak Chinese" (83)—cannot overcome the cultural forces of adaptation operating in Choy and Chinatown, as the boy notes that "there were other ways to be Chinese" (242). Nonetheless, his imagination also makes the return trip. Though he loves *Snow White and the Seven Dwarfs* and is actually given a hand puppet of his favorite, Dopey, he needs to remodel the doll before he can actually play with it effectively. Thus, the sleepy-eyed dwarf is adorned with "a Chinese warrior's gilded cape by safety-pinning one of Mother's embroidered handkerchiefs around his thick neck. In his right cloth palm, I taped a thin bamboo skewer Mother had used for cooking, and tied a miniature hand-made pennant to it. Though his eyes remained sky-blue, Dopey was now as Chinese as I wanted" (220). Dopey, thus, becomes part of his treasured collection of Chinese opera dolls.

Wayson Choy appropriates the genre of the Childhood to reexamine his life in an attempt to tease out the one secret kept from him. In the process, perspectives he learned as he was growing up resonate significantly. For example, because his mother wanted to protect him from the tragic endings of many Chinese operas, she would explain that the heroines at the end cried "for happy": "I remember sensing something was amiss; not knowing any better, I grew to dread happy endings. To this day, if I ever wish for anything, I never wish for happiness" (55). Nonetheless, these reworkings of the opera and the fables his mother told him became "a permanent barrier against pessimism, perhaps even against adversity" (56).

The final section of the autobiography is set in the 1990s, as Choy's knowledge of his adoption leads him to explore his family history more systematically, again as though to locate himself in a lineage he knows he does not belong to and also to validate the history of the Chinese in Vancouver. Though the author never solves the mystery of his parentage, except to note that his mother had died and that his father was an opera singer (whom he may have actually seen during those interminable afternoons at the opera), the quest itself becomes the center of the narrative. The shift in his mother's stories—where heroines cry "for happy"—becomes his own ending: an imagined happy ending as part of his palimpsestic storytelling or, conversely, his peeling away of layers of histories and stories. Using the metaphor of "a Chinese box that opens in a variety of ways, revealing different levels, each sliding compartment secret" (337), the document he inscribes, this Childhood, becomes the record of a search and an awareness on the levels of biology and of culture: "like a good mystery novel, I thought to myself, one's life should always be read twice, once for the experience, then once again for astonishment" (333).

Subverting Tropes of Americanization

Boelhower's description of immigrant identity serves as a frame for M. Elaine Mar's process of selfhood: "the immigrant protagonist's identity—insofar as it is based on at least two different cultural systems—equips him or her to act metaculturally in the New World environment. In other words, the autobiographical journey of the immigrant protagonist inevitably leads to the juxtaposition and interaction of two cultural typologies, due to the very mobility of the hyphenated protagonist. As a structural effect of these two cultural spaces, as an epistemological filter (spatial movement is now a schooling process), the protagonist seeks to mediate between two cultural codes in a deconstructive/reconstructive process embodied in a narrative encyclopedia of international frames" (*Autobiographical Transactions* 14–15). Tropes also serve as effective narrative frames in life writing. In *Paper Daughter,* Mar appropriates three of the most classic tropes of Americanization and critically subverts them to deexoticize previously unquestioned markers of ethnic identity. She uses the tropes of food, the English language, and writing to map her own individual process, reading through and against other texts that also wield these metaphors, but teasing out more substantial meaning by challenging the earlier employment of these tropes.

Mar's Childhood is patterned chronologically—from her early childhood in a cramped apartment in Hong Kong, to the basement flat in her aunt's house in Denver to where they move in 1972 when she is about six, to the family's small apartment, and finally, to Harvard. Mar uses the concept of immigration in interesting ways: she shows how her family history may be mapped in terms of successive immigrations—her grandfather's, her family's, and finally, her own move to Harvard as a departure to a place "as far away as another country" (292). Indeed, her epilogue is titled "A Second Immigration," which suggests how her education, as much as the economic difficulties that made them leave Hong Kong in the first place, operates as a tool for family separation. Ironically, the opportunities that her parents sought for her in the United States become precisely the route to alienation from her family and culture.[9]

Mar harnesses the tropes of immigrant stories to oblige the reader to reconsider previously unquestioned issues of representation. Food is perhaps the most notable of these, and the memoir begins with a reference to food as a primary defining element. The first chapter, "Chicken Bones and Mother's Milk," opens with: "my memory begins with the taste of chicken blood. . . . The memory of sweetness before language, desire born before knowledge of the words to describe it" (1). This reference to the first sweetness is actually a subversive tool because the food described rarely evokes pleasant memories. The taste of chicken blood, which the narrator describes rapturously on several occasions, is bound to make the average American reader squirm. But Mar does not capitulate to mainstream standards of culinary acceptability; rather, she describes in positive terms what might reasonably be considered disgusting and inedible. Her negotiation of food in her Childhood is extensive and elaborate: it is her first memory, it marks celebrations and promotes a sense of family cohesiveness, it is a source of income, it affirms her awareness of the consequences of immigration, and finally, the possibility to control food intake gives her a warped sense of dominion over her own life at a point when she needs independence from her family.

As Sau-ling Wong explains, quoting from James W. Brown, because eating is one of the most biologically deterministic and, at the same time, socially adaptable human acts—a meal can be a simple prelinguistic phenomenon or a multivalent sign coded in language, manners, and rites—alimentary images pose particularly intriguing challenges in the interpretation of nonmainstream literature (*Reading Asian American* 18). Food in ethnic literature may be examined as a code that expresses a "pattern of social relations," reading the contents and sequencing of meals as texts with their corresponding form and thematic content (Mary Douglas 61). Moreover, the description of food and meals plays a fundamental role in Asian American literature, as Wong shows in *Reading Asian American Literature,* illustrating how the use of alimentary images shapes the texts' aesthetic and cultural work. The focus, in many cases, is on "how eating and drinking constitute an elaborate and complex sign language which metonymically brackets and informs all aspects of discourse and human experience" (Hinz v). Asian North American autobiographies use food images to support the epistemological process, a supplement to personal and cultural meaning. Moral values and meals are complexly interwoven: the giving, receiving, eating, and serving of food become means of signifying. Moreover, it appears that something about the immigrant situation—perhaps the shock of permanent relocation to a White-dominated society and the daily trials of adjustment—caused the first generation to value efficient eating unquestioningly, "almost as a measure of spiritual stamina" (Sau-ling Wong, *Reading Asian American* 25). In *Paper Daughter,* all the scenes related to food and eating with the family demonstrate how the narrator privileges these rituals as a part of the negotiation of identity and self-affirmation. The text resonates with enthusiastic descriptions of meals—the ritual they called *Yum Cha* (which Americans call dim sum), New Year's meals, and family snacks, among others. This supports Wong's contention that alimentary images, juxtaposed and read as a group, symbolize necessity—"all the hardships, deprivations, restrictions, disenfranchisements, and dislocations that Asian Americans have collectively suffered as immigrants and minorities in a white-dominated world" (20).

Mar's use of food as a trope for immigrant subjectivity recurs in her Childhood. She articulates her realization that she has truly left Hong Kong and now lives in the United States through food imagery. Her description of chicken blood marks her transition from Cantonese child to immigrant child. Describing her favorite meal in Hong Kong, she gushes: "I *liked* everything else. I *craved* chicken wings. A true Cantonese, I never cared about the meat; I wanted the bones. Watching the adults, I learned to crack the thin-shelled, hollow bones with my milk teeth, voraciously sucking out heavy, clotted marrow. In an overcooked chicken, it clumped, soil-brown and mealy, almost not worth the effort. In one done just right, it spilled out bright red, the color of life, rich and smooth on the tongue. I hungered for that fertile interior where blood cells begin: I wanted to eat the bird's soul" (17). Living with her Aunt Becky in Denver, "[they] ate bland lunches. Sandwiches and cans of Spaghetti-Os that Aunt Becky had taught [her] mother to prepare. Food that erased memory and leached [her] body of desire" (49). When served a meal of chicken wings in front of her Chinese American cousin, San, she devours the meat and ravenously begins to crunch the bones in search of the marrow. San reacts in horror at watching her eat the bones. "I wasn't sure what I had done wrong," Mar remembers, "but I didn't like his reaction. Breathing back tears—regretfully—I reminded myself to behave as San did. No more chicken bones. I lived in America now" (49). Using the child's limited perspective, she traces her transition through the reevaluation of these tropes in her experience.

Closely related to the place of ethnic food in the American imaginary, the Chinese restaurant has become an eloquent location in the Asian American consciousness. The restaurant her father, later her mother, and even herself works at becomes the center of family life—it is their source of income, an epitome of exploitation of Asian immigrant workers, and the location of her first sexual encounter. Her experience in the restaurant offers her the concept of food as a consumer product, a manifestation of the acquisitive power of money, which her family and the other workers did not possess. The first time she tastes leftovers at the restaurant, she admits that it was food she would not have eaten in other circumstances: "but tasting it behind the kitchen, I ingested magic. I suddenly understood how it felt to sit in the dining room, to command rather than serve" (177). Watching how the waitresses and her family ate the leftovers, she notes how they became "vultures, bottom feeders," scavenging

years and ten months, I suddenly discovered that I needed food to think clearly" (270). In the end, she reaches a balance in relation to food because she finds a place where she can express herself freely, independently of her parents' impositions. Moving to Harvard gives her the financial independence she needs to break away, leading to a more crucial break with the family and the past.

The narrator of *Paper Daughter* blends the issues of children's culture—particularly the need to be just like everyone else—with questions of race and ethnic identification. Language serves in many instances as the paradigm of her awareness of liminality. Her loyalty to and appreciation of being Chinese—she acknowledges that it will always be her first language and that "there are things [she] know[s] in Chinese—primal, visceral things—that [she] will never know in English" (x)—shifts as she becomes aware of the power granted by possession of English. Mar describes the situation of the young child trapped between two languages—unable to express herself fully in either because of her lack of proficiency in one and because the other simply did not have the words to express her new experiences. When she begins school and cannot express herself in English, she feels "trapped inside [her] body. Language seemed a purely physical limitation" (66). She does not know how to release the thoughts inside her head and remains mute, leading the children to ignore or ridicule her. At home, she is unable to explain these traumatic experiences to her mother because their language, she believes, does not accommodate such a conversation: "the Chinese don't ask their children, *How was school today?* They say, *What did you learn?* and *Do you understand your lessons?* In Cantonese I could only describe the equations we'd solved that day. I was able to show her my spelling list. And I could honestly say that I *did* understand, on paper, at least. It was harder to explain that the kids groaned when I was chosen to be 'it,' that I hated dodgeball, and that I was largely mute" (69). Even as she grows older, the acquisition of vocabulary does not give her the ability to express herself crossculturally: "I didn't know how to describe my life in a way that my friends could understand. Speaking in English, I had the vocabulary, but not the context: The words *family* and *home* would not carry the meanings I intended. Compared to their Chinese correlates, the English words were limited; they didn't imply generations bound up in one identity, rooted in one place. Using English, I couldn't convey my sense of loss" (215). Mar illustrates, through her own experience, the limitations of learning languages—the untranslatable cultural codes that refer to social structures or mores, rather than merely vocabulary. She highlights particular points in her childhood when the separation between her life at home and her increasingly complicated social life outside it weigh heaviest on her precisely because she does not have the words in either language to be able to connect both locations. Again, liminality is heightened by the abyss between the two spaces she occupies.

A key moment in Mar's process of adaptation comes with the acquisition of a new name. The question of her name is crucial in the narrative—the narrator describes in detail in the prologue how the history of the family name, Mar, is confused yet "one thing is certain: 'Mar' is inappropriately transliterated, and it is the spelling of [her] name" (xi). She then makes a discussion on naming a paradigm for the process of acculturation and a sense of rootedness. After they immigrate and her aunt tells her she needs an American name to fit in better, the child resists at first—her name, Mar Man Yee, is important to her. She had been taught the meaning of the two characters—"*Man Yee,* two characters meaning 'intelligence' and 'righteousness,' respectively" (8)— which were expressions of her parents' desires for her: to be clever and as a commemoration of Mao's Cultural Revolution. Also, because they cannot speak English, she worries that neither she nor her mother will know the name. A Mexican American aunt by marriage is asked to think of a name, and she chooses "Elaine," a name change that the child construes as a shift away from previously unquestioned selfhood: "eee-laine. . . . I repeated the sound. So that's who I was. My life cleaved in two" (62).

This linguistic point, giving the child an American name, also signals the birth of another person—the child Elaine who will speak in English and function within that new identity independently of the family. Further, in the prologue, Mar notes the existence of a multiplicity of spellings of her name: different versions are valid for her narrative of childhood, her birth certificate, and tax records. Most often, she acknowledges that she signs "M. Elaine Mar," a hybrid construction that works as "an indication of what [she's] become— the self expressed in English, preceded by the vestige of a name that cannot be written, ending with the mystery of one that will never leave [her]" (xii). With a new name, increasing proficiency in English, and slow adaptation to school, Elaine changes: she seeks acceptance in the world she occupies for most hours of the day. But she is not spared the process of the immigrant child, who finds herself a veritable misfit everywhere. At school, she cannot comprehend why she continues to be singled out: "I spoke English, I played hopscotch, I owned a McMeen Meenie t-shirt. What could be wrong with me? I tried harder. I got one hundreds on spelling tests, I read better than anyone else in my class. Nobody cared. They pushed in front of me in line to the drinking fountain. They pulled up the corners of their eyes mockingly. *Chink eyes, slant eyes, you're so ugly, why don't you go back to where you came from?*" (116–117). In the fall of 1974, classified as a "minority" she is not bused to another district. Along with this category, she learns that she has the talent to spin stories about Hong Kong that fascinate her schoolmates—and that the more exotic the stories, the more attention she received. "That fall," she realizes, "it became fashionable to be Chinese" (140).

At this point, Mar finds herself not only defined as a minority but also an outsider because she does not have the privilege to buy what the other kids have. Though she is proud of how "American" she has become, she continues to try and hide her "foreignness, that combination of ethnicity and poverty. [She] would have given anything to slip into the ordinary" (158). Because of their poverty, she cannot dress like the rest of her friends, or join in all their activities. On occasions, she resorts to lies in order to participate in the normal activities of an American schoolchild, which are incomprehensible and therefore judged unnecessary by her parents. When the school manufactures T-shirts with the mascot on the front, she desperately needs to have one because everyone else does. Her mother does not comprehend her need to be like the rest, reminding her that the important thing is to be a good Chinese daughter. But, Mar notes, in a universal expression of the childhood desire to be part of a group: "I didn't want to be good or clever or obedient. I didn't even want my snack. I wanted to be a McMeen Meenie" (99).

Mar describes the acquisition of English in terms that extend beyond the traditional ones used in ethnic fiction. English isolates the older immigrant generation from the younger, who become more and more comfortable in the new language and use it, consciously or not, to inhabit a world alien to the adults. Elaine, her cousin, and younger brother begin to address each other with their English names and eschew honorific titles altogether, wearing her mother's protests down by disobeying consistently. "Our household existed in parallel worlds" (161), she explains, with English used by the children and neighbors, but not by the Chinese adults. For the children, it became "a code for power, moving [them] closer to the majority culture, further marginalizing [their] parents and memories of [their] past" (161). More importantly, as Elaine becomes proficient in English and enters her teenage years, family roles inevitably shift: "[I became] the American voice of the family, the connection between our basement room and the outside world. I'd accepted a hollow name, an empty construct, and created an identity with it in four short years" (160).

In particular, her relationship with her mother changes as roles alter and the child begins to look critically at her mother: "we were entering a long period of mutual struggle over our identities. I believed that she reflected poorly on me, and vice versa. I thought she should become more stylish—a code for 'American.' She dreamed of a dutiful Chinese daughter with my face, inhabiting my body" (159). The mother's inadequate possession of English makes her need Elaine, and she becomes susceptible to her daughter's manipulation, "a dreadful power" (159) because it reassigned the traditional roles of mother and child. Because her mother needed Elaine's help for shopping, filling out official forms, bank slips, and report cards, the child began to exert power over the household, questioning her own position and feeling insecure.

But the mother continues to try to control her daughter, leading to more alienation and frustration for both. Elaine's anorexia actually stems from her mother's controlling impulse and their poverty. She begins to violate the most sacred of tenets—absolute loyalty to the family.

The final trope that Mar engages is the idea of writing. Many of the Childhoods analyzed in this book privilege the writing child in a metaliterary gesture that allows us to examine the child that will become the author of the book we read. Elaine admits that her fascination with the storying of the world begins before she can even read, with stories heard at Bible school. As an adolescent plagued by the trauma of misunderstanding at home and in school, she battles her insecurities by writing about needing a home rooted in a place, her ambivalent feelings toward her parents, her longing to get away. As with her organization of food intake, writing allows her to control her life: "my emotions were wild and amorphous, but words had limits. They were concrete, markings confined to paper, their edges shaped by the motion of my hand, their meanings bound by dictionary definitions. I wanted similar boundaries for myself, and writing was my way of establishing them. On paper, my life seemed manageable. . . . I wrote and wrote, and I felt safe because I could close the covers on my words. Every day, after I finished writing, I flipped the notebook shut and hid it under my mattress. Muffling myself" (212).

Her ability to write gets her into the TASP (Telluride Association Summer Program), a six-week seminar at Cornell University, yet leads her to face unarticulated truths about her past. When she reads the recommendation letter for her entry into TASP, one sentence stands out: *"vivid descriptions of the characters who inhabit the seedy restaurant where her father is a line cook"* (274). In one of her most eloquent moments of self-realization, she repeats the words "seedy" and "line cook" to herself and revises her memories of her past, strengthening her resolve to leave it behind. Though Mar's Childhood may be read as a success story—acceptance into Harvard is the culmination of the classic Asian Immigrant Dream—this success comes at a great price: "a second immigration . . . with no way to send for [her] family" (292). Though Mar claims to continue to value Chinese culture and identify with it, she has also, consciously or not, chosen to sacrifice her bond with her family through her willing transformation into an "American." This text demonstrates that even the ostensibly successful stories are not unproblematically formulated and require a reexamination of the nature of success, and the price the subject has had to pay for it. This text therefore gestures toward a renewed resistance to prescriptive norms of social conformity and prevailing discourses on the paradigms of the genre.

By creatively harnessing the tropes of North Americanization, these authors allow us to examine the ways in which the processes of assimilation and/or adaptation have been inscribed in evolving contexts. The way Jade

Snow Wong describes food, for example, responds to a particular manner of articulating Chinese-ness, limited by current perspectives on "exotic" fare; Elaine Mar, writing fifty years later, when Americans were more comfortable with international cuisine, tests the limits of this acceptance by her passionate descriptions of even more "exotic" food, like chicken blood. Though both writers use the same trope, Mar takes Wong's project a step further by demolishing any reader expectation of appropriate representation of ethnic food. These strategies, in any case, tell us more about the time the writers were working in than of their own creativity. Similarly, Choy's recollection of his childhood assembles the markers of a 1930s boyhood in Chinatown—opera, cowboys, and English—as tropes that need to be explored in order to reveal secrets. Examining the way these tropes operate within a genre reveals not only writerly strategies, but the ways in which authors generate and multiply meaning.

Chapter 6

In North America

Formulating Experience

In this chapter, I read Childhoods that actively renegotiate the forms of traditional autobiography to show how these writers' cultural work extends
beyond mere ethnographic interventions to reconfigure the form of life writing
itself. Aimee Liu's *Solitaire,* Evelyn Lau's *Runaway: Diary of a Street Kid,* Lynda
Barry's *One Hundred Demons,* and Loung Ung's *Lucky Child* experiment with
narrative form and encourage us to understand how the form of writing itself
signifies. This study has emphasized the cultural work enacted by the texts in
the process of shaping collective memory as well as how Asian North American
texts have promoted the revision of autobiographical form. Noting once again
the role that Kingston's *The Woman Warrior* has played in the development of
autobiographical writing by women and ethnic subjects, I consider how other
texts by Asian North American writers further expand the structures and forms
through which personal experience may be narratologically enacted.

The relationship between the act of narrating a life and the forms through
which a life may be narrated requires examination. Critics of autobiography
have repeatedly discussed the ways in which theme and form interact, and in
what has become the classic statement of poststructuralist criticism on autobiography, Paul de Man asks, "We assume that life *produces* the autobiography as
an act produces its consequences, but can we not suggest, with equal justice,
that the autobiographical project may itself produce and determine the life and
that whatever the writer *does* is in fact governed by the technical demands of
self-portraiture and thus determined, in all its aspects, by the resources of his
medium?" (920–921). This statement highlights the crucial interrelation
between the life and the forms that the narratives of that life embody. For this
reason, we must explore the structures that authors consciously appropriate in
order to understand, from the formulation of the autobiography itself, the paradigms through which particular lives are narratively enacted.

These writers renegotiate form in a variety of ways; the structures have
intimate links with thematic concerns or creative approaches. According to

Judith Varner Gunn, autobiographical writers construct a self through language and writing, and the autobiographical perspective has to do "with taking oneself up and bringing oneself to language" (16). When the structures of language and genre prove to be limited, ethnic writers have challenged prescriptive norms to formulate structures that more adequately represent their experiences. As such, readers perceive a heightened concern with the norms of self-formation and self-narration in these Childhoods, where previous models are judged unsuitable for representing specific pasts. The disruption between established paradigms and the possibilities for revisionary creative expression denotes that the experience itself becomes a motivating factor for the form of the narrative—Liu's story of anorexia establishes the pattern that these autobiographical narratives will take; Lau's diary validates the form as a Childhood; Barry's comics propose a graphic representation that juxtaposes image and words; Ung's relational autobiography uses a doubled perspective to maintain a unified family structure. Importantly, these narrative strategies show that the authors consciously write beyond a specific cultural arena to address a wider audience—these texts are not only about Asian North American experiences: they are sophisticated enactments of self-narration that speak to more than just ethnic groups. They address questions about self-representation that plague all writers of autobiography and fiction, as they negotiate the ways in which one writes (or draws) the "I" into existence. All these Childhoods narrate painful experiences, in the context of class awareness, racial affiliation, or illness, and the authors' use of innovative structures enhances the reader's appreciation of the experience because it invites a critical reading of the form. These texts are therefore doubly self-conscious: as the writers look back on their childhoods, they also choose the forms that will heighten specific experiences of those childhoods and transmit the issues better to both their ethnic community and the reading public in general.

The question of writing personal and communal stories simultaneously—addressing ethnic concerns as well as narrative possibilities—leads the writers to seek what Carol Feldman calls "an interpretive vocabulary for both group and individual stories" (132). As the individual stories inform the communal stories by internalization, Feldman asserts, the individual stories act on the group by projection, obliging us to attend to multiple ways of meaning that the Childhoods offer. Thus, we read these Childhoods not only as the result of particular experiences but as creative sources of cultural production on many levels. In chapter 3, I argued that the writers of the Childhoods were primarily acted upon rather than acting and that the dramatic bellicose conflicts they experienced obliged them to articulate experiences in a preordained pattern.

Here I posit that other Asian North American writers consciously liberate themselves from limited or limiting structures to take control of the narrative and influence the production of life writing in general. This involves a strong liberatory act, one that involves finding a voice or a style that reflects multiple components of identity, plural perspectives, and increased creative freedom. Interestingly, these negotiations become powerful critiques of prescriptive paradigms within the field of autobiography. Feldman says we should note "that genre not only patterns the telling, and affects the form of individual autobiography, but that it also serves as a cognitive structure for experience" (132). The ordering of the experience, the form that the Childhood takes, not only reflects the reality of the individual narrator, but proposes a way of articulating the experience. Indeed, the texts I consider in this chapter may be regarded, in Caren Kaplan's words, as "out-law genres," forms that resist traditional homogenization and "renegotiate the relationship between personal identity and the world, between personal and social history. Here, narrative inventions are tied to a struggle for cultural survival rather than purely aesthetic experimentation or individual expression" (130). I understand the concept "cultural survival" in its widest sense: not merely managing to stay alive but making new approaches beyond the ethnic community's body of works. Precisely because these texts invent new forms or adopt subversive manners of self-expression, we can argue that they take the Asian North American Childhood beyond the merely anecdotal or cultural.

Beyond Ethnicity

Aimee Liu's *Solitaire* and Evelyn Lau's *Runaway* hover at the edge of the definition of a Childhood, as the central part of the narrators' experiences occur during adolescence. Nonetheless, both texts contribute to the development of Asian North American autobiographical strategies because their structures and their negotiation with themes differ from the "traditional" ones ascribed to ethnic writing. Traumatic events shape the narratives on many levels and expand the experiences of Asian North American writers. These texts invite us to read beyond merely "ethnic" negotiations to attend to the challenges faced by adolescent girls in their changing contexts, where social or familial obligations may be misinterpreted, occasionally leading to tragic consequences. The forms of these narratives—Liu's text, in a sense, patterns subsequent memoirs about anorexia and Lau's diary becomes a multilayered form of life writing—influence our reception of these texts and our understanding of autobiographical possibilities. These Childhoods, because of their forms, thus dialogue with mainstream writing: we need to consider the paradigms of narratives of trauma in our reading of *Solitaire* and criticism on the diary as narrative form in our analysis of *Runaway*.

Solitaire, written when Liu was twenty-five, carries the distinction of being the first book on a personal experience of anorexia nervosa published in the United States. Directly and honestly, Liu recounts how, as an adolescent craving power and control but caught in the midst of family tensions, she resorts to incredibly contrived strategies for not eating from the age of fourteen until her first year in college. As she remembers, "Loss of weight had become my personal path to honor; starvation was the goal of my adolescence" (viii). She brutally punishes herself in order to achieve this goal—exercising continually, drinking her coffee black, overdosing on laxatives, and agonizing over whether she should eat on particular days. Food becomes her obsession: "I think constantly of what I can or can't, will or won't eat. I love food, yet deny myself. I hate food for what it does to me, which is to say sustains me. I have to prove to myself and to everyone watching that I, unlike the average human being, need nothing to subsist. I must prove, in effect, that I am truly superhuman" (45). Her fixation on weight loss becomes almost a spiritual struggle, an exercise in discipline and sacrifice that she believes strengthens the soul.

Liu was part of the generation of girls in the 1970s who participated in the national fad of weight loss, unaware that they were suffering from a serious illness. In this context, skinniness became a status symbol. She recounts how she gazes enviously at thinner friends and describes a warped sense of competition to be "thin enough." When her friend Kimmy loses more than thirty pounds one summer, Liu recalls, "I couldn't tell if I was reacting out of competition, guilt, or anger. . . . I could pretend I thought she looked horrible, that such self-destruction appalled me . . . but the truth was that it fascinated and challenged me to follow suit" (117–118).

Analyses of narratives of anorexia in recent years have led us to think more profoundly about this experience, which has been called everything from "disorder" to "pathology" to what Becky Thompson, from a multiracial perspective, considers creative "survival strategies . . . in response to injustices including racism, sexism, homophobia, classism, the stress of acculturation, and emotional, physical, and sexual abuse" (1–2).[1] Though Liu does not consciously negotiate her Asian American-ness—as a mixed race subject, she is not classified strictly as Asian, although she performs Asian-ness on specific occasions—her anorexia stems from a blend of these factors. Her recovery from anorexia happens when she leaves home to go to college. As she begins to consider the world differently, her priorities shift and she understands the self-delusion that had blinded her for so long: "it's dawning on me what a foolish life I've been leading, unnatural and sick. And for what? No one cares, really, about that. About the obsessions and the false intensity, about my contrived substitutions for life" (200, 202). Susan Bordo's analysis of eating disorders highlights how these "reflect and call our attention to some of the central ills of our culture—from our historical heritage of disdain for the body, to our modern fear of loss of control over our future, to the disquieting meaning of contemporary beauty ideals in an era of greater feminine presence and power than ever before" (227–228). She argues that anorexia appears as "a remarkably overdetermined symptom of some of the multifaceted and heterogeneous distresses of our age. Just as anorexia functions in a variety of ways in the psychic economy of the anorexic individual, so a variety of cultural currents or streams converge in anorexia, find their perfect, precise expression in it" (229).[2] Liu's adolescent striving for a place in which to engage her nascent individuality and autonomy finds its first expression in bodily self-control. Later, in an interesting shift of strategies of domination, she writes *Solitaire* to affirm that she has overcome this irrational need.

This account of adolescent angst incurred in a distorted struggle for self-affirmation becomes an important document of the dramatic tensions of processes of maturity and representation—by writing about the experience, she declares that she has left it behind. After understanding the destructive nature of excessive bodily self-denial, Liu opts for the narrative as a strategy for control. The autobiography then becomes more than a testimony: it points to the multilayered possibilities of autobiographical writing. Life writing thus substitutes the anorexic subject's obsessive control over the body with a power over the representation of the self. The sense of dominion that previously existed in the context of eating is transferred to the realm of narrative structure, style, and language. Noelle Caskey suggests that anorexia "involves highly elaborate visual distortion" (181) applied to the body as the person's warped perception of his or her own body leads him or her to want to change it. The process of metamorphosis is narratively enacted when the subject begins to write the experience, transferring the physical domination of the body to creative authority over experience. This form of life writing may be classified as "scriptotherapy," a term suggested by Suzette Henke to refer to how autobiographical writing can become a form of healing as the writers engage in the process of "writing out and writing through traumatic experience in the mode of therapeutic re-enactment" (xv). The autobiography can thus be read as therapeutic, substituting the production of a life narrative, with its possibilities for recreating and ordering, for the strategy of food denial.[3]

While Liu's autobiographical exercise serves a therapeutic purpose as it allows the author to control the representation of her past, the writing of Evelyn Lau's *Runaway* becomes a struggle to control the present. Published in its original diary form, this memoir of two of her adolescent years on the streets requires us to think about the potential of the diary in the context of autobiographical writing. The diary form precludes the complex retrospection and interpretation characteristic of traditional life writing and offers, in turn, urgency and immediacy of experience. We experience "a commentary on life as it *is* lived, that is, on life as process rather than as product. It might be well argued that the diary or journal can rightly be considered the most authentic form of autobiography because it is least subject to outside editing and censorship and because it most fully represents life as process" (Bunkers 191). Moreover, diaries tend to be fragmentary, episodic productions, structured in a manner that sanctions contradictions and continual reformulations, leading to a challenge to psychological unity or even coherent narrative perspective.

Apart from the narrative advantages or disadvantages that the diary offers in the context of autobiography, there is the evident therapeutic purpose of recording one's day-to-day experiences, as they happen, which is precisely what Lau requires. Writing for her signaled rebellion toward her parents' plans for her to be a doctor or a lawyer: "I decided to become a writer when I was six years old. It wasn't a passing whim; it was something I knew I could do well and enjoy. By that age, I had already become an avid reader—reading was like living in a fantasy world; it had become my form of escape. I thought that by writing I could give that same feeling to other people, that they could open one of my books and disappear for a while. Even then, it was important for me not to stay rooted in reality" (xi). Her diary writing, therefore, attests to a double affront toward her parents: running away from home to a life in the streets, and writing about it. Nussbaum suggests that "the marginalized and unauthorized discourse in a diary holds the power to disrupt authorized versions of experience, even, perhaps to reveal what might be called randomness and arbitrariness of the authoritative and public constraints of reality" (136). Lau's autobiography certainly supports these ideas: her writerly act is marginalized because of her parents' prohibition. Moreover, the experiences on the streets that she recounts—her growing addiction to drugs and alcohol, her prostitution, her growing paranoia and repeated episodes of running away from people who want to help her—offers a unique Asian Canadian experience.[4] Interestingly, Lau identifies herself as Chinese only when it signifies a measure of difference, and not sameness or belonging.[5] She stresses her Chinese immigrant parents' culture-specific expectations of her—"I'd been the good little Chinese girl all my life, jumping through every hoop my parents had set up" (31)—and challenges their impositions, blaming control over her on their inability to adapt to Canadian life.[6] The narrative interrogates, in superlative ways, the model minority stereotype and focuses on Lau's obsession with liberating herself from all she considers limiting, specifically her parents. In "The Currency of Visibility," Marie Lo suggests that Lau's running away from her parents is figured as synonymous with running away from the markers of race and ethnicity.

Runaway covers two years of Lau's life, from the ages of fourteen to sixteen, through dated entries from March 1986 to January 1988. In the prologue, she elaborates on her feeling of repression in her parents' home, where her mother constantly punishes her for not studying enough and her unemployed father withdraws more and more into himself. Unable to deal with this tension, she decides to leave. The book opens with her escape from home, her rapid addiction to drugs and alcohol as well as her rape by a man on her second night on the streets. The diary entries then describe her other experiences—escape to Boston, a time in Calgary, return to Vancouver. Elaine Chang states that "to be precise, Lau *runs*—in, out of, to, and away from the city—and she is not always sure why she is running, what she is leaving, or where she is going" (171). She occasionally sees social workers and a psychiatrist, sleeps wherever she can find a bed, and lives at a home for a while, but resists any form of stability except the obsessive act of writing. Indeed, Lau seems to view herself as she writes as the character in a book, "Evelyn the wronged heroine" (167). Nonetheless, her ambition to be a writer and to make a name for herself through writing is part of her longing for stability: "one of my biggest shocks was to realize that when I wanted to be a successful writer, I wanted the love and the acceptance that presumably went along with it. For a long time I thought that when I got a book published, it would be like acquiring a new family, one I wanted. This reasoning bears a remarkable resemblance to why I went on the street—to feel accepted, to find a home. Both ideas are illusions" (294). Consequently there is a strong sense of performance in Lau's obsession with writing—as though Evelyn Lau the writer watches and records the experiences of Evelyn the runaway. This evident self-consciousness colors the narrative with more than suggestions of self-pity and a sense of futility for the life she has embarked on. Her own traumas appear to be largely self-chosen—she often has to force herself to rebel: "wouldn't it be good not to struggle for a change? . . . I don't know, but there's definitely something magical and irreplaceable about a family" (114).

Lien Chao suggests that we can read *Runaway* as an example of the autobiographical genre called *testimonio*, where the narrator's "urgency to communicate" and the "struggle of survival" are "implicated in the act of narration itself" (158).[7] Writing therefore becomes the central point in Lau's narrative performance, and one might even argue whether she consciously engages in sordid experiences in order to write about them. The published product, and Lau's subsequent writings, demonstrates which choice she did make and her achievement of (controversial) success: she is, for example, the youngest poet ever nominated for a Governor General's Award. In another autobiographical text, *Inside Out*, Lau reflects on that period in her life and on having published the diary. Though she notes that she finds herself unable to read more than the occasional passage of the book, she acknowledges how the process of writing it was the only path toward taking control of her own life:

The writing was always larger than I was. I felt it to be a force for which I was merely a mouthpiece. My diary, in which I recorded every conversation, every ingested drug and flailing emotion, was the shield between myself and that life, though oddly it would later be what left me open, unprotected. I remember recording my life compulsively, forsaking sleep in order to do so, even if it was my first night's sleep in days. If I could just pin those events into the page, all that had passed before my eyes, they would cease the clamor inside me. (4)[8]

As Asian North American representations of adolescence (though as I noted both Liu and Lau negotiate ethnicity only as a secondary concern), these texts engage issues that plague young women in contemporary society. Importantly, the structures of the texts heighten the significance of specific topics—Liu's trauma memoir and Lau's diary of an adolescent prostitute are powerful narratives of that particular period in life. They signal, therefore, the necessary engagement with the act of narrative itself as a constitutive element in autobiography. For these women, who went on to have successful writing careers, these exercises in literary exorcism served an invaluable role, permitting them to challenge their crises through narrative.

A Graphic Childhood

Comics, harnessed by graphic artists to convey perspectives on art and representation, arguably offer one of the most imaginative approaches to life writing. In this section, I examine Lynda Barry's artistic project, particularly her use of comics—a thematically and representationally complex form that deploys the strategic juxtaposition of sequential text and image—as the medium for her Childhood.[9] Barry was already a well-known graphic artist when she created her "autobiofictionalography," *One Hundred Demons,* a series of twenty-panel full-color strips first published semimonthly online at Salon.com from April 7, 2000, to January 15, 2001. Her use of comics to recreate her childhood invites us to explore the potential of this graphic form in the context of life writing.

Since the 1960s, comics for older readers have developed a variety of genres and styles, and autobiographical comics in particular are a distinctive and rewarding domain for exploration from a critical cultural and gender perspective. Joseph Witek asserts that comics are currently "one of the most dynamic cultural forms in the United States" and "while some cartoonists do aspire to social and commercial respectability, others turn to comics as a readymade tool for critiquing and subverting the values of mainstream America" (71, 72). I read comics as a sophisticated and developed medium, a set of cultural signifying practices in which the intersections of culture, history, ethnicity, and gender can be effectively negotiated by cartoonists and their adult readers. Barry writes within an increasingly imaginative culture of comics in Europe and the United States. Autobiographical comic creators use a uniquely palimpsestic graphic medium (both visual and textual) to narrate and construct a life story. Paul John Eakin's idea that "the tension between the experiential reality of subjectivity on the one hand and the available cultural forms for its expression on the other always structures any engagement in autobiography" encourages us to critically negotiate Barry's generic choice (*Touching the World* 88). The characteristics of the comic book format, Will Eisner argues, which "presents a montage of both word and image," obliges the reader to "exercise both visual and verbal interpretive skills. The regiments of art (e.g., perspective, symmetry, brush stroke) and the regiments of literature (e.g., Grammar, plot, syntax) become superimposed upon each other. The reading of the comic book is an act of both aesthetic perception and intellectual pursuit" (8).

Autobiographical comics have existed for almost as long as comic art has. Susanna Egan claims that Art Spiegelman's *Maus*, published in 1993, "produced an (auto)biography so powerful that the role of comics in autobiography must now be assured" (16). Spiegelman successfully deployed comics to portray the horror of the Holocaust—to draw the indescribable, so to speak. It has also become a staple in women's comics, with important comic artists such as Jessica Abel, Erika Lopez, Julie Doucet, and Lynda Barry herself expanding the possibilities of the form. Barry, in particular, considers issues of self-representation in the introduction to *One Hundred Demons*, where she introduces the concept of *autobiofictionalography* to describe her project, interrogating the limits between truth and necessary invention or elaboration: "is it autobiography if parts of it are not true? Is it fiction if parts of it are?" (7).[10] These graphic artists have demonstrated the flexibility of the comics to literally represent memory, dreams, and possibilities, as well as engage the idiosyncrasies of the present. Interestingly, Trina Robbins explains that "big chunks of women's comix tend to be about the artist's dysfunctional family, miserable childhood, fat thighs, and boyfriend problems. Although [Aline] Kominsky seems to have invented the form, the autobiographical comic actually harkens back to the confessional style of mainstream romance comics" (91).[11] Robbins' perspective links women's graphic autobiography with earlier forms, even as she notes that these contemporary women significantly transcend the limits of those earlier texts—artistically, thematically, representationally.

Barry's use of comics as autobiography illustrates Egan's assertion that "every occasion for mixing genres demonstrates how distinctive sign systems can intersect and merge to signify meanings at which neither one could arrive alone" (21). This form highlights the interaction between drawing and language, and its ostensible simplification is actually a complex strategy of representation. Scott McCloud explains this strategy when he describes "cartooning as a form of *amplification through simplification*. When we *abstract* an image through cartooning, we are not so much *eliminating* details as we are *focusing on specific details*. By *stripping down* an image to its essential '*meaning*,' an artist can *amplify* that meaning in a way that realistic art *can't*" (30). This approach to understanding graphic art is structurally related to one of the constitutive elements of the Childhood, where specific details acquire heightened meaning. The process of memory inscribed in the Childhood often involves the symbolic interrogation of particular artifacts, sensory detail such as the taste of specific food or the smell of a childhood home, brief conversations or episodes that resound emotionally in the author's memory. Often in the Childhood, the specific event or detail gives meaning to the whole, as with the comic, where the simplest drawing might acquire the most meaning.

Graphic narratives are particularly effective *künstlerroman* because the subject of the autobiographical comic is, most often, a graphic artist him- or herself. The reader is privileged to participate in the performance of both memory and art, and the complex interaction between them. In *One Hundred Demons*, Barry sets out to exorcise the "demons" of her past, believing that, as a Zen monk named Hakuin Ekaku in sixteenth-century Japan explained, painting one's demons was the way to control them. Graphic representation confers a multilayered performativity to Barry's text: we simultaneously *read* and *see* the story, words and images coalesce to produce, in Joseph Witek's words, "an inextricable narrative *gestalt*" (74). The juxtaposition of visual and verbal constructs gives the author fuller control of her self-as-subject as her text incorporates actual, though stylized, self-portraiture. It deftly exhibits the hallmarks of Barry's powerful storytelling aesthetic: her deliberately "naive" graphic style —almost childlike but highly stylized—complements the brutally honest musings of its young narrator and the often harsh subjects of the strips themselves (De Jesús, "Liminality" 220).

Barry controls the entire book production: she draws everything in the text, including the copyright information. Her signature style consists of large, colorful, crowded panels drawn with Asian-style brushes, some on yellow legal pads. The graphics are collages, creative inventions that invite careful deciphering of the many elements on each page. The structure of Barry's book is typical of most comic books—short titled narrative pieces that form a larger whole. In spite of the ostensibly fragmentary characteristic of the narrative strategy, the text exists as a coherent whole, irrevocably linked by the protagonist/narrator and by a series of motifs, issues, and strategies, notably the concept of the "demon" and the need to paint it in order to master it. Barry's "demons" are the objects, events, or concepts that remind her of the difficult emotional stages of her young life. Indeed, the first part of each chapter title reads: "Today's

Demon," followed by a specific subtitle: "Head Lice," "Dancing," "Common Scents," "Resilience," "Hate," "The Aswang," "Magic," "San Francisco," "Magic Lanterns," "Dogs," "Girlness," and "The Election," among others. In a very clear sense, therefore, this work is a self-help book, with the narrator as the first object of that help. The book ends with satisfactory closure, with the narrator fulfilling her dream of becoming a writer and with an epilogic "Outro" that encourages the reader to "Paint Your Demon" (219).

Barry reflects on elements in her childhood and early adulthood that marked her indelibly, as she notes in "Lost Worlds," which recalls the often violent games of kickball she and her friends played on the street: "who knows which moments make us who we are? Some of them? All of them? The ones we never really thought of as anything special? How many kickball games did I play?" (36). In "Dancing," for example, she explains how she, along with her entire family, loved to dance. But a casually cruel comment from a neighborhood girl she admired made her self-conscious and removed all her pleasure from dancing. Painting this experience allows her to relive the pleasure of dance and conclude that "[she is] grateful to those who are keepers of the groove. The babies and the grandmas who hang on to it and help us remember when we forget that any kind of dancing is better than no dancing at all" (48). This retrospective musing recurs in all the stories, as Barry reenacts the experience from the child's perspective and then uses her adult position to comprehend, learn, reproach, censure, or atone for mistakes. In one of the most poignant stories, "Magic," she recalls her friendship with a neighborhood girl two years younger than her. She remembers climbing to the roof of their school with Ev and "talking about infinity" (106). With adolescence, she begins to ignore Ev and stops playing with her: "it wasn't that she was younger. Something had happened inside of me. I didn't have a name for it. Maybe it was the thing that hits you when you stop believing in magic. One day you notice something is gone. Possibility is gone. It's so gone that everyone around you seems like an idiot or a liar. There is a mood that sets in" (104). Years later, Barry remembers that feeling of cosmic incomprehension and tries to reach out. Placing a picture of them in the final panel of the story, she writes, "This is Ev. This is Ev and me in a photo book in a Woolworth's a thousand years ago. Ev, if you're reading this, hello, it's me" (108). This story evidences a strong metaliterary quality to Barry's project: as she paints her demons, she not only struggles to get rid of them but uses the process to heal herself.

Barry negotiates her ethnic position mostly through her Filipino family and their customs and, importantly, by intersecting issues of race and class. As Melinda De Jesús explains, Barry explores issues of identity and liminality that have particular resonance for Filipino Americans from the perspective of a mixed race Filipina caught between her physical appearance—she draws herself as a rather unattractive freckled redhead—and her racial identity as a mixed race subject ("Liminality" 220). By presenting her loving Filipina grandmother and her beautiful but distant *mestiza* mother, Barry negotiates complex relational bonds between these three generations. In the context of ethnic representation, the full color graphics of *One Hundred Demons* enable the reader literally to "see" Barry's world as she does and thus enter it even more fully; it also invites us to "read" further, "as the striking *visual* contrast of Lynda to her Pinoy extended family throughout *One Hundred Demons* signifies and reinforces the distances she, as a red-haired, fair-skinned *mestiza* Filipina in America, must travel in order to find herself and to find her way back to her family" (223). Further, Barry explores issues of maternal legacies and Filipina identity in "Girlness," which dramatizes her and her mother's discord as rooted in the mother's tragic experiences during World War II and in "The Aswang," which uses a Filipino folktale to explore three generations of grandmother/granddaughter bonding and maternal estrangement in her family.

The intersection between gender and class is explored in "Girlness," where Barry depicts the contrast between the tomboyish girls in her working-class neighborhood with the "girlish girls" whose dolls "had pretty clothes, teeny toys and long comable fixable hair. If I had these things, would I have been a girlish girl too?" (185). Questions of class and privilege that plague children as they approach adolescence connect with issues of self-representation as girls. One graphic shows Barry trying to trade an empty Band-Aid box for one of the girlish girl's pretty dolls. As always, these recollections of vulnerability and insecurity are healed by the lessons learned from experience and from the act of painting the past. Looking back and remembering her grandmother in their "smelly" house, Barry decides that "if they could get that into a spray can, I'd buy it!" (60). In "Girlness," meeting a friend who was not afraid to be herself helps Barry overcome her own self-consciousness about what she should or should not like.

The final comic in the book, "Lost and Found," most clearly represents her process of becoming a graphic artist. She begins describing how she loved to read and made up stories based on classified ads. Again, her insecurities haunt her: "when I read about writers' lives, there are usually stories about writing from when they were little. I never wrote anything until I was a teenager, and then it was only a diary that said the same things over and over again. Writers talk about all the books they read when they were children. Classic stories I never read because I was scared it was proof I wasn't really a writer" (212). Her difficulty lay in how she believed a real writer should be—understanding concepts like story structure, arc, and plot points—and her own personal reading preferences, such as the *Reader's Digest* series "I Am Joe's Lung/Large Intestine" and "Hints from Heloise." She notes how her trouble ended when she started making comic strips because "literary types" didn't think you had to be very advanced to do it: "nobody feels the need to provide deep critical insight to something written by hand. Mostly they keep it as short as a Want Ad. The worst I get is 'Too many words. Not funny. Don't get the joke.' I can live with that. Especially because I'm sure that the nine-year-old version of me who made up all those 'classified stories' would think that this one had a very happy ending" (215–216).

This final story provides a multiple perspective on the particular project Barry develops. First, by concluding her graphic narrative with her own accomplishment as an artist, she allows the reader to participate in her artistic itinerary. Second, after proposing to draw her own demons in order to rid herself of them, she acknowledges that the operation has been a success; her book posits that the healing process has indeed taken place. Third, as an artist in dialogue with her community, her invitation to readers to "paint their demons" interpellates persons who experience racial, ethnic, gender, or class problems to engage them directly, using art and creativity to dominate even those circumstances that appear unchangeable. Barry's project, therefore, reads as the success story of an artist who engages her art personally and culturally.

Relational Lives

Loung Ung's experiences in the killing fields of Cambodia, *First They Killed My Father,* were narrated in the traditional chronological form of autobiography. I suggested, in chapter 3, that this Childhood was structured by the experience of war, that political events framed the narrative in fundamental ways, making the child protagonist an observer rather than active architect of her own life. Ung continues her story in *Lucky Child,* which opens where *First They Killed My Father* ends: with her immigration to the United States at age ten, as a dependent of her older brother, Meng, and his wife, Eang. Here, Ung deploys an innovative form of life writing: this text narrates her early years in the United States juxtaposed with the story of her sister Chou, the one closest to her in age and affinity and who was left behind when Meng had to make his choice about which sibling (he was allowed to take only one) to bring along. He chose Loung because she was younger and spunkier, not realizing how difficult separation would be for the sisters and that the family would not be able to reunite for more than a decade. In this text, Loung attempts to bridge those years of separation by narrating, in alternating chapters, her story along with that of her sister's. Using the first person for herself and the third for Chou, Loung Ung produces a text that illustrates recent theories of intersubjective autobiographies and the relational quality of life writing by ethnic subjects.

Relational approaches to life writing complicate notions of self-representation by privileging the intersubjective rather than the merely individual. The Asian American challenge to the pervasive notion of the individual as the prime subject of autobiography begins with Kingston's *The Woman Warrior,* which illustrates how the first person in autobiography is, as Paul John Eakin argues, "truly plural in its origins and subsequent formation," as it addresses "the extent to which the self is defined by—and lives in terms of—its relations with others" (*How Our Lives* 43). Several recent critical studies on autobiography have emphasized a new discernment in inscribing the self-in-relation. The relational configuration of autobiography controls the shape of the text, leading to originative formal choices. Eakin defines the most common form of what he calls the "relational life" as those autobiographies "that feature the decisive impact on the autobiographer of either (1) an entire social environment (a particular kind of family, or a community and its social institutions—schools, churches, and so forth) or (2) key other individuals, usually family members, especially parents" (69). The writing subject therefore views and inscribes his or her story from the prism of intersecting lives. Susanna Egan, defining her eponymous operative term, "mirror talk," argues that this process begins "as the encounter of two lives in which the biographer is also an autobiographer. Very commonly, the (auto)biographer is the child or partner of the biographical subject, a relationship in which (auto)biographical identity is significantly shaped by the processes of exploratory mirroring" (7). These perspectives require us to revise our perceptions about identity and strategies of self-representation on diverse levels, as well as the possibilities of signifying for the writer of the autobiography, specifically the formal remembering and reimagining of intersecting lives.[12]

Relational life writing challenges the fundamental paradigm of the unified self of traditional autobiography, as well as the concept of monologic representation. Philippe Lejeune suggests that "a *life* (that is, a written and published story of a life) is always the product of a transaction between different postures" ("Autobiography of Those" 197). In a sense, this form of autobiographical inscription corresponds to a logical reality, as Michael Jackson explains, "Life stories emerge in the course of *inter*subjective life, and intersubjectivity is a site of conflicting wills and intentions. Accordingly, the life stories that individuals bring to a relationship are metamorphosed in the course of that relationship. They are thus, in a very real sense, authored not by autonomous subjects but by the dynamics of intersubjectivity" (23). Indeed, the renewed aesthetic experience of these autobiographical texts stems precisely from the unique tension created by this complex dialogue, the performance of intersubjectivity. One of the constitutive thematic/textual markers of this life writing exercise involves an emphasis on the intersection of biography and autobiography, locating the narrating subject most often in the context of a community—family or ethnic group. This relational component, already limned in Kingston's text, continues to mark the development of much subsequent Asian American life writing.[13] This concern operates on a formal level as well, proposing a renewed aesthetic that subverts the concept of the individuality of the narrator and revising our perspective on the intersection between experiential authenticity and narrative coherence.

The dialogues enacted in relational texts foreground the collective nature of memory. In Asian North American texts, where a negotiation with structures of power often guides the representational impulse, the dialogue between two people often becomes a debate between two binary positions. Eakin considers the most common form of the relational life as "the self's story viewed through the lens of its relation with some key other person, sometimes a sibling, friend, or lover, but most often a parent—we might call such an individual the *proximate other* to signify the intimate tie to the relational autobiographer" (*How Our Lives* 86). In some cases, the writer presents the biography of the other as part of his or her own life writing exercise, occasionally to the point of writing the "autobiography" of that other. When this happens, the narrators' authority must be established for rhetorical reasons, based primarily on the validity of the autobiographical pact. We also need to consider the role of the writer in relation to that of the subject. In the relational lives I consider here, "the story of the self is not ancillary to the story of the other, although its primacy may be partly concealed by the fact that it is constructed through the story told *of* and *by* someone else. Because identity is conceived as relational in these cases, these narratives defy the boundaries we try to establish between genres, for they are autobiographies that offer not only the autobiography of the self but the biography *and* the autobiography of the other" (58). The voices elicited in these texts are often posited as mirroring, highlighting the intersubjective, and postulating the advantages of double voicing in the process of experiential authenticity.[14] When the life writer goes a step further and appropriates not only the *story* but the *voice* of the proximate other, the implications for life writing multiply.

As relational approaches to life writing become more prevalent, we observe interesting experiments with this frame. In the context of writing about Cambodian Americans, Adam Fifield's memoir of childhood, *A Blessing over Ashes: The Remarkable Odyssey of My Unlikely Brother,* uses his relationship with his adopted Cambodian brother as the central structuring device. Though Fifield is not an Asian American writer, his text may be located within the discussion of Asian American lives. The narrative opens as the Fifield family—parents, eleven-year-old Adam and the younger Dave—await the arrival of fourteen-year-old Soeuth, who had already been living with another family. Soeuth's incorporation into this middle-class WASP family alters their lives, and the text is Fifield's attempt to engage his "unlikely" brother's past and present. After two introductory chapters that describe how the well-meaning family tries to welcome Soeuth, Fifield narrates in alternating chapters his boyhood in Vermont and Soeuth's in the killing fields of Cambodia to explore the nature of childhood, of family, and of brotherhood. Though Fifield chronicles the sections about Soeuth in third person, he appropriates the story and develops this parallel to the point of their shared lives. The narrative ends when Fifield accompanies Soeuth back to Cambodia to visit the intact family left behind, a journey that reveals their mutual ambivalence toward the experience of adoption and the manner in which historical circumstances modified both their families. Fifield, who tries to collect Soeuth's story from his parents, makes Soeuth's parents face the reality of what happened to their son when they allowed him to be taken away by the Khmer Rouge and demonstrate their remorse.

Fifield regards Soeuth's arrival as a disruption of the organized harmony in his family life: the nuclear unit was, in a sense, invaded by a character whose tragic history challenged their comfortable complacency, requiring them to reexamine their perspectives on Asia. By inscribing this doubled life story, Fifield recognizes that the revisitation of his own past—and his own process of identity—is tinted by the destabilizing lens of his older brother's history. By allowing his brother to reconstruct both their histories, Soeuth becomes a protagonist in Adam's life story—the insistent concern with brotherhood in this text highlights the implications of the term for adoptive families, the recovery of the biological family, and ultimately, decisions about personal location. To Fifield's credit, he tries to avoid oversimplifying these issues, as well as American cultural stereotypes about Asians and the situation in Asia. Discursively, this text widens the possibilities of the Asian American canon; this can arguably be categorized as an ethnic text if we attend to its discussion on the consequences of American interventionist policies in Asia as a contextualization of sociopolitical factors surrounding international adoption, and issues of identity, race, ethnicity, and marginalization. It also serves as a paradigm for the kind of effect that the number of refugees in the United States has on the "mainstream" population. Here, we view the reconfiguration of a family, a microcosm for society itself, as it changes necessarily in order to accommodate its new configuration.

While Ung's *Lucky Child* evinces the same strategy as Fifield's text, her purpose differs: Fifield writes about his adopted brother's life in Cambodia in order to link their histories, to *create* family; Ung writes her sister's life to *preserve* family when it has been split by immigration and the difficulties of reunification. Importantly, this text implies that Asian North American subjects cannot ignore the real presence of Asia in their lives. Ung's itinerary of selfhood lies in intersubjective identification with the sister and the history she left behind, which foregrounds the need for mutual recognition by the protagonists of the life writing exercise. As Jessica Benjamin explains, "the idea of mutual recognition . . . implies that we actually have a need to recognize the other as a separate person who is like us yet distinct" (qtd. in Egan 8). Moreover, Ung needs to keep her sister in her life, which she can only do through the narrative act years later because they were out of touch for several years after immigration. American laws prevented the immigrants from communicating directly with Cambodia; in fact, Chou did not know her brother and sister were alive until three years had passed.

This text proves that Ung understands she can never really leave the past and her family behind. Though she struggles to become an assimilated American, the nightmares that plague her and the constant reminders of her siblings in Cambodia keep the past alive. For that reason, *Lucky Child* (the title emphasizes her perspective on her position and the responsibility that privilege entails) serves a therapeutic purpose: by writing Chou into her own story, she textually juxtaposes their histories and heals through narrative the wounds of separation. As Ung explains in the prologue: "it would be fifteen years before I would be reunited with my sister again in 1995. Fifteen years of her living in a squalid village with no electricity or running water. Fifteen years of me in the United States living the American dream. It is my obsession with these fifteen years that has taken me back to Cambodia over twenty times" (xiii). This "obsession" structures her particular autobiographical strategy, as she explains: "For no matter how seemingly great my life is in America or France, it will not be fulfilling if I live it alone. . . . Living life to the fullest involves living it with your family" (237).

Ung alternates chapters about herself and her sister to show the different worlds they lived in at the same time. "Here are our stories," she explains, "mine as I remember it and Chou's as she told it to me" (xiv). Writing her sister's story gives Chou the voice that living in Cambodia denied her. Ung collates their radically different experiences, creating a composite portrait of two young sisters united by bonds of love and suffering, but separated by political circumstances. Their stories are dramatically opposed: while Meng pays for their food with food stamps, Chou scrounges for rice; Loung learns to draw cartoons, rollerskate, and swim as Chou hauls wood and water; Loung is haunted by flashbacks of the war as Chou hides from the Khmer Rouge; Loung agonizes about fitting in at school, while Chou cannot go to school because she takes care of her baby cousin; Loung worries about her first teenage crush as Chou's marriage is being arranged; as Loung admits that "all [she cares] about is becoming an American" (108), Chou fights to stay alive. For a time, when it seems that the family will never reunite, Loung begins to think of herself as Meng's only sister, even though she remembers her large family, because "missing them [had] become too difficult. . . . That life is gone and no matter how [she wished] it, it [would] never be so again. This thought [made her] feel like the small dead critters [she saw] on the road—crushed, flattened, and alone" (139). Though imagining herself alone serves as a survival strategy for a time, writing the relational memoir becomes an even more effective operation.

At many moments in her narrative, Ung stresses her need to remember her family members who died and who were left behind: "when I look into the mirror, I don't see the girl they see. Instead, my hands pinch and pull at my features to bring forth Ma's nose, Pa's eyes, Keav's smile, and Chou's lips. I crave to hold their image in my hand and stare at their faces until their imprints are permanent in my brain. But we do not have a single picture of them and my face is now the only image I have to remember them by" (22–23). Watching *The Brady Bunch* even before she understands English takes her back to when she was part of a large family. Yet she resists her sister-in-law's attempts to raise her as a proper Cambodian, wanting to assimilate as soon as possible. She refuses to talk about Cambodia to her new friends and finds that in her friend Beth's house, she gets "to have [her] American family" (102). Ung's childhood ambivalence is logical: torn between the crushing memories of the past and the peaceful possibilities of the present, her instinct is to shelter herself in the new world and forget the past. But because four of her siblings remain in Cambodia, there is no way to completely sever those ties.

One of the strongest connections she has with Cambodia is the sense of dread that follows her after years of living in fear: "I know that in my new home, there is no war, hunger, or soldiers to be afraid of. Yet in the quiet recesses of my mind, the Khmer Rouge lurks and hovers in dark alleys, waiting for me at the bend of every corner" (27). The festive fireworks at a Fourth of July celebration bring on a terror attack; watching the film *The Killing Fields* makes her understand that she will never be able to "leave the war" (124). Though her brother reminds her constantly that they are safe and that she does not have to fight anymore, she knows that "in [her] mind the war rages on" (69). Until the family can be together again, she will not find the peace that this land can bring. Indeed, when she once overhears someone saying that it was fortunate that she was so young when the war happened, as she could more easily forget and move on, she reacts angrily: "they are wrong. I *do* remember. I just don't have the words to tell them about it. And although most of the time I'm silent about the war, it's never silent to me. . . . And I'm sick of it all. I'm tired of waiting for the pain to heal. I want it cut out of my body" (179). Her desperation leads her to try to commit suicide. Finally, she begins to write her story in an attempt to exorcise the memories of the Khmer Rouge and the loss of her family members, suggesting that these two-hundred-odd pages of desperate narrative written at the age of fourteen became the genesis of her first *Childhood*, *First They Killed My Father.* Just before her high school graduation, she finds those pages again and thinks about herself at that point in time.

> If the war is a distant story, the girl who wrote these pages is a stranger to me now. . . . I remember how when the girl started to write, she couldn't stop. The story was like toxic poison that demanded to be purged out of her body, forcing her to write during breakfast, in class, and at night after everyone had gone to sleep. . . . For six months, the girl wrote until her fingers cramped and grew calluses, and her forearm ached at night. When she was done, there was a beginning, a middle, and an end, and she believed that her story was finished. She understood then that she didn't want to die, but that she just didn't know how to live with the ghosts. (191)

The publication of Ung's first *Childhood* clearly expelled many of the "demons" of her past, but the second book is, in a sense, equally necessary. Ung needs Chou's story to complete her own—there is a constant sense of something missing that pervades her narrative. Even as she wants to adapt to America and dreams of having friends who are "not Asians, who aren't 'different'" (59), she sees her sister Chou, "with all her sweetness, friendliness, and generosity" (67) in her friend Li, also a Cambodian immigrant. Both Loung and Chou's accounts make constant references to each other, to their parents, and their sisters, Keav and Geak, both of whom died in the war. Loung also seeks to justify the fortunate choice that allowed her to leave Cambodia for a new life and even, after a while, for the guilt of recognizing that she hates "because [she knows] that somewhere in Cambodia, Chou is waiting for [her], but [she does] not want to join her" (84).

The completed relational auto/biography, which foregrounds the link between the sisters and by extension, the Ung family, serves as an important cultural document that resonates in immigrant communities. By privileging the relational quality of their lives, and positing processes of identity in the context of intersubjective identification, Ung enacts a paradigm of identification based not on unalloyed cultural heritage, but on the dynamic constituted by changing cultural contexts. Loung tells her own story by telling that of her sister's, *through* Chou's story as well. Unlike traditional autobiography, in which the author *of* the text is squarely the protagonist *in* the text, Loung is found *in relation* to the other central character. This strategy posits identity as inseparable from history, culture, and family, and negotiated precisely in the stories learned from others and that occasionally need to be transformed to accommodate current demands.

What writers such as Liu, Lau, Barry, and Ung ultimately enact in their narratives are models for complex ethnic and personal identity, formulated precisely through generic renovation. Though this study has argued that Asian North American writers revise the structure of the Euro-American Childhood, these writers move further by experimenting more freely with form and proposing new ways of articulating selfhood. Life writing therefore involves the form of the text as much as the theme.

Chapter 7

● **The Childhood for Children**

The Cultural Experience of the Early Reader

This study, which reads autobiography as a writerly project that creates a reader and enhances cultural memory, needs to consider the important role played by children's literature. As a cultural product, autobiographical writing for children is an independent but interdependent literary artifact that can promote renewed perspectives on history and society.[1] Moreover, I argue that an analysis of Asian North American life writing for children expands the paradigms of research in Asian American autobiography. Broadening the frontiers of scholarship that critically reads ethnic autobiography, an analysis of this form of self-representation illuminates originative strategies. Katharine Capshaw Smith asserts that "children's literature allows readers a means to reconceptualize their relationship to ethnic and national identities. Telling stories to a young audience becomes a conduit for social and political revolution" (3). Tracing the evolution of ethnic children's literature in the last two or three decades, one notes the way literature functions as a cultural product that reflects and shapes the cultures of those who live it—and the way that "consumers" or beneficiaries can in turn play a role in the production culture's literary artifacts (Carpenter 53).

Children's literature, moreover, is evaluated by a multiple audience, which includes adults involved in education—teachers and librarians—as well as parents who supervise their children's reading. This literature "becomes a particularly intense site of ideological and political contest, for various groups of adults struggle over which versions of ethnic identity will become institutionalized in school, home, and library settings" (Katharine Capshaw Smith 3). An Asian North American author of an autobiography for children makes us rethink the role of life writing within the context of identity formation, reconfiguring the genre with insurgent possibilities.

Asian North American children's literature highlights the value that society attributes to history, national and ethnic affiliation, intercultural relationships, and communities. The target audiences of these texts—"mainstream" and "ethnic" children—are addressed in doubled ways: Asian North American children, for example, would be encouraged by the authors to resist "pejorative categorizations by asking the reader to reimagine herself, to identify herself with the text's cultural models"; readers from other ethnic groups would be encouraged to overcome prejudice and stereotypes through crosscultural understanding (Katharine Capshaw Smith 4). For these children today, issues of history, heritage, peer communities—cultural and scholastic—and the possibility (or imperative) of self-formation serve as impetus for processes of empowerment and agency. As Carole Carpenter argues, the most successful children's books reject the assumption that children are merely receivers of culture, presenting them as "creative manipulators of a dynamic network of concepts, actions, feelings and products that mirror and mold their experience as children" (57). Though children's existence and experience as cultural beings must be negotiated critically by readers, meaning in effective literary texts lies, at least in part, through the traditions and experience of collective children's culture that each of them experiences individually (Carpenter 56). By addressing children generally, the narratives also admit reflection on multiple claims of identity that many young Americans and Canadians encounter. Meaning arises, therefore, from the text's involvement with the nature of childhood, more than simply with the experience of ethnicity.

Nonetheless, when the network of concepts involves ethnic appreciation, autobiographical texts play operative roles in articulating the contexts within which children can enter in a process of self-formation. The evolution of recent ethnic autobiography for children has been toward historical realism and intercultural narratives that emphasize the varied cultural influences a child growing up in the United States or Canada experiences. This new historicism in children's literature, according to Mitzi Myers, helps "integrate text and socio-historic context, demonstrating on the one hand how extraliterary cultural formations shape literary discourse and on the other how literary practices are actions that make things happen—by shaping the psychic and moral consciousness of young readers but also by performing many more diverse kinds of cultural work, from satisfying authorial fantasies to legitimating or subverting dominant class and gender ideologies" (42). Many of these texts, for example, focus on historical events that are not taught in North American school curriculums. By incorporating historical information in autobiographies, writers not only present the events of history in ways that encourage identification and understanding, but offer all North American children perspectives on the past. The potent issue of authenticity in life writing therefore endorses "the didactic imperatives both embedded in the texts and imposed contextually by adult arbiters" (Katharine Capshaw Smith 6). These Asian North American Childhoods therefore present a revisionary range of possibilities for child readers to help them become more intelligently aware of what it means to be Asian or of Asian descent in the United States and Canada. Discursively, the increasing number of texts about Asian or Asian American children allows them to claim a space for themselves in America's own history and in its stories about its children.[2]

Two related phenomena help us understand how authors deploy autobiographical writing for children and how these texts function didactically and culturally. First, several of the writers in question have, after the successful publication of autobiographies for adults, rewritten these texts for a child audience. Specifically, Younghill Kang, Adeline Yen Mah, Yoshiko Uchida, and Da Chen have produced versions for children of their previously published autobiographies, the first three of them converting their more comprehensive accounts of their lives into Childhoods, ending these narratives earlier than in the original work.[3] These literary decisions were, I believe, enacted precisely because of the authors' consciousness of the effective cultural work that children's texts execute. By addressing a young readership, these autobiographical narratives formulate widened patterns of experience for Asian North American readers. Precisely because these texts were successful among adult audiences and became part of the network of cultural narratives that aided the creation of a historically and socially conscious readership, the imperative to offer these narratives to young readers existed. Moreover, the actual rewriting of the text implied more than just "simplifying" the content or vocabulary of the original autobiography. In each of these cases, the writer positively reimagined the story's formulation, negotiated new metaphors, images, and specific experiences in order to make the story resonate more effectively with the implied child reader.

The second phenomenon stems from the concept of bibliotherapy, which involves using specific texts to help people understand particular situations.[4] Parents and teachers use bibliotherapy to help children face potentially difficult situations such as a new sibling, the beginning of school, peer pressure or, in many cases, dealing with the awareness of difference that may arise in the case of international adoption or the dawning of ethnic or racial consciousness. The use of literature thus offers children access to experiences that they undergo but cannot talk about, and gives them the opportunity to explore their heritage culture on their own terms. Because, as Jann Pataray-Ching and Stuart Ching explain, children "identify with characters that look like them, that participate in shared cultural traditions and daily experiences, and that know the struggles of their families' pasts" (479), making the representation of the reality of ethnic history and characters in autobiographical texts instructive as well as fortifying. Because these texts are presented as autobiography, readers discover that other children have shared their experiences, learn positive coping strategies, and find opportunities for positive cultural identification (Lu 476). Although, fortunately, recent Asian North American literature engages in more balanced ways the realities of the ethnic experience, the responsible use of life writing allows for a more effective challenge to stereotypical representations of Asians, errors or misconceptions, and a devaluing of heritage culture. From this perspective, we understand how successful autobiographies for children empower their readers.

This chapter's structure is based on the paradigms I set for the analysis of the Asian North American Childhood: the presentation of a pre-American life and an engagement with Asian history and the story of immigration, adaptation, and socialization. The settings of these autobiographies vary: Asian countries, internment camps, and urban spaces are the locations from where these Asian American adults reconfigure their childhoods. The children in the Childhoods I read make decisions regarding cultural affiliation and develop as individuals and within interpersonal relationships, underscoring the diversity of childhood and contradicting any tendency to essentialize the "Asian" or "American" subject. Having a child as the central narrating character and choosing to focus primarily on the preadult years becomes a significant critical gesture: it makes the process of identification easier for the reader who encounters a real story that can resound more effectively in his or her consciousness. Also, I will engage specific literary choices the writers make to highlight the literary nature of these texts.

Pre-American Lives

A notable number of Asian North American Childhoods for children are set in Asian countries and focus primarily on the protagonist's preimmigration life.[5] Apart from validating a non-American childhood setting for the Asian American subject, these texts reconfigure America's image of its children, or at least of its citizens' pasts. Importantly, these Childhoods give readers access to many of their parents' or grandparents' historical or cultural stories, or if they are immigrants themselves, it validates their experiences in the North American literary context. These autobiographies for children also illustrate a palimpsestic itinerary of location and affiliation, complicating in effective ways the traditional fixed representation of the American child's awareness of position. And, finally, they posit Americanization as an individual process, rather than an inherited patrimony. These Childhoods set outside North America, therefore, suggest to Asian North American children that itineraries of affiliation are personal and unique, and attest to a multiplicity of experiences as constitutive of citizens' lives, including the experience of a childhood in an Asian country.

Adeline Yen Mah's *Chinese Cinderella* and Lu Chi Fa and Becky White's *Double Luck: Memoirs of a Chinese Orphan* are stories of unwanted children set in China. Mah's story, which recounts her experiences until the age of fourteen, appropriates a fairytale character, Cinderella, as a structuring device and operative metaphor. The autobiography reproduces the paradigmatic characters of the original story—the characters of Mah's Childhood are, as in the intertext, an "evil" stepmother and an "innocent" child. Mah states her didactic intentions clearly: she dedicates the book to adults "who were also unwanted children [so that they] may be encouraged" and she communicates her solidarity with them. She asserts that she wants to convince child readers that they have "within [themselves] something precious and unique" and that they can "transcend [their] abuse and transform it into a source of courage, creativity, and compassion" (xii). This sentimental and arguably consumerist approach unfortunately undermines a valid second purpose: to educate her implied readers— (Asian) American children—about China's language, history, and culture. She achieves this in effective ways: her chapters are numbered and titled in both English and Chinese, she gives explanations and illustrations on how Chinese names are written and used in family contexts, and she clarifies cultural beliefs and practices. She also explains the metaphor of Cinderella in cultural terms as well, arguing that Ye Xian, a character in a story collected by Duan Chengshi in the ninth century, is the "original Chinese Cinderella" (199). She thus relocates the origin of this beloved children's story to introduce the richness of Chinese culture to American readers and encourage appreciation of cultural legacies.

The book traces Mah's struggle to be loved by her family. Her mother dies when she is born, the fifth child of an affluent Chinese family, an event that marks her as cursed or "bad luck" (3). When her father remarries soon after that, her stepmother, Niang, displays overt animosity toward the children from the first marriage, clearly favoring her own son and daughter. Adeline's father is a distant figure whose indifference—he forgets her name and birthday, and abandons her in a convent school when they leave China—wounds her deeply. The child's suffering is acute and incessant; the narrative enumerates experiences of rejection, abuse, and neglect. Mah uses specific episodes to illustrate her stepmother's manipulative cruelty: she cannot receive visits from friends, she has to walk to school and is often left behind there, her stepbrother's dog kills her pet duck, and Niang's cutting remarks undermine her sense of self-worth. The child finds solace in her relationship with her grandfather, Ye Ye, and her Aunt Baba, but she is separated from them. Finally, Adeline understands that academic success will gain her her father's favor and give her independence. The story ends when her proud father allows her to go to study medicine in England. Academic success becomes a gateway to a new life. The writer ends her story with a letter from her Aunt Baba, which tells the inspiring story of the Chinese Cinderella: "like Ye Xian, you have defied the odds and garnered triumph through your own efforts. Your future is limitless" (197).

While Mah's narrative is problematic on several levels—the portrayal of the stepmother is too stereotypical, and the representation of the child's victimization smacks of an overindulgent exercise in self-pity and blatant self-validation[6]—the book introduces important aspects of Chinese culture and life, as well as the country's transition in the mid-twentieth century. Two appendices provide significant cultural and historical grounding: in the first one, Mah recounts her research on the figure of the Chinese Cinderella and reproduces the Chinese text, written during the Tang Dynasty (618–906 AD). The second appendix consists of a short historical note that contextualizes China's recent history and serves as the background to the narrative action, enticing readers to consider the ways in which history intersects with daily life. Mah's cultural appreciation and her intelligent manner of inviting child readers to learn about heritage encourage a sense of community with many Chinese people who also, for different reasons, have opted for immigration to the West. Moreover, as a book about an Asian child who becomes a successful Asian American adult— Mah's postscript recounts her eventual success as a doctor and immigration to California—it offers a privileged glimpse of a successful Asian North American trajectory. If we elide the problematic aspects of Mah's representation, we can appreciate her cultural work in the creation of a young American or Canadian reader who might be receiving his or her first introduction to Chinese culture.

Lu Chi Fa's autobiography also traces the complicated and oftentimes distressing itinerary of a Chinese orphan who achieves the American dream of success. Lu's parents die when he is three, and he spends the rest of his childhood shuffling between more or less caring relatives, with no real place to call home. His sister-in-law sells him for five bags of rice to a communist couple who treat him like a slave; returning to his family, he is starved and beaten. Due to the upheavals in China, he escapes to Hong Kong with another sister-in-law and nephew, where he begins to support his family with the money he earns from begging. Chi Fa eventually strikes out on his own and immigrates to the United States.

Though his story is filled with more physical suffering than Mah's, his account is less self-indulgent and more hopeful. The theme of luck runs through the text: when his sister must leave him at their uncle's, she tells him to always remember that he is a good boy and that he is lucky—this thought sustains him. His determined hopefulness in the face of worsening circumstances illustrates the characteristic that will bolster him until he achieves the ultimate goal: America and success. The epilogue describes his first return visit to China to see his sister, almost fifty years after leaving. He explains that he owns a successful restaurant in California: "over the years, I have found America to be everything that I had heard as a child and much more. I eat three times a day, and, indeed, am too full to swallow sorrow." As though to take comfort that her words to a young orphan boy have come true, his sister repeats to him, "You are lucky, Chi Fa. Good fortune has found you" (206).

The positive tone of his text contrasts vividly with Mah's self-pity. Lu never presents himself as a victim, nor does he seek superficial compassion. Rather, he posits his trajectory as a learning experience. Interestingly, his chapter titles are doubled: each states where he lives and, parenthetically and in italics, the lesson he learned there. Thus, Chapter 1, "Sister's House," also reads (Be Strong); Chapter 7, "The Stranger's House," reads (Be Kind); and Chapter 12, "Beggar Boy," reads (Be Humble). The epilogue, "Two Days with Sister," significantly reads (Be Fulfilled). The strength of the book lies in Lu's optimism. The author engages his own suffering only to illustrate a more important process: his personal struggle for virtue and his determination to rise above his circumstances. Ultimately, that is the message the text offers along with a confirmation of the reality of the American dream for this immigrant. The fulfillment of that dream appears to be the reward for his determination, tenacity, and positive approach to life. Indeed, the author presents his Americanization as, in a sense, the culmination of a process of development that had begun in China. As a life writing exercise that defines success as economic prosperity, this text offers a positive role model for the story of the immigrant. Though it may be considered at some points stereotypical or simplistic in its depiction of China and Chinese customs, the author's artless manner of narrating liberates the novel from any cheap pathos. Again, historical events in China are the background of the story, inviting readers to see how these were lived by ordinary people and explaining the imperative of many to emigrate.

Nostalgia prevails in *The Land I Lost: Adventures of a Boy in Vietnam,* Quang Nhuong Huynh's idyllic account of his childhood in Vietnam.[7] The separate but interrelated stories about growing up in a hamlet in the central highlands of Vietnam center on discrete memories of his childhood adventures with animals—particularly his water buffalo, Tank—his family, and friends. Aimed at an audience of young children, Huynh blends pathos and humor, as in the story about his opera-loving, karate-expert grandmother, who saved her family from bandits. He also recounts the danger in the animals—monkeys, snakes, crocodiles—of the region and his Huckleberry Finn–type escapades with his cousin, blending local legend and folktales with his memories. By setting his stories in approximately an entire year's cycle, Huynh offers an engaging portrait of a childhood in rural Vietnam and explains the way the seasons evolve in the country. This portrayal locates the protagonist in a setting that validates a peaceful Vietnam for American child readers whose only probable idea of that country might arise from stories about the Vietnam War. By focusing on the landscape, myths, customs, and traditions, and by recounting them with humor, Huynh offers readers a vision of a prewar country where peace prevailed and children played.

A farmer's child who worked in the fields from the age of six, Huynh learned from his father how to survive in the jungle and care for animals, and how to dream of an education in order to improve the village situation. But the last story, titled "Sorrow," radically alters the tranquil rhythm of their lives. Here, he narrates the death of his beloved Tank, killed by a stray bullet during fighting between the French forces and the Resistance led by Ho Chi Minh. By introducing the tragic consequences of the war, the author alludes to the historical circumstances that led to the massive immigration out of the country. The animal's death symbolizes the loss of something greater—the peaceful life of the hamlet, lost with the war, leading to mass death and exile. In the introduction, Huynh says that he "planned to return to [his] hamlet to live the rest of [his] life there. But war disrupted [his] dreams. The land [he loves] was lost to [him] forever" (xi). His nostalgia serves an important didactic purpose: as the author captures a lost past, it offers child readers another perspective on Vietnamese refugees and immigrants, victims of war, who continue to long for the country they were forced to leave behind.

Engaging Asian and North American History

Though Mah, Lu, and Huynh's narratives are clearly situated geographically and temporally, they focus primarily on personal stories. The dramatic events in China and Vietnam in the mid- to late-twentieth century are a significant background but are by no means the center of the stories. Other texts privilege historical events more predominantly and limn the ways history directly reconfigures family relationships and lives, peer groups, and perspectives on issues such as nationhood and citizenship. Historical events shape autobiographies of childhood by Yoko Kawashima Watkins, Sook Nyul Choi, Song Nan Zhang, Ji-Li Jiang, and Da Chen, whose texts also teach Asian history of the twentieth century, which most children in the United States or Canada do not have access to in the current school curriculum. This knowledge helps explain much recent immigration, as these narratives ostensibly end with their authors/protagonists' immigration, due primarily to the circumstances narrated in the texts.

Several autobiographies center on the consequences of war in Japan and China in the mid-twentieth century. Yoko Kawashima Watkins's two-volume account of her childhood in Korea and Japan introduces child readers to that history by focusing on a colonial family that has to survive relocation and adapt to life in their own country.[8] *So Far from the Bamboo Grove* is the first account of the Japanese experience in Korea during World War II written for children, an important contribution to the canon of juvenile literature. It narrates the story of the Kawashima family, happily settled in Korea, from the point of view of eleven-year-old Yoko, whose father was a Japanese government official working in Manchuria. The portrayal of their life in Nanam, in the north of Korea close to the Chinese border, in the early 1940s is happy; they live as Japanese and admit that they consider themselves separate from the Koreans. Comfortable in their colonial existence, symbolized by the eponymous bamboo grove, they do not consider that the Koreans might desire their independence.[9] The narrative opens in 1945, shortly before the end of World War II, when the Koreans want to regain control over their homeland and as Russian communist troops enter North Korea to overturn the Japanese occupation. When violence escalates that summer, Yoko (called "Little One" by her family), her teenaged sister, Ko, and their mother make their difficult way back to Japan. In the process, they lose everything they own and undergo severe trials: hunger, injury, witnessing violence and death, and eventually, when they do return to Japan, losing their family home to allied bombers, the death of their mother, and crippling poverty. Yoko and Ko survive through the kindness of strangers and their admirable resilience and resourcefulness, and the first book ends with their reunion with their older brother, Hideyo.

Watkins' story of war is told in stark, realistic detail that does not spare the reader any of the pain she experienced. She narrates straightforwardly her memory of witnessing a rape and scavenging through garbage cans for food. The account of their escape is loaded with dramatic details: a newborn baby on the Red Cross train must be bathed in urine because there is no water, the shrapnel that leads to her hearing loss, the selfishness and cruelty of some of the struggling refugees. Her mother's death is narrated simply, free of cheap sentimentality or sensationalism. Interestingly, Watkins constructs a doubled account of the family's escape from Korea: she alternates chapters in first person with a third-person narration of her brother's journey. Jean Fritz, in the foreword to Watkins' book, notes that it is the story of Yoko's "victory," which includes "her struggle to master English and record the nightmare of her private war story" as a "demonstration of the persistence and will she showed as a little girl, escaping from Korea and learning to survive when—as she says—she was 'in the most bottom of the bottom'" (para. 4). In the narration of these events, the reader witnesses a profound change in Yoko. From a spoiled youngest child, she develops into a strong, resilient girl who places family above all and endeavors to rise above the poverty and rejection experienced in Japan. The child, though often on the brink of desperation, manages to sustain her optimism and continue to privilege the important things—family bonds, the need to stay together, the desire to continue living and making something of oneself, small acts of kindness that change people's lives.

The family story continues in the award-winning *My Brother, My Sister, and I,* which takes up the story immediately after the first one ends.[10] A fire in the factory they are living in leaves Ko wounded and crippled, and Yoko and her brother have to work to survive. The story also focuses on Yoko's attempts to succeed in school, despite her classmates' taunting. This story ends with a reunion with their father who had been interned in a Siberian prison camp, six years after leaving Korea. In her afterword, Watkins explains how she later married an American and immigrated to the United States, where she was eventually joined by Ko. Both these texts open up new vistas on the war in Asia for American readers who have been taught that the United States "won" World War II. Here, the story is told from the point of view of the "losers" and recounts what happened to the Japanese after the war, a strategy that conveys to readers ideas about the real victims of war.[11]

Sook Nyul Choi's autobiographical trilogy—*Year of Impossible Goodbyes, Echoes of the White Giraffe,* and *Gathering of Pearls*—contrasts with Watkins' texts as she presents the Korean perspectives on the war. As an educator—she has taught creative writing in high schools—Choi has noted the lack of knowledge about Korea by Americans and consciously writes to help fill that gap and foster a better understanding of Asia and Asian Americans. As she explains, "I also feel it is important to create literature about Asia and Asian American experiences for young Asian Americans to learn about their heritages and to feel that there is a voice for them to relate to" ("Sook Nyul Choi" 47). This evident didactic purpose locates her autobiographical novels in a dialogue with other writing, notably with Watkins' books. Taken together, these texts provide a rounded perspective to the conflict in the Pacific around the time of World War II. By focusing on the child's experiences, these texts serve to humanize the official stories told about the Japanese colonization and the war; they also show children that war is not just a matter of taking sides, but results in suffering for everyone.

Year of Impossible Goodbyes narrates the events of Korean history during World War II and its aftermath. Ten-year-old Sookan Bak lives in Pyongyang and struggles to preserve her Korean identity from the intentions of the Japanese colonizers to eradicate it. She describes incessant humiliation at the hands of the Japanese, who deliberately destroy everything that gives them a sense of self-worth and pride: the Koreans cannot profess any religion apart from Shintoism and are forbidden to speak their language; things of beauty are confiscated (e.g., the family is denied the aesthetic pleasure of a pine tree in their garden); young women forcibly serve as "spirit girls" for the Japanese army. Their fear makes her even doubt her pride in being Korean: "I thought of the Japanese children who went to the special school and live in pretty houses that Koreans used to own. The Japanese could have whatever they wanted in Korea" (30). On her first day at school she has to sing the "Kimigayo," the Japanese national anthem, to pledge loyalty to the emperor and, most traumatic of all, respond to her Japanese name, Aoki Shizue, which makes her confused and afraid: "I knew I had no choice. My baptismal name and my Korean name would only be used at home from now on. Here I would have to answer to this strange Japanese name; I was someone I did not want to be and I had to pretend" (73). When the Japanese lose the war in 1945, the exhilaration over freedom the Koreans feel—flying the Korean flag, speaking openly in Korean, dressing in the colorful *hanbok,* listening to Korean and Western classical music—does not last long. The Russian takeover promises to be even more dangerous and Sookan's mother—alone, as her older sons are in jail and her husband detained in Manchuria—decides to leave for the American-controlled south with her young children, Sookan and seven-year-old Inchun. This dramatic journey, which includes the children's separation from their mother and their desperate flight to cross the border to the south, eventually leads them to their father.

The text conveys the young girl's thoughts—her fears and anxieties, her little victories and dreams—as well as the details of daily life during colonial occupation and war. Choi uses small details to unveil the characters' deepest emotions: the children bathing their grandfather's feet and discovering that his toenails had been pulled out under torture by the Japanese; the shame of Korean schoolchildren who urinate at their desks because they are not allowed a break from reciting Japanese propaganda; the desperation of the girls dragged out to be raped by Japanese soldiers. Sookan's pride in her Korean heritage, cultural identity, and family are at the center of the novel. In the context of narratives of war for children, this text illustrates how civilians become the helpless victims of political struggles, but how family bonds continue to be essential for survival. The "goodbyes" of the title refer to the family's exile and the end of Sookan's childhood as the story concludes with the family reunited in Seoul, trying to begin a new life.

The family's story continues in *Echoes of the White Giraffe,* where Sookan, now fifteen, her younger brother, and their mother leave everything behind in war-ravaged Seoul to live in a mountaintop refugee hut in Pusan. Once again, they are separated from their father and brothers, this time because of the Korean War. The novel centers on the family's poverty and the sense of alienation typical of refugees. Though she tries to maintain an illusion of normalcy —attending a makeshift school, developing friendships—the separation from the rest of the family also weighs heavily on her. Choi's second book examines the consequences of war on those who grow up in its shadow. Sookan begins to show signs of independence, struggling with her personal feelings in the face of tradition and customs. She also experiences her first romance, a "forbidden" relationship with Junho, who shares her love for poetry and music. Junho eventually enters the priesthood and Sookan applies for admission into an American university. The effect of war on these young people is portrayed, in general, in positive terms; they have to accept the consequences of the events, including the death of close family members and the sense of displacement brought about by constant relocations and loss of a history. Their resilience, determination, and confirmation in their faith in God and their families lie at the core of the autobiography. This is evidenced by the character Baik Rin (White Giraffe), a poet who, though dying of tuberculosis, greets everyone cheerfully each morning from the top of his mountain, reminding the refugees to appreciate each new day. This optimism serves as a symbol of hope to those who hear him. Where *Year of Impossible Goodbyes* centers on the child's narrative of rapid and dramatic historical events, *Echoes of the White Giraffe* engages the emotional struggle of coping with tragedy, of making history part of each person's configuration of their own path in life.

The final book in the trilogy, *Gathering of Pearls,* recounts Sookan's immigration to the United States in 1954 and her experiences as a freshman at Finch College in New York. It expands on some of the themes introduced in the previous book, specifically Sookan's willingness to challenge tradition and live an independent life. At the center is her process of adaptation to her new life and her connection with her family in Korea, dramatizing her evaluation of both cultures and her own position between them. By describing her relationships with new friends, Sookan navigates new possibilities and rethinks traditional values and forms. Here, Choi presents the typical dilemma of the young immigrant who has to negotiate her responsibilities against individualism and a newfound sense of independence, traditional values against freer perspectives. The text concludes with Sookan's "gathering of pearls," remembering and treasuring her mother's teachings, after her mother's death, realizing that she had been given the strength to forge a new life. Though the third volume is less engaging than the first two, the trilogy describes an important story of the Asian diaspora through an evolving child/young adult character faced with significant choices.

Choi's writing negotiates history and the consequences of Asian immigration by illustrating the choices and difficulties faced by Korean children in Asia and in the United States. Her perspective is generally positive, and she notes the difficulties of the situation in ways that suggest possibilities for children and young adults, and allow them to attend actively to the realities of Asian Americans. Both Watkins and Choi narrate their autobiographical accounts in third person, unlike the first person generally used by other authors. Yet, the autobiographical pact exists: the girl protagonists have the same names as the author, confirming the authenticity of the narrative through personal testimony. Their voices are valid perspectives on historical situations and provide readers with access to traumatic events of the past through personal accounts. Texts like these offer child readers, parents, and educators new dimensions and psychological insights into children's responses or memory of wartime trauma. Importantly, the authors are concerned with stressing the humanity of all the sides presented in the conflict: Watkins' account, for example, offers a privileged glimpse of the suffering of the "returnees" to Japan, a group previously criticized for their colonization of Korea.

Perspectives on China's Cultural Revolution are negotiated by Song Nan Zhang, Ji-Li Jiang, and Da Chen. Zhang, a Chinese Canadian artist, wrote and illustrated *A Little Tiger in the Chinese Night: An Autobiography in Art,* which narrates his idyllic experiences in China after World War II, his idealism during the "Great Leap Forward," and his growing disillusionment with the regime due to physical and psychological repression. The title of the story comes from an episode when three-year old Zhang, hiding with his family from Japanese-occupied Shanghai, sees a tiger in a forest. Seeing a tiger is considered a lucky omen, but it seemed to cause the opposite effect, as Zhang experiences a dramatic shift from innocent happiness to a reeducation process that includes building dams and attending self-criticism meetings, culminating in immigration to Canada. He recounts his first trip away from China, to France, where the country's wealth makes him realize that "everything [he] had been told, everything [he] had believed, was a lie" (34). His artistic talent allows him to leave the country to study; he is in Montreal when the events at Tiananmen Square take place, and remains there. Zhang's artistic and didactic purpose to his Childhood is clear: he writes and paints to "give others some insight into the human dimension of China over the past half century. For one billion lives are made up of a billion individual lives, each as important as any individual life anywhere in the world" (5). He supports his intention by providing maps and a concise historical outline so that readers may contextualize the narrative.

The juxtaposition of narrative and colorful illustrations adds an artistic dimension to this work. The use of illustrations multiplies the levels of meaning in the narrative—the almost idealized coloring and shapes in the paintings appear to contradict some of the dramatic events recounted. Though Zhang was trained in China, his paintings blend two cultural ways of representing reality through art, providing readers with a doubled perspective on illustration. For example, though he describes many hardships he endured, his paintings always show characters smiling and well fed. The manner of Zhang's paintings suggests the nostalgia or the inaccuracy of memory or, more probably, signal the influence that communist-style idealistic realism in art had on him. These elements contribute to the specific aesthetic pleasure experienced in Zhang's book, a tension between the manner of drawing and the harrowing events described. Interestingly, the narrative voice in the text appears to be detached and rational; the drawings convey more emotion and invite identification.

Both Ji-Li Jiang and Da Chen are children of landowning families, which condemn them to being despised by their neighbors, schoolmates, teachers, and community leaders. Jiang's *Red Scarf Girl* traces her trajectory of self-awareness as she learns the real meaning and consequences of the Cultural Revolution.[12] Her narrative opens with her description of life before the Revolution: "I was happy because I was always loved and respected. I was proud because I was able to excel and always expected to succeed. I was trusting, too. I never doubted what I was told: 'Heaven and earth are great, but greater still is the kindness of the Communist Party; father and mother are dear, but dearer still is Chairman Mao'" (1). The Cultural Revolution begins when she is twelve. She describes her evolution from an enthusiastic follower of Mao's dictum to abolish the Four Olds—old ideas, old culture, old customs, and old habits—to a thoughtful teenager who, having witnessed numerous indignities forced on family members and neighbors, elects loyalty to her family over the proletarian dictatorship.

Jiang's narrative reveals the confusion and fanaticism that resulted from the cult of Mao encouraged in the late 1960s. To make this political story more effective, Jiang centers on the radical choice that she has to make between dedication to the Revolution and love for her family. At a time when children who betrayed their parents were praised as heroes, she comes close to changing her name in order to dissociate herself from her landowning family. But in a telling episode when members of the Dictatorship Group search her house for a letter that "proves" the family's landownership, she deliberately lies to protect her family. At this point, she realizes that "[she] would never do anything to hurt [her] family, and [she] would do everything [she] could to take care of them. [Her] family was too precious to forget, too rare to replace" (262–263). At the end, she concludes: "once my life had been defined by my goals: to be a *da-dui-zang* [student council president], to participate in the exhibition, to be a Red Guard. They seemed unimportant to me now. Now my life was defined by my responsibilities. I had promised to take care of my family, and I would renew that promise every day. I would not give up or withdraw, no matter how hard life became" (263). Looking back on her childhood, Jiang notes with pain how the Chinese people were victims of a power struggle between members of the

Party. Jiang explains how memories of her childhood never left her, even after moving to the United States. She decided to write her autobiography because, as she explains, "I wanted to do something for the little girl I had been, and for all the children who lost their childhoods as I did" (266). This strategy for empowerment communicates to child readers the healing power that literature can play in each person's life, particularly when burdened with a traumatic history. Though Jiang makes positive choices she is still burdened by the historical context that oppresses those who wish to think freely.

In David Henry Hwang's foreword to Jiang's autobiography, he explains how Mao's strategy brought "untold suffering to those very masses in whose name the battle was waged, as well as disabling an entire group of young people who are now known as the 'lost generation'" (xvii). Another member of this lost generation is Da Chen, also a grandson of landowners, whose family was systematically persecuted. Chen's *China's Son* is set in a remote rural village, Yellow Stone, also subject to the consequences of the Cultural Revolution. His father is repeatedly interned in labor camps and his siblings leave school to become farmers. Da understands that excelling in school is the only way he can climb out of the hole they have placed him in: "I shone, despite their efforts to snuff me out" (37). But he eventually also has to leave school in the face of constant humiliation. His narrative includes humor, particularly in his account of his relationship with a gang of older boys—a kind of extended family who ignores his privileged background and teaches him to smoke and gamble. After Mao's death, Da realizes that an education is the only way to overcome the stigma his family suffers and he prepares for college exams, eventually getting accepted into the Beijing First Foreign Language Institute. The general content of this story reiterates *Colors of the Mountain,* and Chen's rewriting strategy consists mostly of highlighting the events of his childhood and stressing interpersonal relationships with his peers. He also emphasizes his family relationships and school. Chen does not present himself as an ideal child—compared to Jiang, for example, who seems much more mature at an early age. Chen is oftentimes childish and irresponsible, frustrated at the dead ends that the government imposes, and almost gives in to desperation. Fortunately, he manages to find a place for himself when he decides to take schooling seriously, paving the way for his version of the success story.

Taken together, these autobiographies paint a multilayered picture of China's recent history though representations of the lives of the country's children. Several threads link these very different accounts: all the protagonists are fiercely loyal to China and mourn the destruction wrought by the abuse of power. Chen chooses to retitle his adapted memoir "China's Son," which symbolically foregrounds his perception of himself. Similarly, Jiang's title highlights the emblem of the Youth Pioneers that she proudly wears, until she becomes aware of the ultimate conditions of the regime. Further, neither of the protagonists wants to leave the homeland but understands that immigration becomes the only option. As Jiang explains, "I was willing to take on the struggle to establish myself in a new country because I knew that was the price I would have to pay for the freedom to think, speak, and write whatever I pleased" (271). Zhang's immigration to Canada happens almost accidentally, when he does not return after Tiananmen. Zhang, Jiang, and Chen also acknowledge the need to write their books as evidence of their survival and to humanize China's Cultural Revolution. Zhang tells his story, he says, in the hope that "it will give others some insight into the human dimension of China over the past half century" (5); Chen characterizes his book as "a book about love in the face of hate, a book of hope for the hopeless" (viii); Jiang also hopes that her book will contribute to her mission "to promote cultural exchanges between the United States and China" (271). For child readers, these narratives provide access to the experiences of other children who have to make difficult choices and overcome harrowing odds to survive, as well as to individual stories behind immigration. They emphasize that immigration was a strategy for survival, not a lack of loyalty. The China represented in these texts is, and always will be, *home* for the protagonists—a place they look back to with longing and sorrow. This notion offers an important cultural perspective to American readers, who can then understand, through autobiographical texts, how and why the heritage country continues to live in the consciousness of immigrants.

American and Canadian history are another central concern of Asian North American autobiographies of childhood for children because creatively interpreting history has proven crucial to the process of legitimization by ethnic writers. For many of these writers, engaging history is critical to their strategy for staking a claim in the country they feel themselves a part of but that had often rejected them in its official version of itself.[13] As Stephen Slemon points out, among the various challenges to inherited concepts of history is the attempted imaginative recovery of "those aspects of culture that have been subject to historical erasure" (165). The problem of history becomes particularly important for the ethnic writer who has to deal with official and nonofficial versions of events and the danger of obliteration from mainstream memory. Ethnic children's writers often "work consciously to respond to prejudiced narratives of ethnicity through signification, allusion and confrontation. Texts recoup lost heroes, fill the gaps of historical memory, subvert ethnic stereotypes, and advance revisionary versions of cultural identity" (Katharine Capshaw Smith 6). For Asian North Americans, literary incursions into their role in the development of the country provide more than mere insight into a concealed past. As these writers struggle to inscribe the truth about their historical situations, trying to do justice to Asian American history, they do justice to American history.

Making Asian North American history the subtext for children's autobiography is part of the process of decoding past collective experiences and reimagining possibilities for the future. These historically informed texts highlight the sense of collective identity that the protagonists of the stories share, as well as provide a critical source of knowledge and meaning within the Asian North American experience. A number of Asian North American writers have engaged diverse moments and aspects of the history of the Asian presence in the United States, foregrounding stories of immigration, heritage culture, racism, and acculturation. A proactive concern that American and Canadian children, of Asian descent or not, learn the lessons of history impels much of this writing. As Smith points out, "Because works often narrate and explain details of a traumatic past, like the internment of Japanese Americans or the enslavement of African Americans, to an audience innocent of historical knowledge, the stakes are high: adult mediators recognize the gravity of their role as gatekeepers to history and arbiters of ethnic identity. Scholars of ethnic literature will therefore find much complexity in the ways writers construct history and negotiate the demands of various audiences (4).

Jeanne Wakatsuki Houston, Shichan Takashima, and Yoshiko Uchida's Childhoods negotiate the relocation and internment of Japanese North Americans during World War II. These autobiographies privilege the perspectives of Americans and Canadians of Japanese descent in the writing of American and Canadian history, empowering them to recount stories of government-sanctioned racism. Houston's *Farewell to Manzanar,* coauthored by her husband, begins with her childhood in California before the internment, an event that dramatically changed the course of her life: "the start of World War II was not the climax to our life in Ocean Park. Pearl Harbor just snipped it off, stopped it from becoming whatever else lay ahead" (40). Because she was a young child when this event occurred, she does not engage political aspects in great detail, centering rather on the experience of her large family. In particular, she uses the story of her father's psychological disintegration as a metaphor for the insidious effects of racism on longtime Japanese residents and on young Japanese American citizens. As she says of her father's arrest, "He didn't struggle. There was no point to it. He had become a man without a country. The land of his birth was at war with America; yet after thirty-five years here he was still prevented by law from becoming an American citizen. He was suddenly a man with no rights who looked exactly like the enemy" (6).

Because she was so young when they were interned, she recognizes the gap between her perception of the camps and that of the adults around her. She guesses that for some people, like her older brothers and sisters, moving to camp gave them a feeling of relief from the anti-Japanese sentiment that occasionally exploded into violence. But for the older Issei, such as her mother, the issue of privacy, for example, was fundamental, and the crowded sleeping arrangements, communal mess halls, and open toilets were perceived as "an open insult to that other, private self, a slap in the face you were powerless to challenge" (24). Houston's account of life in the camps is tinged with psychological reflection on how this event changed the very structure of the Japanese American family: "my family, after three years of mess hall living, collapsed as an integrated unit" (27). The father's traditional role as head of the household and the strong filial feeling that governed their families shifted as each of the family members began seeking out their own positions—as soldiers, teachers, and more independent persons who could no longer count on their father to provide or make decisions for them.

Critics have noted that Houston's autobiography is as much about her father (and by extension, about the Issei generation) as it is about herself. Fifty years old when the war began, her father crumbles under the accusation of disloyalty: "for a man raised in Japan, there was no greater disgrace. And it was the humiliation. It brought him face to face with his own vulnerability, his own powerlessness. He had no rights, no home, no control over his own life" (52). The tragedy of her father's story nonetheless opens up possibilities for hers. Using the image of her father's cane, which he needed after a stroke, and comparing it to a samurai sword, a "virtue and a burden," she notes that "it helped [her] understand how Papa's life could end at a place like Manzanar. He didn't die there, but things finished for him there, whereas for [her] it was like a birthplace. The camp was where [their] lifelines intersected" (34). With the resilience of the young, she adapts easily to life in camp and suggests that this experience allowed her to grow in ways that may not have been possible elsewhere, or which were simply exacerbated in this context. It appears that this is where her father's life "ended" and hers "began"—a perspective that Elaine Kim disputes by arguing that the lives of father and daughter actually intersect when the girl rejects her father in favor of acceptance by Whites, limiting him, in a sense, to the role of the Japanese father that frightens off White boyfriends (*Asian American Literature* 85–86).

Importantly, Jeanne recognizes that her experience of Manzanar was different from that of her mother or siblings: "at seven, I was too young to be insulted. The camp worked on me in a much different way" (25). Because she, too, "looked exactly like the enemy," her trajectory in this autobiography consists of positioning herself in her temporal and geographical context, and the book chronicles her efforts to deal with the insidiousness of external and internal racial rejection. Manzanar became "a world unto itself," while it existed:

"in time, staying there became far simpler than moving once again to another, unknown place. It was as if the war was forgotten, our reason for being there forgotten. The present, the little bit of busywork you had right in front of you became the most urgent thing. In such a narrowed world, in order to survive, you learn to control your rage and your despair, and you try to re-create, as well as you can, your normality, some sense of things continuing" (72). When, at the age of ten, she learns they are to be released, she begins to feel a dread— "the foretaste of being hated," she recalls, "and I would have stayed inside the camp forever rather than step outside and face such a moment" (95). To an important extent, Houston internalized certain racist attitudes, even accepting some negative attitudes toward people of Japanese ancestry: "I knew ahead of time that if someone looked at me with hate, I would have to allow it, to swallow it, because something in me, something about me deserved it" (95). Ironically then, internment at Manzanar embodied the racism that prompted Houston's desire to be acceptable to the very people who incarcerated her (Kim, *Asian American Literature* 86). Linda Trinh Moser suggests that during internment, Houston begins to devalue her Japanese heritage, following the example of the larger American society (130). "The fact that America had accused us, or excluded us, or imprisoned us," Houston writes, "did not change the kind of world we wanted. Most of us were born in this country; we had no other models" (72).

In a sense, it may have been easier for her to accept the negative stereotypes of the Japanese and desire to adhere to the model of a typical "American" (read "mainstream / White") life. Unfortunately, though she does well in school and sports, she is not allowed to become a Girl Scout and some parents forbid their daughters from socializing with her. Instead of challenging these prohibitions, she faults herself, viewing them as "the result of [her] failings. She was imposing a burden on *them*" (115). Elaine Kim notes that Houston "discerns that her past was governed by what she calls a 'dual impulse'—the desire to disappear completely and the urge to fight invisibility" (*Asian American Literature* 84). At one point, in an effort to be accepted, she tries on different disguises to *be* like everybody else by *looking* like everybody else: she twirls a baton and dresses as a majorette—the "one trick I could perform that was thoroughly, unmistakably American" (79)—she wants to wear a nun's habit, or dress like a princess for confirmation. She also vies for the title of Carnival Queen, winning it after she "decided to go exotic, with a flower-print sarong, black hair loose and a hibiscus flower behind [her] ear" (124). Nonetheless, as Patricia Sakurai explains, though this figuration of the "exotic" Asian female allows her "a certain amount of dubious 'at-homeness,' her attempts at playing the all-American girl allows her no sense of 'at-homeness' whatsoever, further emphasizing the specific form of femininity and sexuality she is expected to enact as an Asian American woman. None of her attempted identities proves fitting" (167).

Jeanne Wakatsuki Houston's autobiography narrates a search for individuality and identity in the context of a country that imprisoned its own citizens. She explains that writing the text was a healing exercise for her, as she confronted her own tragic history. But the text is also a psychological incursion into the complex racial perspectives and political events of Japanese American history. As Houston notes, "Much more than a remembered place [Manzanar] had become a state of mind" (140). This location becomes the central metaphor of the child's experience of physical and psychological liminality. Moreover, in a text that highlights ironic contradictions, Houston realizes that "one of the most amazing things about America is the way it can both undermine you and keep you believing in your own possibilities, pumping you with hope" (111). Her story enacts a significant project of self-acceptance in the context of rejection. For Asian American children learning about this history, Houston's account offers a positive vision that does not elide the ambivalence felt by Japanese Americans. As a cultural artifact, this Childhood serves as a document that narrates a process of self-inscription into history.

Takashima's *A Child in Prison Camp* is formulated as a series of diary entries by a Japanese Canadian girl who is eleven years old when "overnight" their rights as Canadians are taken away (5).[14] The text contains Takashima's illustrations, delicate watercolors that capture scenes from camp life, from the wait for the train to take them to camp to the *obon* festival they celebrate. These diary entries cover between March 1942 and September 1945, which manifestly locates the narrative in the years of relocation in Canada. A brief epilogue dated June 7, 1964, narrates the inauguration of the Japanese Canadian Cultural Center in Toronto. Takashima thus chronicles not only the history of the Japanese Canadian relocation but also notes the efforts of the Canadian government to redress those wrongs. The author was already a well-known artist in Canada when her Childhood was published, and this text reveals the multilayered meaning of her artistic production, as the drawings enhance in dramatic ways their verbal narratives. Moreover, the potential of the drawings produces a highly dynamic text, as opposed to the more static words-only text, highlighting the dialectic between text and image that provides creators with a wider range of artistic and imaginative possibilities. Paul John Eakin's idea that "the tension between the experiential reality of subjectivity on the one hand and the available cultural forms for its expression on the other always structures any engagement in autobiography" encourages us to critically ponder Takashima's strategy (*Touching the World* 88).

Because of the diary format and the inclusion of drawings, Takashima's text has an immediacy that the other Childhoods for children lack. The sense of continual present that a journal provides allows the reader to identify with the evolving action in significant ways. The events Takashima narrates are similar to those in other memoirs of relocation, but the narrative structure becomes a successful tool for communicating the difficulty of the experience. Discursively, the idea of a diary to recount the difficulty of war has become part of children's literature since the publication of *The Diary of Anne Frank*. But Takashima takes her text a step further, with paintings that distinctly convey not only the specific situation, but the feelings of the painting subject. The pastel colors used in the *obon* festival depiction transmit feelings of joy and good wishes; the relatively monochromatic blue-greens of the wait for the train signals the characters' boredom; the light browns and ochres in the bathhouse scene convey the serenity of the evening ritual; finally, the rainbow colors of the painting of Shichan and her mother rinsing clothes in the river for the last time communicate their hope and happiness at the thought of leaving the camp. Takashima provides the child reader not only with an account of the camp experience, but with diverse options for artistically negotiating this experience. By ending the narrative with information about the government's official apology and compensation, this text becomes part of the personal process of healing that the artist has undergone, linking the personal process with the official action.

There is a more evident didactic and artistic impulse in Yoshiko Uchida's *The Invisible Thread,* a *künstlerroman* that stresses her process of artistic development and describes the genesis of her future literary endeavors.[15] Uchida, one of the most prolific Asian American writers for children, has turned repeatedly to the theme of the Nisei in the internment camps in both her fiction and autobiography. In 1982, after decades of successful writing for children, she published her autobiography, *Desert Exile: The Uprooting of a Japanese-American Family,* that depicts her family's experiences in Topaz. Her purpose was primarily didactic: she wanted to help Japanese Americans find a "sense of continuity with their past. . . . But [she] wrote it as well for all Americans, with the hope that through knowledge of the past, they will never allow another group of people in America to be sent into a desert exile again" (154). This explains her motivation to rewrite the memoir for children, retitling it to stress the metaphor of connection with Japan. The ten-year gap between the first and second texts evidence how "the perspective of years and the unfolding of the movement towards a national recognition of the injustice to the Japanese Americans brings a new strength to her narrative" (Kapai 378).

Uchida's account of her childhood in *The Invisible Thread* shows an "American" child growing up in the early decades of the twentieth century in California. The markers of her childhood are those of children's culture: sibling rivalry with her older sister, Keiko; games with neighborhood children; piano lessons; school; the death of a pet. The early chapters of the book depict an almost ideal childhood, with compassionate and loving parents, where her only real problem seems to be dissatisfaction at always having to wear hand-me-downs. A seemingly innocuous reference to a custom the sisters hated—"all the company that seemed to come in a never-ending stream, mostly from Japan"—limns the difference between Uchida's childhood and that of her neighbors. The awareness that "a long invisible thread would always bind Mama and Papa to the country they had left behind. And that thread seemed to wind just as surely around Keiko and [Yoshi] as well" (5) signals the child's nascent awareness of ethnic identity. The eponymous thread—the shifting meaning of her relationship with the land of her parents—becomes a leitmotif. The text itself, on a discursive level, becomes the enactment of the invisible thread that she admits links Japanese Americans to each other and to Japan.

Uchida juxtaposes her perception of herself as an American child with that of America's classification of her as a foreigner. The shifting paradigms of her vision of herself, which she repeatedly compares to or contrasts with those of the people around her, address the complicated process of affiliation for the Asian North American child in the process of acquiring self-esteem and knowing his or her position in the world. Her relationships with her peers is represented positively, although she recognizes that her own insecurity might have prevented her from developing more relationships: "unfortunately, society had caused me to have so little self-esteem and to feel so inferior, I was careful to close myself up to insure against being hurt" (55). In the chapter titled "Unhappy Days," Uchida engages more specifically her growing awareness of ethnic division in California and the racism against Asians. Reference to an episode when a photographer, taking a picture of the Girl Reserves for the local paper, tries to "ease [her] out of the picture" (55) indicates the official portrait of itself that mainstream American desired at the time, which denied the presence of Asians. Her friend Sylvia, understanding the photographer's aim, pointedly draws Yoshi in, and "standing together in [their] white middies and [their] blue Girl Reserves ties," the girls smile (55). Yoshi's perception of the nature of the American gaze becomes more acute as she recounts the story of their internment: to the government, they were "aliens and nonaliens"; to the army, they were simply "prisoners," a word she stretches ironically as she defines their new situation. From law-abiding citizens, the Japanese Americans had been converted into "prisoners of [their] own country" (69, 73, 74). Her childhood questions about her identity reverberate significantly: "how could America—my own country—have done this to us?" (79).

The Invisible Thread may be classified as a *künstlerroman* because of Uchida's emphasis on her development as a writer and its performance of writing as a strategy for survival. Uchida narrates her almost accidental discovery of the power of the written word. At the age of eleven, after the death of their dog, Brownie, inventing an ending for Brownie's story becomes a liberating moment: "I had also discovered that writing in the booklet was a means, not only of holding on to the special magic of joyous moments, but of finding comfort and solace from pain as well. It was a means of creating a better ending than was sometimes possible in real life. I had discovered what writing was all about" (30). Interestingly, as she writes about animals and other people, she recognizes that "it never in [her] wildest dreams occurred to [her] to write about a Japanese American child" (32). The absence of literary engagements with ethnicity for children was, at first, an unconscious restraint upon her own creativity. Having no Japanese American literary models became, upon reflection, the impetus for Uchida's later endeavors to create those characters for Japanese American children. Uchida states her metanarrative purpose in inscribing her memoir, as she reviews her life and her work and analyzes the creative impulse behind her writing. She explains: "in my eagerness to be accepted as an American during my youth, I had been pushing my Japaneseness aside. Now at last, I appreciated it and was proud of it. I had finally come full circle." Her writing becomes her attempt to pass on that legacy of ethnic appreciation to the Sansei—the third generation Japanese Americans—"to give them the kinds of books [she'd] never had as a child. The time was right, for now the world too, was changing. . . . [She] wanted to give the young Sansei a sense of continuity and knowledge of their own remarkable history [and] hoped all young Americans would read these books as well" (131). This perspective validates Uchida's decision to rewrite her memoir in order to reach a larger audience and achieve more significant didactic purposes and wider cultural appreciation.

Living in North America

The increasing visibility of Asian Americans in the public sphere has led to a number of life writing texts that engage their lives. Figure skater Michelle Kwan's autobiography, cowritten by Laura M. James, is notable in this context on several levels.[16] The skater recounts her life in chronological order, stressing her motto—"Work hard, be yourself, and have fun"—as well as the support she received from her family, coaches, and mentors. She openly shares her sense of determination and love of competition, as well as the joy of winning and disappointment of losing. As someone who at the age of sixteen became the Women's World Champion, Kwan has become an example of perseverance and dedication for many (Asian) American children. Her autobiography, though it does not engage her ethnicity significantly, offers a viable model for many children. Her obvious Asian-ness, as well as her clear identification as an American, posits a trajectory of successful socialization, integration, and success for children.

Sing Lim's *West Coast Chinese Boy* describes the life of the Chinese in Vancouver in the early decades of the twentieth century. Lim grew up in a prison-like apartment building, built after anti-Asian rioters had smashed all the windows of other buildings in the district. The new building, meant to protect them "in case of future riots," also seems to be built to keep them in: "it had only one entrance with an iron gate that could be closed in an emergency, like a prison or a fort" (12). Lim tells his family's story through a series of vignettes about different characters, customs, or episodes, linking them with the history of the early Chinese in Canada, with the First Nations peoples, with other Asian groups, and with the White majority. He also explains traditional Chinese customs—births, funerals, foodways, festivals, the opera—and highlights colorful characters in Chinatown: the herbalist, the poultry shop owner, and so on. There is no clear plot pattern in his narrative; the recollections appear to be random snapshots of the life around him, independent of chronology or a specific climax.

Lim engages the question of identity in specific ways. The vignettes titled "School and School" and "Being Chinese" negotiate his ambivalence with the two systems he finds himself between. His parents, because of the "racial intolerance" they had suffered, did not want to assimilate to Canadian culture and obliged the children to speak only in Chinese. Yet, Lim notes, "the older Chinese looked down on us who were born in Canada. They called us 'siwash' and 'half bread' (half-breed). The word 'siwash' was what the whites called the Indians. . . . When an older Chinese used it, he meant 'native, without Chinese culture.' It was not a nice name to be called, whatever its exact meaning" (22).

Lim's art becomes a recurring theme in the narrative. He notes the first time he sees Western art in a neighbor's apartment building and how his teachers encourage him to draw. He presents two forms of drawing in his book: simple line drawings on almost every page and more elaborate watercolors in the middle pages. The childlike line drawings are often accompanied by handwritten explanations that accompany the narrative and complement the information revealed. The colored paintings are more complex, and some are arranged to illustrate specific episodes. These paintings are monotypes; Lim paints on glass, then blots paper on top to make a print: "only one painting results, and it must be right or it is thrown away. Like a spontaneous drawing, it cannot be corrected" (61).

Lim uses his drawings in a manner similar to Takashima's, illustrating how the structural connection between the writing of childhood and graphic art lies in the manner in which both forms negotiate complementary ways of perceiving. The issue of perspective is crucial to how we read both memoirs and illustrations, as the forms themselves require the reader to strategically position him- or herself in order to comprehend the performance enacted. Childhood memoirs similarly focus our attention on specific ideas and forms of understanding the world, the writers' individual itinerary of selfhood. Noting intersections in these modes of inscription, we must approach contemporary drawing in memoirs as increasingly sophisticated forms of inscribing the past. For child audiences of these texts, the drawings center readers' attention and highlight the essential. Further, metaliterary elements serve as signifying strategies and these texts engage, in particularly effective ways, the writers' perception of themselves. These narratives that include drawings are particularly effective *künstlerroman* because the subject of the autobiography, most often, is an artist him- or herself. The reader is privileged to participate in the performance of both memory and art, and the complex interaction between them.

The idea of writing about Asian North Americans to provide (Asian) American children models that would widen their processes of ethnic or interethnic appreciation also lies behind Laurence Yep's artistic itinerary. A prolific writer for children since the 1970s, Yep presents, in the autobiography of his childhood and early adulthood, *The Lost Garden,* two separate but mutually enhancing stories: the account of his growing awareness and understanding of himself as a Chinese American, and his process of becoming a writer.[17] Born a clumsy, asthmatic son to an athletic family, Yep spends his early years feeling like "a changeling, wondering how [he] wound up born into the family. [He] felt not only inadequate but incomplete—like a puzzle with several pieces missing" (12). The image of a puzzle serves as a metaphor for his personal and cultural insecurity; a misfit in his family, he also perceives himself a misfit in his predominantly African American neighborhood. But Yep needs to recognize his liminality before he can begin to engage it productively. The itinerary of his struggle to belong is articulated through his definition of himself as a puzzle solver, suggesting that he has developed the creative agenda that sets him on a path to self-knowledge, which involves an imaginative negotiation with memory as a tool for agency.

The narrative foregrounds Yep's process of becoming a writer. From the beginning, he notes certain events or situations that lead to his vocation, notably the awareness of how his ethnicity and experiences in the multicultural neighborhood shaped his character and imagination. As Yep explains, "I don't know, though, if I would have become a writer if my life had been allowed to follow a conventional, comfortable track" (23). The dramatic change in his neighborhood, from predominantly Chinese to African American when Yep was seven, turning him into "an outsider in what had once been [his] own home turf" (37), makes him aware of ethnicity as a social marker. In the chapter titled "The Owl," Yep narrates the development of his ethnic consciousness and his approaches toward overcoming the gap between his vision of himself and that presented by his racial features. Recognizing himself as "the neighborhood's all-purpose Asian . . . made me feel like an outsider more than ever in [his] own neighborhood. It was like suddenly finding that the different pieces of a jigsaw puzzle no longer fit together" (38). The writer engages emblematic Asian American literary themes—such as his growing awareness of his Chinese-ness and his ambivalent relationship with Chinatown—in a manner appropriate for children. His relationship with his maternal grandmother, one of the strongest influences in his life and on his writing, marks his developing comprehension of ethnicity. "My grandmother," he says, "represented a 'Chineseness' in my life that was as unmovable and unwanted as a mountain in your living room. Or rather it was like finding strange, new pieces to a puzzle that made the picture itself take a new, unwanted shape" (46). Importantly, she initiates his process of reciprocal appreciation of ethnicity: "I knew she accepted her strange, American-born grandson—far better than I accepted my China-born grandmother. In many ways, she came to embody what I came to consider my 'Chineseness'—that foreign, unassimilable, independent core" (2).

One of the most fascinating aspects of his autobiography is the manner in which he discusses the inception of his different books: the way family members inspired characters, how his literary imagination developed, and how research blends with creativity to make fiction. He describes his evolving understanding of what it meant to be Chinese in San Francisco in the 1950s and early '60s: the pressure to conform, the ridicule at being different. He recalls the contradictory feelings of shame at not being able to speak Chinese and his struggle to deny his ethnic background. The concluding chapters describe Yep's strategy of utilizing memory to write. Though most of his work is fiction, he has repeatedly acknowledged that he writes about himself: "In writing about alienated people and aliens in my science fiction, I was writing about myself as a Chinese American" (104). His writing exploits his growing comprehension of the consequences of ethnicity and the place he carves for himself in the complex (Chinese) American society. The central component of Yep's itinerary for selfhood involves—more than just consciousness of his liminal position in American society—recognizing and appropriating his heritage "to know its strengths and understand its weakness" (43). Yep thus undertakes a physical and imaginative journey that reverses that of his parents: his forebears left China to explore America, and the writer enters Chinatown in search of pieces of the puzzle of his life. The text, as an Asian North American autobiography for children, blends the story of Yep's journey toward self-knowledge and creative expression, offering a positive vision of ethnic identity and stressing (textually and contextually) the empowerment offered by the act of writing.

These Childhoods for children develop notable strategies of meaning in the context of generic revisions of autobiography and the cultural work performed by ethnic texts. By addressing a child audience, the authors widen the sphere of the receptors of ethnic history. Providing personal accounts of trajectories of selfhood by Asian North American protagonists allows the children of the United States and Canada to recognize these experiences as an integral part of their societies. Asian North American children can thus identify with the stories of their heritage cultures; children of other ethnicities can learn about diverse cultural histories and perspectives. As a manner of motivating cultural and collective memory, these texts realize invaluable designs that function beyond the merely political to engage the aesthetic, highlighting the redemptive qualities of art in individual processes of formation and representation.

Conclusion

Rewriting the Childhood

Asian North American autobiographers who engage their childhood experiences influence the development of the forms life writing takes and the culture that receives these texts. This multilayered process functions in the contexts of literary practice and cultural mobilization, connecting with Lisa Lowe's assertion that "the making of Asian American culture includes practices that are partly inherited, partly modified, as well as partly invented; Asian American culture also includes the practices that emerge in relation to the dominant representations that deny or subordinate Asian and Asian American cultures as 'other'" (65). The writers discussed in this study appropriate and subvert an established Euro-American genre to negotiate complex questions about self-representation and the construction of cultural memory.

These Asian North American texts illustrate a more general pattern of cultural dynamics in our time. Importantly, as Michael Fischer notes, "Ethnic autobiographical writing parallels, mirrors, and exemplifies contemporary theories of textuality, of knowledge, and of culture. Both forms of writing suggest powerful modes of cultural criticism. They are post-modern in their deployment of a series of techniques: bifocality or reciprocity of perspectives, juxtapositioning of multiple realities, intertextuality and inter-referenciality, and comparison through families of resemblance. Insofar as the present age is one of increasing potentialities for dialogue, as well as conflict, among cultures, lessons for writing ethnography may be taken from writers both on ethnicity and on textuality, knowledge, and culture" ("Ethnicity and the Post-modern Arts" 230). For this reason, we need to consider these texts in context and, importantly, in dialogue with literary tradition. My emphasis on Asian North American Childhoods as *writerly* acts foregrounds the importance of the text as artifact that stems from and modifies existing literary and cultural traditions. For immigrants or racialized subjects in the United States and Canada, the production of the autobiography of childhood gestures toward a beginning—narratologically, phenomenologically, culturally.

As interventions in the literary history of autobiography, these texts high-

light the ways in which the Asian North American self may be written by signaling narrative strategies, formal structures, tropes, and metaphors. Indeed,
as I have shown, in many cases narrative choices actively construct the self-in-
text, as the autobiographer configures the past into a shape that takes its formal
design from established or renewed modes. Because autobiography has a history, these creative interventions influence later texts formally and contextually.
These autobiographical occasions become sites where literary strategies and
cultural purposes intersect, as the writer's agency confers validity on historical or cultural experiences. Thus, by attending to the formal strategies of these
Asian North American Childhoods, we discern community-building strategies
and address the intersection of literary genre and cultural position to formulate
a renewed appreciation of childhood in contemporary American and Canadian
societies.

Apart from a dialogue with literary history, these texts operate a revisioning of the narratives of history, particularly those of Asian history and the
experiences of Asian subjects in North America. The didactic purpose to these
texts is enacted through a privileging of microhistories, which may contrast or
complement official versions. Importantly, these narratives help validate the
experiences of Asian immigrants for both the Pan-Asian community and mainstream United States and Canada by promoting their visibility and making history itself a part of community development.

Reading these texts together clarifies a series of literary and cultural devel-
opments. Formally, the texts evolve from a traditional chronological structure
to more experimental patterns that challenge stereotypical representations and
posit original forms of self-representation. The use of graphics in comics and
picture books, the narrative enactment of relational lives, the appropriation of
the diary, the blending of prose and verse, among others, signal a strong liberatory impulse in the writer. No longer must the autobiographers adhere to
established forms; their particular experiences of North America necessitate
renewed forms of self-inscription. Culturally, these Childhoods dialogue with
existing autobiography, fiction, and poetry and serve a strong community-
building purpose. By recounting experiential history, they establish community
narratives that fill in gaps in personal or group remembrance and address a
wider audience of mainstream American or Canadian subjects.

At the end of *Lost Names,* Richard Kim, who had earlier realized that "we
are all in the making of history together" (187), takes to heart his father's
charge, "It is your world now" (195). This quotation exemplifies this study's
central conclusion: that Asian North American Childhoods, creative interventions in literary history and community building through examination of memory, are actually directed toward the future. The community that receives these
texts not only perceives how narratives of cultural or collective memory vali-

date their history, their positions, and even their political agendas, but also harness the texts' utility in projecting future literary and cultural projects. Carolyn Steedman's questions, quoted in the introduction to this book—"Who uses these stories? *How* are they used, and to what ends?" (28)—receives multilayered replies. These Childhoods, I argue, are used by authors to create a reader that can renegotiate the narratives of his or her community histories through specific literary intervention or by examining the history of Asians in North America. This process reminds us of the increasingly collective nature of memory and its ability to share a social past. These Childhoods oblige readers to reevaluate established literary forms and implicate them in the processes that create meaning. They interpellate an implied audience for culture and history, challenging them to take on an active role in validating, disseminating, or as the case may be, canonizing a given text as emblematic of an ethnic identity or position.

Clearly, therefore, the Asian North American autobiographer who functions within a developing discourse of memory and self-inscription writes not just *about* him- or herself but to engage a larger communal project. The Childhood evolves from a passive act of witnessing to dynamically reconfigure audience reception. The writers revise their childhoods as imaginative structures that allow them to explore their positions in history, society, and culture, as well as lay out designs of community configurations. These documents operate significant modifications in the ways we read and write autobiography and reimagine Asian North American communities. As they gesture toward an understanding of the problem of a search for forms of self-representation, they participate in a process of collective and cultural memory that reshapes our perspectives on narratives of history, society, and selfhood.

Notes

Introduction: Revisiting the Childhood

1. I will not analyze in detail contemporary theories of autobiography, a task which has already been done excellently by scholars such as Paul John Eakin, Susanna Egan, Françoise Lionnet, Laura Marcus, Sidonie Smith, and Julia Watson, among others. I owe many of my perspectives on autobiography to their work, which I cannot acknowledge in detail. For ideas on ethnic autobiography, I'm grateful for the work of Betty Bergland, William Boelhower, Michael Fischer, Shirley Lim, Sau-ling Wong, and Traise Yamamoto.

2. I use the term "autobiography" to refer to a life narrative text (or serial) in which the author, narrator, and protagonist are the same person: the autobiographical pact as described by Philippe Lejeune. I deliberately adhere to a traditional reading of the genre, even as I recognize that the forms of autobiography are changing (discussed in this study).

3. I do not want to simplify the complex differences between Asian American and Asian Canadian writing, which have been dealt with in detail in studies by Guy Beauregard, Iyko Day, Donald Goellnicht, Marie Lo, and Roy Miki, among others. Specifically, for example, in the case of Asian Canadian cultural discourse, there is an important engagement with Canada's colonial history that Asian American criticism does not share. Asian subjects in the United States, in turn, have to negotiate the difficult formulations of race relations in connection with the history of African Americans (indeed, we generally agree that the political impetus that led to the development of Asian American studies came from the atmosphere created by the civil rights movement, which raised the consciousness of Asian Americans to the nature of racism in their own lives and in the institutions they were part of, notably the university) and Hispanic subjects, particularly in the West. Important as well, Asian American literary studies developed institutionally in the 1960s and 1970s, before Asian Canadian criticism, which has been examined in relation to diaspora studies, postcolonial literature, and Asian American literary criticism at diverse points in recent years. See Goellnicht's "A Long Labour: The Protracted Birth of Asian Canadian Literature" and Beauregard's "The Emergence of 'Asian Canadian Literature': Can Lit's Obscene Supplement?" for a historical discussion of the the-

oretical development of the field, particularly in relation to Asian American Studies and Canadian literary studies. Another difference may be noted as Asian Canadian literary criticism often negotiates its paradigms in relation to other ethnic groups, notably the First Nations. See Marie Lo's "Native-Born Asian American Model Minorities" for a discussion of imperialism as an object of critique and as a basis for Asian Canadian–First Nations coalitions. At diverse points in this study, I will make references to specific issues that are relevant to these concerns. For the purposes of a more inclusive discussion, I will generally refer to this writing as "Asian North American."

4. "The Childhood, over and above everything else, is a form of *literature;* and as such it follows the inviolable laws that govern any purely literary text: the law of readability, and the law which decrees that the truth of the imagination shall take precedence over the truth of fact" (Coe, *When the Grass* 84).

5. Yet Coe himself acknowledges that the genre's literary status is debatable: it should be "not literature but a sort of documentary" (*When the Grass* 3). It is worth noting that Coe's study was published in 1984, relatively early in the rapidly growing field of ethnic autobiography criticism. Yet, this perspective leads organically, in the context of ethnic writing, to the idea of the historical and cultural implications of the form.

6. See my *Transcultural Reinventions: Asian American and Asian Canadian Short Story Cycles* for an analysis of how writers have appropriated this genre, as well as my coedited volume, *Literary Gestures,* for perspectives on the aesthetic in Asian North American criticism.

7. See Shirley Geok-Lin Lim's *Approaches to Teaching Kingston's* The Woman Warrior, among others, for perspectives on the reception of this text. See also Sauling Wong's "Ethnic Dimensions of Postmodern Indeterminacy: Maxine Hong Kingston's *The Woman Warrior* as Avant-garde Autobiography." Kingston's seminal text has been analyzed extensively from a variety of perspectives, which I will not engage in this study. Specifically, though important parts of her text focus on her childhood, I contend that *The Woman Warrior* is not strictly a Childhood because of the complex use of biography in her life writing exercise and her collagic construction. For that reason, I do not include her in my catalogue of Asian American Childhoods, although her work illustrates many of the characteristics of the genre.

8. Further, Stone argues,

> Because of its several often subtle and submerged connections to different dimensions of public life and private consciousness, an autobiography is, in the language of psychoanalysis, an overdetermined document. Its statements and implications must be explained in more than a single set of terms. As an account of past actions and gestures, autobiography asks to be judged skeptically as a version of history. As a deliberate pattern of words and the imitation of a distinctive voice, it is a story which seeks a sympathetic ear. As the articulation of past and present motives, impulses, and ideals, autobiography becomes a kind of case-history as well as a spiritual confession, with the reader as invited priest-psychia-

trist. Finally, as a more or less trustworthy linguistic bridge between one self or soul and others, autobiography recreated a model of literate culture itself and the social circumstances in which individual personality is discovered, asserted, and confirmed (or denied) and community potentially established. (5)

9. Indeed, autobiographies, and especially ethnic autobiographies "can be conceived 'politically,' as Antonio Gramsci has pointed out: 'autobiography therefore replaces the "political" or "philosophical" essay: it describes in action what otherwise is deduced logically. Autobiography certainly has great historical value in that it shows life in action and not just as written laws or dominant moral principles say it should be'" (qtd. in Bergland, "Representing Ethnicity" 70).

10. I take my cue from Françoise Lionnet's approach in her work on autobiography: "but I try never to impose a theoretical grid on the text; instead, I draw from it the means of theorizing its own process of production. This technique might be labeled a noncoercive feminist practice of reading, since it allows text and reader to enter a dialogue that does not follow the usual rules of linear, agonistic, and patriarchal discourses. To read noncoercively is to allow my self to be interwoven with the discursive strands of the text, to engage in a form of intercourse wherein I take my interpretative cues from the patterns that emerge as a result of that encounter" (27–28).

Chapter 1: To Begin Here

1. Though Coe's work is admirably comprehensive, it generates problems for readers and scholars today. For example, he limits his mention of ethnic Childhoods to those written by Maya Angelou, Alfred Kazin, Maxine Hong Kingston, Joy Kogawa (though he notes that *Obasan* is not really an autobiography and only shares some characteristics of the genre), N. Scott Momaday, Philip Roth, and Jade Snow Wong. Considering that most of the texts I consider were written in the last two decades of the twentieth century, his limited list is understandable, as ethnic writing and criticism was in an early stage of development when he was writing. Nonetheless, apart from the lack of focus on ethnic or postcolonial writing, some of his categorizations are too generalized and disputable. See Marianne Gullestad's "Modernity, Self, and Childhood in the Analysis of Life Stories" (3–6) for a more thorough discussion of some of the debatable issues in Coe's work, such as the unconvincing concepts of the "trivial" and "magic."

2. See my *Transcultural Reinventions*.

3. I use the term "performative" as Sidonie Smith does to refer to autobiographical storytelling as "always a performative occasion" ("Performativity, Autobiographical Practice" 18). I agree with Helen Buss when she notes that the term "'performance,' which implies both scripting and improvisation, as well as the possibilities of variations in incremental performances over time, also suggests these senses of the self as 'awareness in process' and 'energy,' rather than self as a fixed entity" (20). Further, Roger Porter's perspective on autobiography as an *activity* is

illuminating in this context as he focuses on "the function autobiography appears to serve for a given writer with the activity itself, especially with the ineluctably complex presentation of the pleasures, necessities, sorrows, or reluctances of the autobiographical act" (xii).

4. See Alicia Otano's *Speaking the Past* for an analysis of the use of child perspective in several Asian American novels. Her study on fictional narrative strategies engages issues such as speech acts and shifting perspectives, which have been very useful for my reading of several texts in this book.

5. "When they rise to the surface," Coe explains, "they do so in the form of themes, or symbols, or images which recur in the works of writers or artists having contact with one another in space or time. . . . There is strong evidence to suggest that the myths reveal an alternative, and profound relationship: not one of determinism, but rather one of symbiosis" ("Reminiscences of Childhood" 2–3).

6. In *When the Grass Was Taller,* Coe speaks of the

> exotic-schizophrenic childhood—the narration of an experience of the past self, in which two incompatible cultural backgrounds clash so violently that the eventual writing of the autobiography becomes something of an exercise in psychotherapy, an attempt to rescue the adult self from the void to which the contradictory, self-canceling forces have consigned it. . . . In particular, the schizophrenic trauma is liable to occur (to judge from our evidence) among second-generation emigrant children, themselves born and brought up in the new country, but their parents and families still ineradicably held by the old . . . the most impressive analysis of this aspect of the exotic from the child's point of view is to be found in Maxine Hong Kingston's *The Woman Warrior.* (228–229)

Though this term might reasonably be used in this discussion of Asian North American Childhoods, I choose not to use it, as the term "schizophrenic," which has a specific meaning in psychiatric studies, is confusing if used to describe the experiences of many of these children.

7. Recent criticism by Amy Ling and Floyd Cheung suggests that these texts are actually more complex than they appear. I will discuss these perspectives in chapter 2.

8. Mar's issues with names and naming will be discussed in more detail in chapter 5.

9. See Marie Lo's "The Currency of Visibility" for a discussion of the complex configurations of model minority discourse in the United States and visible minority status in Canada. See also Eleanor Ty's *The Politics of the Visible* for issues of racial in visibility in Canada.

10. Although there are clear differences in the history of Asians in the United States and Canada, Goellnicht notes that "in the treatment of Asian immigrants, Canada's pattern of behaviour was very similar to that of the United States, with the exploitation of Chinese labour in the nineteenth century, when cheap labour was in demand (for gold mining, railway building, etc.), and the exclusion of immi-

grants during most of the first half of the twentieth century; with the internment and 'repatriation' of Japanese Canadians during World War II; with the exclusion of immigrants from India from 1908 to 1951; and with the disenfranchisement of all these groups" ("A Long Labour" 9).

11. Importantly, the diversity of these texts also allows us to understand the inadequacy of the umbrella terms "Asian American" and "Asian Canadian," though they continue to be necessary for political mobilization and community building.

12. In the last two decades, we have witnessed an important rereading of the founding autobiographies of the Asian American canon. Specifically, note Shirley Lim's work on Jade Snow Wong; Traise Yamamoto on Monica Sone, Jeanne Wakatsuki Houston, and Yoshiko Uchida; Rachel Lee's analysis of Carlos Bulosan; Amy Ling and Floyd Cheung's articles on Yan Phou Lee; and Georgina Dodge's article on humor in Etsu Sugimoto's autobiography. These studies of early texts suggest that the writers' autobiographical strategies and issues may not have been adequately understood in their time. In a sense, we can argue that time has unveiled (or developed) a more perceptive implied reader for these early texts.

13. See Eakin's *How Our Lives Become Stories* and Egan's *Mirror Talk* for a discussion of the relational component of life writing. In chapter 6, I discuss Asian American relational life narratives in more detail in the reading of Loung Ung's *Lucky Child*.

14. Eakin asks: "what counts as a relational life? While acknowledging the relational dimension that makes its presence known in any life, I want to preserve the usefulness of the label by applying it to those autobiographies that feature the decisive impact on the autobiographer of either (1) an entire social environment (a particular kind of family, or a community and its social institutions—schools, churches, and so forth) or (2) key other individuals, usually family members, especially parents" (*How Our Lives* 69).

15. In her dissertation, Kate Douglas studies the manner in which readers engage British and Australian Childhoods by analyzing the increasingly predominant mode of responding autobiographically to these texts by both "professional" and "recreational" readers. She explores the textual position of readers through "reader address, disclosure, and reference" by examining critical responses to Childhoods by book reviewers and "customer comments" from Amazon.com to explore the investments and judgments that are being made about Childhoods. Her strategy reveals fascinating results, but these are beyond the scope of my project.

16. On a similar note, William Boelhower speaks of the "documentary level" of autobiography: the level of the collective subject, which determines the historical substance of the individual level and explains the horizon within which the individual unconscious works. Documentary meaning, therefore, refers to the identical homologous pattern underlying a vast variety of cultural creations (*Autobiographical Transactions* 23).

17. In its most exacerbated form, the shift of perspective regarding the nature of memory is highlighted by the debate over the status of remembering within the

era of *postmemory,* as theorized by Marianne Hirsch. See Winter and Sivan's "Setting the Framework" and Hynes' "Personal Narratives and Commemoration" for interdisciplinary perspectives on history and collective remembrance.

18. Paula Hamilton distinguishes between different modes of public ("official" or "historical"), private, and personal memory. Other forms of memory she discusses include "national memory," that constructed and remembered by particular national groups; "popular memory" and "counter memory," which posits memory as a social product that relies on general participation, although "popular memory" often includes "individual or group stories that refuse to fit the dominant historical narratives" (19, 23).

Chapter 2: The Asian Childhood

1. See Stanley's "Is There Life in the Contact Zone?" for a complete discussion of this perspective on Pratt's propositions in *Imperial Eyes: Travel Writing and Transculturation.*

2. Other early autobiographies that introduce Asian countries to American readers are Etsu Sugimoto's *Daughter of a Samurai* and Lin Yutang's *My Country and My People.* See Elaine Kim's chapter "Early Asian Immigrant Writers" in *Asian American Literature* for a discussion of this approach.

3. Coe's list of archetypal endings include: "a death (most frequently of a mother or grandmother); leaving home, getting a first job, breaking with the family; leaving school, going to university, graduation; engagement or marriage; going off to war or military service; losing faith or discovering a vocation; publishing the first book or writing the first poem" (*When the Grass* 77).

4. The texts discussed in this chapter are all Asian American texts; I have not found any Asian Canadian Childhoods that focus on a pre-Canadian life, except Kwan's *Things That Must Not Be Forgotten,* which will be analyzed in chapter 4.

5. Floyd Cheung suggests that Lee's text end abruptly "because it was designed to focus on his childhood in China, but also quite possibly as a result of tampering during the publication process" (51). The extent of the publisher's control of the text may also be noted in the way some of the illustrations do not seem to correspond with the text, as Amy Ling observes ("Reading Her/Stories" 82–83). In another article, Ling also notes that we can safely assume "that the topics of his book—the Chinese calendar, domestic architecture, cooking, schooling, religion, games, and the social position of girls—were largely dictated by his editor, who undoubtedly sought a certain uniformity and coherence for the volumes in the series" ("Yan Phou Lee" 274).

6. See Seiwoong Oh's "Ilhan New" for a discussion on contemporary reviews on his text.

7. Some of the questions Ling sees Lee positing include: "where is home? Where do my loyalties lie? What forces are stronger in the shaping of my identity—biology or culture? By choosing one culture, am I betraying the other? Must I forever be a bridge between worlds, a mediator between cultures and races? Can I get

out of the ethnic box and join the mainstream, or is that turning my back on my people?" ("Yan Phou Lee" 274).

8. This book has a fascinating publishing history. Thomas Wolfe personally championed its publication at Scribner's and the review he wrote is believed to be the only book review he ever published (Oh, "Younghill Kang" 154).

9. Bulosan's autobiography, *America Is in the Heart,* deals with his immigration as a young adult and his life as an itinerant laborer, his tuberculosis that led him to spend years in a sanatorium but allowed him to enter the world of American literature, his participation in early labor movements, and so on. See Elaine Kim's *Asian American Literature* and Rachel Lee's *The Americas of Asian American Literature* for readings of Bulosan's text.

10. See Oh's "Younghill Kang" for an overview of reviews of Kang's autobiographies. See my "Etsu Inagaki Sugimoto" for an idea on how a similar text of this time was received and praised mostly for contrasting East and West "with a smile" and how her book "does not plead any 'cause' nor discuss vexing questions" (332).

11. A more comprehensive perspective on Kang requires an analysis of *East Goes West,* which is unfortunately beyond the scope of this chapter. See Oh and Elaine Kim for discussions on this text.

12. See Slatin's "Blindness and Self-Perception: The Autobiographies of Ved Mehta" and John Stotesbury's "Blind Visions of Childhood: Autobiography and Unseen Worlds" for analyses of Mehta's negotiation with his blindness, as well as issues of language.

13. I will not discuss this last text in detail, as it is not strictly an autobiography of childhood. Mehta's autobiographies include *The Stolen Light* and *Up at Oxford, Remembering Mr. Shawn's New Yorker: The Invisible Art of Editing, All for Love, Dark Harbor: Building House and Home on an Enchanted Island,* and *The Red Letters: My Father's Enchanted Period.*

14. The idea of "facial vision" is explored conceptually in more detail in *Sound-Shadows of the New World.*

15. See my *Transcultural Reinventions* for a discussion on the autobiographical short story cycle.

16. In her essay "Finding Your Voice," Tham explains the connection between her background and her development as a poet.

> I subscribe to the Western concept of identity in the sense of the individual, but I also believe that identity is rooted in tradition like a plant that takes its nourishment from its soil and shapes itself from its many nutrients. One cannot see a shape without a contrasting background. Only after a person has examined, by writing, her or his experiences and ideas, the rejected as well as the integrated parts, can she or he have the understanding of self that is identity. Family history, myths, legends, the "forgotten" immigrant grand/great-grandparents' cultures, all feed into a writer's mind and make good mulch for growing poems. . . . Writing poems has been my way of exploring and reaffirming my identity. Many of my poems are memories revisited. Each time I write a poem retelling myths,

legends, value systems, customs—I examine what I believe in, what I have discarded, what I have chosen to retain. With each poem, I gain a stronger sense of myself, of who and what I am. (para. 5)

17. See Kathleen Uno's "Afterword" to Kuramoto's autobiography for a contextualization of *Manchurian Legacy* as a narrative of the consequences of the Japanese history of colonization.

18. The Western presence in Asia at the time included the British in India and Hong Kong, the Dutch in the East Indies, the Americans in the Philippines, and the French in Indochina.

19. The only other writers who had published literary works before writing their Childhoods were Wayson Choy, whose *The Jade Peony* won Canada's Trillum Award; Lynda Barry, a syndicated graphic artist who had published four comic books before *One Hundred Demons;* Hilary Tham, who had produced five books of poetry before *Lane with No Name;* Michael David Kwan, already a well-known playwright before publishing his Childhood; and Yoshiko Uchida and Laurence Yep, prolific and award-winning writers of children's literature. The remaining authors in this study produced their Childhood as their first book. Some writers such as Younghill Kang, Ved Mehta, Kien Nguyen, Da Chen, Aimee Liu, and Evelyn Lau then proceeded to write sequels to their Childhoods or engage other literary genres, such as the novel or short story.

20. Regarding the issue of the factuality of the information in *Lost Names,* Kim states that "everything in the book actually happened. It happened to me" (Masalski para. 1).

21. Montye Fuse points out that the text "demonstrates the dynamic relationship between Koreans (and Korean Americans), memory, and Korean national history. Indeed, Kim's memoir was published sixteen years after he left Korea and twenty-five years after the end of the Japanese occupation. Kim's memoir reconstructs Korean history and national identity from the perspective of those whose voices were silenced during the thirty-six years of colonization. It also demonstrates Kim's and other Korean Americans' enduring connection to the Korean peninsula and its history, no matter where they might find themselves within the Korean diaspora" (161).

22. The book is, in many ways, a portrait of Kim's father, "a prominent Korean resistance leader who has suffered greatly for his convictions—he was expelled from a Japanese university, and imprisoned for years—he is also a just and humane man, equally devoid of hatred for the Japanese oppressor and of self-righteousness towards those Koreans who are a part of the Japanese system" (Goar 465).

Chapter 3: Cultural Revolutions and Takeovers

1. The idea that texts lead to others is attested to by online bookstores' strategy of recommending books on similar topics. For instance, after any book search done on Amazon.com, the website provides a list titled "Customers who bought

this item also bought . . . ," a list thematically similar to the book being viewed. This affirms the probability that people who read autobiographies about war in Asia, for example, would continue to do so, creating both a collective appreciation of the experience being rendered (or of the preferred literary genre) and sustaining the community that reads the text, in turn producing more texts.

2. Jiang's *Red Scarf Girl*, a text for children, will be discussed in chapter 7.

3. Parts of Chen's autobiography severely test the reader's suspension of disbelief as the author represents himself as almost impossibly perfect: the child who lives in poverty with little access to education knows novels by heart; becomes an accomplished flutist, violinist, and ping pong player; can carry his father on a bicycle for miles; and is never questioned by his concerned mother when he returns home late smelling of smoke and alcohol.

4. Chen's narrative continues in his *Sounds of the River,* which recounts his four years at college and ends with his immigration to the United States.

5. I am grateful to Zhou Xiaojing for explaining the meanings of the character "*zao*" as a product of the combination between the sound character and the conceptual radical in Chinese ideograms.

6. Chen's is the only Childhood I have identified where the photograph on the cover is not of the author. This may be explained by the obvious nonexistence of photographs of Chen's childhood, or as a more universalizing literary gesture: Chen identifies with many Chinese children who also suffered during the Cultural Revolution. Considering the aesthetic presentation of this book cover, it is less important to actually have a picture of Chen than to understand the dynamic of the Chinese character "*zao*" and the photograph of two children reading eagerly.

7. See Molyda Szymusiak's Childhood, published originally in French, *The Stones Cry Out: A Cambodian Childhood, 1975–1980.* Szymusiak's story is similar to Ung and Him's, except in the end, where she travels to France and, together with two of her cousins, is adopted by Polish exiles Jan Szymusiak, an academic historian, and his wife, Carmen, rather than being reunited with family members in the United States. Hyok Kang's *This is Paradise!,* originally written in French, focuses on his childhood in North Korea and engages similar issues about hunger, repression, and deprivation. For a contextualization of this form of life writing, see Teri Shaffer Yamada's "Cambodian American Autobiographies: Testimonial Discourse," which explores how these texts signify, as "a painful testimony of cultural genocide and dislocation, [which] recenters the ideological discourse of American autobiography from a national debate on the parameters of American identity to an international application of American values in the form of global human rights" (144).

8. For a more thorough discussion of trauma in autobiography, see Gilmore's *The Limits of Autobiography: Trauma and Testimony* and Tal's *Worlds of Hurt.*

9. Further, Tal explains, "Traumatic experiences are written and rewritten until they become codified and narrative form gradually replaces content as the focus of attention. For example, the Holocaust has become a metonym, *not* for the actual series of events during World War II, but for the set of symbols that reflect the formal codification of that experience" (6).

10. In 2005, Ung published a second Childhood, *Lucky Child,* which narrates her first years in the United States and her reunion with her sister, Chou. I discuss this text in chapter 6.

11. Him's preoccupation with giving the reader information extends to a rather unusual practice: the use of explanatory footnotes which, though helpful and enlightening, often distracts from the reading.

12. The VVAF cofounded the International Campaign to Ban Landmines, which won the Nobel Peace Prize in 1997.

Chapter 4: The Liminal Childhood

1. I cannot engage here in detail the development of contemporary theories of race and its representation, which has been done very successfully in other contexts and in other studies. In particular, Michael Omi and Howard Winnat urge academics to examine the ongoing development of the concept of race, rather than think of it as an ideological construct or objective condition. Their theory of *racial formation* examines the connection between discourse and practice, signaling how processes of racial formation occur "though a linkage between structure and representation" and are contingent on social meanings continually being revised by changing political climates (56). Interestingly, as Stephen Ropp notes, "in the emerging literature of 'multiracial' studies, there is this reluctant but almost inevitable use of such terms as multiracial, biracial, and mixed-race even when trying to deconstruct or write against racialized thinking. Even when attempting to transcend race it is necessary to continue to refer to radical categories and racial logic which leads to a reinscription of race, albeit in more sophisticated hybrid and multiplied forms" (3). See Helena Grice's *Negotiating Identities* (pp. 121–155) for a comprehensive discussion on race and biraciality in Asian American women's writing.

2. Fictional engagements with biraciality beyond stereotypical representations of a supposedly "double" self include Aimee Liu's *Face,* Sigrid Nunez' *A Feather on the Breath of God,* Shawn Wong's *American Knees,* and Brian Ascalon Roley's *American Son.* Critical studies on these texts include Eleanor Ty's "Abjection, Masculinity and Violence in Brian Ascalon Roley's *American Son* and Han Ong's *Fixer Chao,*" my reading of Nunez in *Transcultural Reinventions,* and studies on *Face* by Ibarraran and Simal González.

3. For further studies on the Eaton sisters and biraciality, see Amy Ling's chapter "Pioneers and Paradigms" in *Between Worlds* (pp. 21–55); Helena Grice's "Facing/De-Face-ing Racism" and her chapter on "Writing Biraciality" in *Negotiating Identities,* and Carol Roh-Spaulding's articles.

4. Further, Spickard argues that multiracial Asians have to defend themselves against two ironically contrasting forces: "the *dominant discourse* imposed by White America, in order to establish control of their own identity" and the "*subdominant discourse* imposed by Asian Americans," who often also reject the mixed race person who might not identify completely (or enough) with the Asian ethnicity in question (45).

5. Some autobiographies appear to exploit the issue of biraciality, in both Asian and American contexts. A notable case is Elizabeth Kim's *Ten Thousand Sorrows*, which generated loud controversy among Korean Americans because its numerous cultural and historical inaccuracies made critics suspect that the narrative was bad fiction, rather than autobiography. They accused Kim of trying to take advantage of the current interest in autobiographies, particularly those that involved violence against women (which she focuses on) and international adoption. See Charse Yun's "Fact or Fiction?" and Hillel Italie's "Fact or Fiction of a Memoir" for reasons readers rejected the text, as well as Kim's defense of her memoir.

6. There is an increasingly vocal mixed race or *hapa* community in the United States that tries to make the general public aware of current issues. For information, see The Hapa Forum (http://www.hapaissuesforum.org) and Eurasian Nation (http://www.eurasiannation.com). See also "No Passing Zone," a special issue of *Amerasia Journal* edited by Velina Hasu Houston and Teresa K. Williams; and Jeffrey Santa Ana's "Affect-Identity: The Emotions of Assimilation, Multiraciality, and Asian American Subjectivity" for notions on the marketing of multiethnicity.

7. Delman's "Author's Note" provides a brief historical overview of the Bene Israel. Jael Silliman's *Jewish Portraits, Indian Frames,* a memoir of four generations of Jewish women in Calcutta, presents another perspective on the Jewish community in Asia.

8. Maria Root charts four different ways in which a mixed race person might identify.

> a) People might identify as other people identify them, which carries implicit applications of rules of hypodescent (e.g., a person of Eurasian ancestry identifies as Asian American, a person of Afroasian ancestry identifies as African American); b) people might carry a similar identity but derive it from feelings of kinship having been isolated or raised within a single community or in a particular family; c) people identify as both or all (e.g., Chicano and Filipino American); d) people refuse to identify according to the established categories of race. An important part of this conceptual model was that no endpoint is necessarily better than the other. Contextual and historical experiences guide the formation of these identities which are malleable over one's lifetime. (35)

9. Reyes' uncritical acceptance of the American assimilationist politics is problematic from our twenty-first-century perspective. But we must understand that his position was the rule, rather than the exception, for middle- or high-class Filipinos of the time who benefited economically and socially from the American occupation. Reyes also buys in quite happily into the ideal of the American "melting pot" (3).

10. By "colonial mentality," I refer to a term that Filipinos use to speak of their own preference for foreign ways, customs, and products, rather than local effects.

11. For perspectives on American colonization, education, and languages in the Philippines in the years since independence from Spain, see Brainard and Litton's *Journey of 100 Years: Reflections of the Centennial of Philippine Independence.*

12. Interestingly, Reyes' memoir omits a crucial part of his life: the events from his capture by the Japanese on Corrigedor and his resurfacing in Manila in 1947. During some of those years, at least, he was forced to work, along with other allied POWs who were radio professionals, in enemy propaganda broadcasts from Radio Tokyo in Japan such as "Zero Hour." One of his colleagues was Iva Ikuko Toguri, a Japanese American from California who was later tried for treason, accused of being the infamous "Tokyo Rose." Apart from doing important work to sabotage these radio broadcasts, Reyes testified in her defense at her trial. For details on what Reyes omits from his memoir, see Masayo Duus's *Tokyo Rose: Orphans in the Pacific.* I'd like to thank Edgar Krohn for leading me to this source and the fascinating supplementary information.

13. The Dutton edition of *Memories of My Ghost Brother* is marketed as fiction. Yet I believe that there are enough textual markers to be able to classify this as autobiography, such as the autobiographical pact. Fenkl has stated explicitly that the book is not a novel, but the story of his childhood in Korea "drawn from life but told in such a way that there is a clear aesthetic consciousness behind it" ("The Interstitial DMZ" para. 2). The decision to call it a novel was made by the publisher's marketing department. Fenkl concludes that "given the current state of literary theory, I was comfortable calling my work either thing—a novel (because of its literary style, its use of tropes, its collaging of time and character) or a memoir (because nearly everything in it is true, in the factual sense, within the realm of flexibility for that form)" (para. 5).

14. Alicia Otano's *Speaking the Past: Child Perspective in the Asian American Bildungsroman* analyzes the use of dual narrative perspective in Fenkl's text, the nuances of the homodiegetic narrator, as well as the use of linguistic strategies and metanarrative. Her study discusses speech acts and shifting perspectives, which have been useful for my reading.

15. Hutcheon's article, "Crypto-Ethnicity," discusses the situation of subjects in Canada "whose avoidance and repression of their ethnicity can go publicly unnoticed" (30) and her own place as a crypto-ethnic Italian Canadian professor of English in the context of the changing multicultural dynamic in Canada. She ends the article with "And the crypto-ethnic marker I once valued as a protective mask I now appreciate as a reminder of the constructedness of all forms of ethnic identity" (32).

16. See Robert S. McKelvey's *The Dust of Life: America's Children Abandoned in Vietnam* for a thorough discussion on the children of American servicemen and Vietnamese women.

17. Though the Vietnamese terms for half-breed are known and used quite commonly in cultural studies, Nguyen uses the English expression, perhaps in order to convey to non-Vietnamese readers a rhetorical connotation that is lost when he uses the Vietnamese expression. In any case, Nguyen, as the son of a White American, is still privileged over other biracial children. As a shopkeeper tells his mother, "I tell you, your children are lucky that they are White. At least they have a chance to live. The burnt-rice [half-Black children] have only bad luck" (179).

18. After the successful publication of his memoir, Nguyen has written two historical novels about Vietnam: *The Tapestries*, based on stories about his grand-father's life, and *Le Colonial*, the story of three French missionaries in the eighteenth century. These texts might discursively represent Nguyen's attempt to claim a part of Vietnamese history for himself and establish, within the cultural politics of Asian American writing, his authority to inscribe the history that he was denied.

19. This particular metaphor points to the implied audience of Nguyen's Childhood—primarily an American public who would understand the reference.

20. He has also published *Broken Portraits: Personal Encounters with Chinese Students* and *The Chinese Storyteller's Book: Supernatural Tales*. His unpublished "A Season in Purgatory" won the 1995 DuMaurier National Playwriting Competition and "The Undaunted," an unpublished screenplay about Chinese laborers in Canada in the 1890s, won the 1999 Praxis Screenwriting Award. *Things That Must Not Be Forgotten* received the Kiriyama Pacific Rim Book Prize in 2000. Kwan passed away in 2001.

21. Though he would have had the right as the son of an American citizen to citizenship, he did not claim that right before his eighteenth birthday, as stipulated by law.

22. One might also suggest that, given the increasingly critical perspectives deployed by scholars regarding the role of the United States in Korea, in the Vietnam War, and in the Philippines, these "insider" accounts of first-hand experiences nuance the paradigms of the dialogue. Moreover, these texts are the first known of their ethnicities that explore the biracial situation, another facet of American intervention in these Asian countries.

Chapter 5: Citizens or Denizens

1. Boelhower explains:

> What Sollors and myself have tried to do with the two vectors of consent and descent, however, is to treat them as cultural constructs, as two structurally related ways of encoding identity and interpreting it in situational contexts. The terms themselves, in other words, prove most helpful as tools of cultural analysis when they are understood as pragmatic principles rather than as categories that yield a definable and easily measurable set of substantive traits. . . . As constructuring terms for interpreting autobiographical identity, they can best be appreciated for the type of semiotic space they produce and the positions of reading they allow. In this context, relational fluency, or the positive ability to move back and forth between the two different semiotic intentionalities of descent and consent, is foremost. ("Making of Ethnic Autobiography" 131)

2. Texts on the Japanese American relocation and internment—Houston's *Farewell to Manzanar,* Monica Sone's *Nisei Daughter,* George Takei's *To The Stars,* and Uchida's *Desert Exile* and *The Invisible Thread,* among others—also foreground

the group experience. These writers emphasize the importance of belonging to a group and preserving group identity, while simultaneously gesturing toward membership in mainstream society.

3. Criticism on Wong has highlighted many of these issues and the caveats I noted, as the discussions on Yan Phou Lee and Ilhan New apply to Wong as well. Her Childhood, published in 1945 when she was only twenty-four years old, is one of the first texts written by a Chinese American woman who was naturally subject to the cultural and critical prejudices prevalent at the time. Subsequent readings of Wong's text tend to be enacted from perspectives that Wong had no access to, simply because perspectives on racial, cultural, or genre identity were not as politically sophisticated as they are today. In particular, as Fu-jen Chen explains, ethnic critics have challenged Wong's "reluctance to blame racist prejudice, her ignoring historical facts, and her sacrificing her own ethnic community in exchange for a position in the American mainstream" (394). For many, her status as a pioneering Chinese American woman writer has shifted negatively, and she is now regarded by many as an "accomplice of racism, and her book is labeled a propaganda" (395). See Karen Su's article "Jade Snow Wong's Badge of Distinction in the 1990s" for a discussion of how criticism on Wong has evolved according to the shifting paradigms of Asian American critical perspectives.

4. Wong begins using the third person in No Chinese Stranger, her second volume of autobiography, written twenty-five years after Fifth Chinese Daughter. The shift from third to first person happens upon the death of her father. In fact, the title of Part 2 of this autobiography, "First Person Singular," denotes a clear emphasis on the author's autonomy.

5. See Elaine Kim's Asian American Literature, Shirley Lim's "The Tradition of Chinese American Women's Life Stories," Fu-jen Chen's "Jade Snow Wong (1922–)," and Karen Su's "Jade Snow Wong's Badge of Distinction in the 1990s" for a more thorough discussion of the representation of patriarchy in Wong's autobiography.

6. It would be unfair to say that Wong was merely reinforcing preexisting stereotypes of the Chinese. As Grace Chun suggests, her text actually challenges the "assimilationist perspective that assumes that ethnic subjects typically aspire to blend in with the norms of mainstream America. In fact, [Wong and Pardee Lowe] chose to accentuate their cultural differences, albeit selectively, thereby maintaining their integrity as ethnic persons rather than becoming indistinguishable from the rest. While they did enjoy the prestige and social standing that came with being native informants who could adroitly manage the orientalist system, they were actually anthropologists in their own right, generating views about China, its people, and Chinese America that differed in important ways from the prevailing, dominant discourse about the Chinese" (43).

7. Kim criticizes what she considers Wong's "sketchy and incomplete" representation of the "Chinatown bachelor," a distinctive figure of Chinese American history. Uncle Kwok, the protagonist of Wong's eponymous chapter, Kim claims, is presented only as "a hopeless dreamer and a pathetic fool, a mysterious part of

the Chinatown scene about whom Wong is only a little curious" (*Asian American Literature* 92). Kim's primary critique of Wong's representation is that she expresses little interest in this emblematic figure beyond its decorative value as a character sketch that forms part of the "descriptions of customs, festivals, and artifacts that make up the Chinese American community they present for the reader's edification" (91). Once again, as with the historical reconsiderations of the texts by Lee and New, we have to take into account the context of Wong's inscription of her autobiography and note the possibilities, intentions, and purpose of her text.

8. The third section of *The Jade Peony* is narrated by Jung-Sum, the second brother, adopted by the family at the age of four after his mother's murder. Throughout the story, this boy is presented as "different" and, at the end, he discovers that he is gay, in a way similar to Choy's account, in *Paper Shadows,* of his own discovery of his sexual orientation.

9. In many ways, Mar's journey mirrors Richard Rodríguez' story. In *Hunger of Memory,* he considers how education often separates the working-class child from his family. The section titled "The Achievement of Desire" narrates his awareness of this increasing separation. As with Mar, Rodríguez' departure to Stanford only made "physically apparent the separation that had occurred long before" (57). See this chapter of Rodríguez' autobiography for a discussion on the repercussions of children's higher education on the families of immigrants.

Chapter 6: In North America

1. See Noelle Caskey's article "Interpreting Anorexia Nervosa" and Greta Olson's *Reading Eating Disorders: Writings on Bulimia and Anorexia as Confessions of American Culture* for criticism on the representation of anorexia.

2. See Bordo's *Unbearable Weight: Feminism, Western Culture, and the Body* and Leslie Heywood's *Dedication to Hunger: The Anorexic Aesthetic in Modern Culture* for sociological and psychological perspectives on anorexia nervosa.

3. After *Solitaire,* Liu wrote several novels—the award-winning *Face, Cloud Mountain,* and *Flash House. Face* deals with biraciality and the trauma of rape, while *Cloud Mountain* rewrites her family's history in the United States, both of which can be understood as ways of dealing with the past. See my "Aimee Liu" in the *Dictionary of Literary Biography* for a discussion of her work.

4. Regarding the intersection of ethnic representation, commodification of women, and postcolonial issues in Lau's text, see Rita Wong's "Market Forces and Powerful Desires" and Elaine Chang's "Run through the Borders." Jennifer Kornreich, in her review of *Runaway,* defines the book as a "simply whiny . . . adolescent pout about the cruelty of established authority. . . . Lest one forget why Lau cannot bear to return home to her family, she reminds us: 'whenever my jaw aches or my arms fall asleep, whenever a man takes forever to come, I tell myself it is much better than vacuuming the house for my parents . . . confined to my bedroom studying again.' Oh dear. Even Cinderella wouldn't resort to such hyperbole" (18).

5. Sau-Ling Wong and Jeffrey Santa Ana classify *Runaway* as one of a series of recent diasporic texts where "sexuality is deployed, whether inarticulately, deliberately, defiantly, or in celebration, to counteract images of Asian American men and women as the asexual model minority" (194).

6. The promotion for the book appeared to offend the Chinese Canadian community who argued that it presented the Chinese in Canada in a very negative light, reinforcing racial and cultural stereotypes of Chinese, and particularly women. Rita Wong suggests that "the general tendency to disavow or avoid race in Lau's writing yields a number of possible readings: one is a refusal to be pigeonholed as an 'ethnic' writer, and another is to consider this work as a yearning for acceptance that translates into assimilation, which is then accordingly validated and rewarded. In the absence of racialized characters, the normalized power relations at work tend to default her characters into whiteness" (130). See also Marie Lo's "The Currency of Visibility" for a discussion of the deracinated nature of Lau's work and her position as an ambivalent figure in Asian Canadian criticism.

7. Chao argues that the book is a blend of "autobiography and testimony" (158). Though I agree with her points about the book's testimonial value, her distinction between these two terms is less clear, partly perhaps because she does not consider the theoretical implications of the diary in autobiographical studies.

8. Interestingly, because Lau's first piece was autobiographical, her subsequent writing (much of it erotic) continues to be read autobiographically; critics rarely separate the accounts of her years on the streets from her more sophisticated poems, such as those in *You Are Not Who You Claim* and the stories in *Fresh Girls* and *In the House of Slaves*. Lien Chao, for example, notes that "Lau's street experience as a prostitute and drug addict more or less constitutes the essence of her poetry and prose, the public and the media seem to be more interested in her than in her writing" (156). In any case, Lau herself has titillated the media and public's attention. She attracted notoriety by publishing in *Vancouver Magazine* the details of her three-year affair with the writer W. H. Kinsella, forty years her senior, leading to one of the most dramatic scandals in the Canadian literary scene. Her essay "Anatomy of a Libel Suit," in *Inside Out,* narrates the court battle that Kinsella initiated after her exposé.

9. The term "comics" is itself subject to debate. It was first used as a plural form to describe graphic narratives published in newspapers. Some critics have argued that "comics" sounds juvenile and its most colloquial synonym, "funnies," detracts from the form's thematic and artistic complexity, and should be replaced. Will Eisner proposes the use of the terms "sequential art" or "graphic sequential art" in his study *Comics and Sequential Art*. Art Spiegelman introduced the term "commix" as a way of suggesting the crucial "co-mixing" of words and pictures that distinguishes the comics from other types of visual narratives ("Commix" 61). I use the word "comics" as Scott McCloud defines it: "n. plural in form, used with a single verb. 1. Juxtaposed pictorial and other images in deliberate sequence, intended to convey information and/or to produce an aesthetic response in the viewer" (9). I will also refer to "comics" synonymously as "graphic narratives."

10. See Melinda L. De Jesús's articles, "Liminality and Mestiza Consciousness in Lynda Barry's *One Hundred Demons*," and "Of Monsters and Mothers: Filipina American Identity and Maternal Legacies in Lynda J. Barry's *One Hundred Demons*" for thoughtful discussions of Barry's autobiographical strategy, issues of race, ethnicity, nationhood, class, and the mother/daughter relationship.

11. Robbins also points out that "so many women's autobiographical comics are depressing, and so many are about dysfunctional families, that it becomes tempting to believe that dysfunctional families breed women cartoonists" (127). For information on the ways women graphic artists have developed comics, see Robbins' *From Girls to Grrrlz*, among others.

12. See Michael M. J. Fischer's "Autobiographical Voices (1,2,3) and Mosaic Memory: Experimental Sondages in the (Post)Modern World" for more perspectives on the relational component to life writing.

13. Important Asian North American collaborative or relational autobiographies include Sara Suleri (Goodyear)'s *Meatless Days* and *Boys Will Be Boys*, Garrett Hongo's *Volcano*, May-lee and Winberg Chai's *The Girl from Purple Mountain*, Clark Blaise and Bharati Mukherjee's *Days and Nights in Calcutta*, and Helie Lee's *Still Life with Rice*, among others. For analysis of *Meatless Days* and *Volcano*, see my *Transcultural Reinventions;* for a reading of *Days and Nights in Calcutta*, see my "Performing Dialogic Subjectivities"; I read the relational strategies in *Boys Will Be Boys, The Girl from Purple Mountain,* and *Still Life with Rice* in "The Self in the Text versus the Self as Text." Multigenerational auto/biographies such as Connie Kang's *Home Was the Land of Morning Calm* and Duong Van Mai Elliot's *The Sacred Willow* may also be read effectively in this context.

14. In certain cases, Asian American writers have reconstructed the life story of proximate others in books marketed as novels. Among these are Milton Murayama's *Five Years on a Rock*, which tells his mother's story of a young picture bride brought to Hawai'i, and Kien Nguyen's *The Tapestries*, presented as the inscription of the author's grandfather's stories. Frances and Ginger Park also inscribe a fictionalized version of their parents' story in *To Swim across the World*.

Chapter 7: The Childhood for Children

1. Several recent journal issues attest to the growing awareness of the role of ethnic children's literature: on multiethnic literature for children in general, *MELUS* (Summer 2002, edited by Katherine Capshaw Smith) and *Children's Literature Association Quarterly* (Summer 2003, edited by Roberta Seelinger Trites); *The Horn Book*'s three-part series on the development of multicultural literature in the United States (2002–2003, written by Barbara Bader); a special issue, "Asian American Children's Literature," in *The Lion and the Unicorn* (2006, edited by Dolores de Manuel and myself). These issues highlight ethnic literature's cultural work, the diverse manners of engaging genre, and the didactic possibilities of the form.

2. Many of these texts are recipients of important literary awards, which I will note in this chapter.

3. In 1995, Joy Kogawa rewrote her 1981 autobiographical novel *Obasan* into a children's story titled *Naomi's Road*. Because of the hybrid nature of this text and the nonexistence of the autobiographical pact, I do not consider either as autobiographies and will not engage them in detail. Nonetheless, the issues I raise with regard to the changes effected in the autobiographies that have been rewritten can be successfully applied to Kogawa's narrative.

4. I would like to thank Kathleen Bergquist for explaining this concept to me and introducing me to useful bibliography. For more information on bibliotherapy, see Freitag et al., Pardeck, Dixey and D'Angelo, and Myracle.

5. Jean Fritz' *Homesick: My Own Story,* the story of an American girl raised in China who returns "home" to the United States at the age of twelve, is an interesting case. Though her text may arguably be considered "Asian American" because of her exposure to both cultures, I will center, in this paper, on autobiographies by persons of Asian descent.

6. The author's postscript describes her family's continuing "conspiracy" against her, which she narrates in excruciating detail in *Falling Leaves.*

7. The book was named an ALA Notable Children's Book of 1982, a 1982 Teacher's Choice Book (NCTE), a Library of Congress Children's Book of 1982, and also won a 1982 William Allen White Children's Book Award.

8. Watkins' *Tales from the Bamboo Grove,* a collection of six Japanese folktales she recalls hearing from her parents in her early childhood, may be read as a companion piece to these two autobiographies.

9. Watkins does not promote, justify, or condemn the Japanese colonization of Korea and Manchuria. Perhaps because of the nature of her children's text, she avoids a political discussion of Japan's imperialist policies and its consequences, focusing rather on her personal story. Her position is, in a sense, coherent with that of herself as a child narrator, who would probably be unaware of the larger political context and unable to criticize what her parents supported and the only life she knew.

10. This autobiography was named an ALA Best Book for Young Adults and a *New York Times* Notable Book.

11. Another interesting autobiography for children in this context is Tomiko Higa's *The Girl with the White Flag* (originally written in Japanese), which recounts the survival of an orphan girl in the streets of Okinawa after the war.

12. This autobiography was named a Notable Children's Book of 1997 by the ALA, one of the Best Books for Young Adults by the ALA, and a Publisher's Weekly Best Book of 1997.

13. See my "Reinscribing (Asian) American History in Laurence Yep's *Dragonwings*" for perspectives on the writing of ethnic history in children's literature.

14. *A Child in Prison Camp* has won the Sankei Shimbun Literary Award (Japan), the VI Premio Europeo di Letteratura Giovanile Award (Italy), and the Canadian Association of Children's Librarians Amelia Frances Howard-Gibbon Medal for Best Illustrated Book of the Year, among others.

15. For a more detailed analysis of Uchida's text, see my "Ethnic Autobiography as Children's Literature: Laurence Yep's *The Lost Garden* and Yoshiko Uchida's *The Invisible Thread*." *The Invisible Thread* was an ALA Best Book for Young Adults.

16. There are a number of interesting biographies about Asian American sports figures such as Kristi Yamaguchi, Michael Chang, and Tiger Woods. Unfortunately, I have not found any autobiographies for children by them.

17. See my "Ethnic Autobiography as Children's Literature" and "Laurence Michael Yep" for a more detailed analysis of Yep's autobiography.

Works Cited

Accomando, Claire Hsu. *Love and Rutabaga*. New York: St. Martin's Press, 1993.

Anderson, Linda. *Autobiography*. New York: Routledge, 2001.

Ang, Ien. "To Be or Not to Be Chinese: Diaspora, Culture, and Postmodern Ethnicity." *Southeast Asian Journal of Social Science* 21.1 (1993): 1–17.

Bader, Barbara, ed. "How the Little House Gave Ground: The Beginnings of Multiculturalism in a New, Black Children's Literature." *The Horn Book* (November–December 2002): 657–678.

———. "Multiculturalism in the Mainstream." *The Horn Book* (May–June 2003): 265–306.

———. "Multiculturalism Takes Roots." *The Horn Book* (March–April 2003): 143–164.

Baena, Rosalía. "Transcultural Autobiographies: The Photograph as Site of Ethnicity." *Sites of Ethnicity: Europe and the Americas*. Ed. William Boelhower, Rocío G. Davis, and Carmen Birkle. Hamburg, Germany: LIT Verlag, 2004. 361–374.

Bakhtin, M. M. *The Dialogic Imagination*. Ed. Michael Holquist. Trans. Carly Emerson and Michael Holquist. Austin: University of Texas Press, 1987.

Bal, Mieke, Jonathan Crewe, and Leo Spitzer, eds. *Acts of Memory: Cultural Recall in the Present*. Hanover, NH: University of New England Press, 1999.

Barros, Carolyn A. *Autobiography: Narratives of Transformation*. Ann Arbor: University of Michigan Press, 1998.

Barry, Lynda. *The Greatest of Marlys*. Seattle: Sasquatch Books, 2000.

———. *One Hundred Demons*. Seattle: Sasquatch Books, 2002.

Beauregard, Guy. "The Emergence of 'Asian Canadian Literature': CanLit's Obscene Supplement?" *Essays on Canadian Writing* 67 (Spring 1999): 53–75.

———. "What Is at Stake in Comparative Analyses of Asian Canadian and Asian American Literary Studies?" *Essays on Canadian Writing* 75 (Winter 2002): 217–239.

Bergland, Betty. "Postmodernism and the Autobiographical Subject: Reconstructing the 'Other'." *Autobiography and Postmodernism*. Ed. Kathleen Ashley, Leigh Gilmore, and Gerald Peters. Amherst: University of Massachusetts Press, 1994. 130–166.

———. "Representing Ethnicity in Autobiography: Narratives of Opposition." *The Yearbook of English Studies* 24 (1994): 67–93.

Bhabha, Homi K. *The Location of Culture.* New York: Routledge, 1994.

Blaise, Clark, and Bharati Mukherjee. *Days and Nights in Calcutta.* 1977. St. Paul, MN: Hungry Mind Press, 1995.

Boelhower, William. *Autobiographical Transactions in Modernist America: The Immigrant, the Architect, the Artist, the Citizen.* Udine, Italy: Del Blanco Editore, 1992.

———. "Immigrant Autobiographies in Italian Literature: The Birth of a New Text-Type." *Forum Italicum* 35.1 (Spring 2001): 110–128.

———. "The Making of Ethnic Autobiography in the United States." *American Autobiography: Retrospect and Prospect.* Ed. Paul John Eakin. Madison: University of Wisconsin Press, 1991. 123–141.

———. "The Necessary Ruse: Immigrant Autobiography and the Sovereign American Self." *Amerikastudien* 35.3 (1990): 297–319.

———. *Through a Glass Darkly: Ethnic Semiosis in American Literature.* New York: Oxford University Press, 1987.

Bordo, Susan. "Anorexia Nervosa: Psychopathology as the Crystallization of Culture." *Food and Culture: A Reader.* Ed. Carole Counihan and Penny Van Esterik. New York: Routledge, 1997. 226–250.

———. *Unbearable Weight: Feminism, Western Culture, and the Body.* Berkeley: University of California Press, 1995.

Brainard, Cecilia Manguerra, and Edmundo F. Litton, eds. *Journey of 100 Years: Reflections of the Centennial of Philippine Independence.* San Francisco: Tiboli Press, 1999.

Brennan, Jonathan, ed. *Mixed Race Literature.* Stanford: Stanford University Press, 2002.

Browdy de Hernandez, Jennifer. "On Home Ground: Politics, Location, and the Construction of Identity in Four American Women's Autobiographies." *MELUS* 22.4 (Winter 1997): 21–38.

Brown, James W. *Fictional Meals and Their Function in the French Novel 1789–1848.* Toronto: University of Toronto Press, 1984.

Brown, Wesley, and Amy Ling, eds. *Visions of America: Personal Narratives from the Promised Land.* New York: Persea Books, 1993.

Bruss, Elizabeth W. *Autobiographical Acts: The Changing Situation of a Literary Genre.* Baltimore: Johns Hopkins University Press, 1976.

Bulosan, Carlos. *America Is in the Heart.* 1946. Seattle: University of Washington Press, 1973.

Bunkers, Suzanne L. "Midwestern Diaries and Journals: What Women Were (Not) Saying in the Late 1880s." *Studies in Autobiography.* Ed. James Olney. New York: Oxford University Press, 1988. 190–210.

Buss, Helen M. *Repossessing the World: Reading Memoirs by Contemporary Women.* Waterloo, Ontario: Wilfrid Laurier University Press, 2002.

Carpenter, Carole H. "Enlisting Children's Literature in the Goals of Multiculturalism." *Mosaic* 29.3 (September 1996): 53–73.

Caskey, Noelle. "Interpreting Anorexia Nervosa." *The Female Body in Western Culture.* Ed. Susan Rubin Suleiman. Cambridge, MA: Harvard University Press, 1988. 175–189.

Chai, May-lee, and Winberg Chai. *The Girl from Purple Mountain: Love, Honor, War, and One Family's Journey from China to America.* New York: Thomas Dunne Books, 2001.

Chang, Elaine K. "Run through the Borders: Feminism, Postmodernism, and Runaway Subjectivity." *Border Theory: The Limits of Cultural Politics.* Ed. Scott Michaelson and David E. Johnson. Minneapolis: University of Minnesota Press, 1997. 169–194.

Chang, Jung. *Wild Swans: Three Daughters of China.* New York: Simon & Schuster, 1991.

Chao, Lien. *Beyond Silence: Chinese Canadian Literature in English.* Toronto: TSAR, 1997.

Chen, Da. *Colors of the Mountain.* New York: Anchor Books, 2001.

———. *China's Son: Growing Up in the Cultural Revolution.* New York: Delacorte Press, 2001.

———. *Sounds of the River.* New York: HarperCollins, 2002.

Chen, Fu-jen. "Jade Snow Wong (1922–)." *Asian American Autobiographers: A Bio-Bibliographical Critical Sourcebook.* Ed. Guiyou Huang. Westport, CT: Greenwood Press, 2001. 389–396.

Cheng, Nien. *Life and Death in Shanghai.* New York: Grove, 1986.

Cheung, Floyd. "Early Chinese American Autobiography: Reconsidering the Works of Yan Phou Lee and Yung Wing." *a/b: Auto/Biography Studies* 18 (2003): 45–61.

Chin, Frank, and Jefferey Paul Chan, eds. *The Big Aiiieeeee! An Anthology of Chinese American and Japanese American Literature.* New York: Meridian, 1991.

Choi, Sook Nyul. *Echoes of the White Giraffe.* Boston: Houghton Mifflin, 1993.

———. *Gathering of Pearls.* Boston: Houghton Mifflin, 1994.

———. "Sook Nyul Choi, Memoirist and Novelist." *Yellow Light: The Flowering of Asian American Art.* Ed. Amy Ling. Philadelphia: Temple University Press, 1999. 46–54.

———. *Year of Impossible Goodbyes.* Boston: Houghton Mifflin, 1991.

Choy, Wayson. *The Jade Peony.* Vancouver: Douglas and McIntyre, 1997.

———. *Paper Shadows: A Chinatown Childhood.* Toronto: Viking, 1999.

Chu, Patricia P. *Assimilating Asians: Gendered Strategies of Authorship in Asian America.* Durham, NC: Duke University Press, 2000.

Chun, Gloria Heyung. *Of Orphans and Warriors: Inventing Chinese American Culture and Identity.* New Brunswick: Rutgers University Press, 2000.

Coe, Richard N. "Childhood in the Shadows: The Myth of the Unhappy Child in Jewish, Irish, and French-Canadian Autobiography." *Comparison* 13 (Spring/Summer 1982): 3–67.

———. "Portrait of the Artist as a Young Australian: Childhood, Literature and Myth." *Southerly* 41 (1981): 126–182.

————. "Reminiscences of Childhood: An Approach to a Comparative Mythology." *Proceedings of the Leeds Philosophical and Literary Society* 19.6 (1984).

————. *When the Grass Was Taller: Autobiography and the Experience of Childhood.* New Haven, CT: Yale University Press, 1984.

Cosslett, Tess, Celia Lury, and Penny Summerfield. "Introduction." *Feminism and Autobiography: Texts, Theories, Methods.* Ed. Tess Cosslett, Celia Lury, and Penny Summerfield. New York: Routledge, 2000. 1–21.

Coveney, Peter. *The Image of Childhood.* London: Penguin, 1967.

Davis, Rocío G. "Aimee Liu." *Dictionary of Literary Biography, 312: Asian American Writers.* Ed. Deborah L. Madsen. Detroit: Bruccoli Clark Layman/Gale, 2005. 218–222.

————. "Ethnic Autobiography as Children's Literature: Laurence Yep's *The Lost Garden* and Yoshiko Uchida's *The Invisible Thread.*" *Children's Literature Association Quarterly* 28.2 (Summer 2003): 26–33.

————. "Etsu Inagaki Sugimoto." *Asian American Autobiographers: A Bio-Bibliographical Critical Sourcebook.* Ed. Guiyou Huang. Westport, CT: Greenwood Press, 2001. 329–333.

————. "Laurence Michael Yep." *Asian American Autobiographers: A Bio-Bibliographical Critical Sourcebook.* Ed. Guiyou Huang. Westport, CT: Greenwood Press, 2001. 401–407.

————. "National and Ethnic Affiliation in Internment Autobiographies of Childhood by Jeanne Wakatsuki Houston and George Takei." *Amerikastudien/ American Studies* (forthcoming).

————. "Performing Dialogic Subjectivities: The Aesthetic Project of Autobiographical Collaboration in *Days and Nights in Calcutta.*" *Literary Gestures: The Aesthetic in Asian American Writing.* Ed. Rocío G. Davis and Sue-Im Lee. Philadelphia: Temple University Press, 2005. 159–172.

————. "Reinscribing (Asian) American History in Laurence Yep's *Dragonwings.*" *The Lion and the Unicorn* 28.1 (2004): 390–407.

————. "The Self in the Text versus the Self as Text: Asian American Life Writing Strategies." *Asian American Literary Studies.* Ed. Guiyou Huang. Edinburgh, Scotland: Edinburgh University Press, 2005. 41–63.

————. *Transcultural Reinventions: Asian American and Asian Canadian Short Story Cycles.* Toronto: TSAR, 2001.

Davis, Rocío G., and Sue-Im Lee, eds. *Literary Gestures: The Aesthetic in Asian American Writing.* Philadelphia: Temple University Press, 2005.

Day, Iyko. "Interventing Innocence: Race, 'Resistance,' and the Asian North American Avant–Garde." *Literary Gestures: The Aesthetic in Asian American Writing.* Ed. Rocío G. Davis and Sue-Im Lee. Philadelphia: Temple University Press, 2005. 35–51.

De Jesús, Melinda L. "Liminality and Mestiza Consciousness in Lynda Barry's *One Hundred Demons.*" *MELUS* 29.1 (Spring 2004): 219–252.

————. "Of Monsters and Mothers: Filipina American Identity and Maternal Legacies in Lynda J. Barry's *One Hundred Demons.*" *Meridians: feminism, race, transnationalism* 5.1 (2004): 1–26.

Delman, Carmit. *Burnt Bread and Chutney: Growing Up between Cultures—A Memoir of an Indian Jewish Girl.* New York: Ballantine Books, 2002.

De Man, Paul. "Autobiography as Defacement." *Modern Language Notes* 94.5 (1979): 919–930.

De Manuel, Dolores, and Rocío G. Davis, eds. "Asian American Children's Literature." Special issue. *The Lion and the Unicorn* 30.2 (April 2006).

Dixey, Brenda, and Angela D'Angelo. "Using Literature to Build Emotionally Healthy Adolescents." *Classroom On-line* 3.6 (2000). Available at http://www.ascd.org/readingroom/classlead/0003/1mar00.html.

Dodge, Georgina. "Laughter of the Samurai: Humor in the Autobiography of Etsu Sugimoto." *MELUS* 21.4 (Winter 1996): 57–69.

Douglas, Kate. *Remembering Childhood: Nostalgia, Trauma, and the Child Self in Recent Australian and British Autobiography.* Unpublished dissertation presented at the School of English, Media Studies, and Art History at the University of Queensland, Australia, 2003.

Douglas, Mary. "Deciphering a Meal." *Daedalus* 101.1 (1972): 61–81.

Duus, Masayo. *Tokyo Rose: Orphans in the Pacific.* Trans. Peter Duus. Tokyo: Kodansha International, 1979.

Eakin, Paul John. *How Our Lives Become Stories: Making Selves.* Ithaca, NY: Cornell University Press, 1999.

———. *Touching the World: Reference in Autobiography.* Princeton, NJ: Princeton University Press, 1992.

Egan, Susanna. *Mirror Talk: Genres of Crisis in Contemporary Autobiography.* Chapel Hill: University of North Carolina Press, 1999.

Eidse, Faith, and Nina Sichel, eds. *Unrooted Childhoods: Memoirs of Growing Up Global.* London: Nicholas Brealey Publishing/Intercultural Press, 2004.

Eisner, Will. *Comics and Sequential Art.* 1985. Tamarac, FL: Poorhouse Press, 2003.

Elbaz, Robert. *The Changing Nature of the Self: A Critical Study of Autobiographic Discourse.* London & Sydney: Croom Helm, 1988.

———. "Language and the Self in the Marginal Text." *Imagined Childhoods: Self and Society in Autobiographical Accounts.* Ed. Marianne Gullestad. Oslo, Norway: Scandinavian University Press, 1996. 159–178.

Elliot, Duong Van Mai. *The Sacred Willow: Four Generations in the Life of a Vietnamese Family.* New York: Oxford University Press, 1999.

Espiritu, Yen Le. "Possibilities of a Multiracial Asian America." *The Sum of Our Parts: Mixed-Heritage Asian Americans.* Ed. Teresa Williams-León and Cynthia Nakashima. Philadelphia: Temple University Press, 2000. 25–33.

Feldman, Carol Fleisher. "Narratives of National Identity as Group Narratives." *Narrative and Identity: Studies in Autobiography, Self, and Culture.* Ed. Jens Brockmeier and Donald Corbaugh. Amsterdam, Holland: John Benjamins, 2001. 129–144.

Fenkl, Heinz Insu. "A Few Notes on *Memories of My Ghost Brother*." Available online at http://www.geocities.com/Area51/Rampart/2627/haunting.html (accessed August 9, 2004).

————. "The Interstitial DMZ." Available online at http://www.artistswithoutborders.org/why/the_interstitial_dmz_1.html (accessed December 1, 2004).

————. *Memories of My Ghost Brother.* New York: Dutton, 1996.

Fifield, Adam. *A Blessing over Ashes: The Remarkable Odyssey of My Unlikely Brother.* 2000. New York: Harper Perennial, 2001.

Fischer, Michael M. J. "Autobiographical Voices (1,2,3) and Mosaic Memory: Experimental Sondages in the (Post)Modern World." *Autobiography and Postmodernism.* Ed. Kathleen Ashley, Leigh Gilmore, and Gerald Peters. Amherst: University of Massachusetts Press, 1994. 79–129.

————. "Ethnicity and the Post-modern Arts of Memory." *Writing Culture: The Poetics and Politics of Ethnography.* Ed. James Clifford and George E. Marcus. Berkeley: University of California Press, 1986. 194–233.

Freitag, R., et al. "Deriving Multicultural Themes from Bibliotherapeutic Literature: A Neglected Resource." *Counselor Education and Supervision* 3.2 (1999): 120–133.

Friedman, Susan Stanford. "Women's Autobiographical Selves: Theory and Practice." *The Private Self: Theory and Practice of Women's Autobiographical Writing.* Ed. Shari Benstock. Chapel Hill: University of North Carolina Press, 1988. 34–62.

Frisch, Michael H. "American History and the Structures of Collective Memory: A Modest Exercise in Empirical Iconography." *Memory and History: Essays on Recalling and Interpreting Experience.* Ed. Jaclyn Jeffrey and Glenace Edwall. Lanham: University Press of America, 1994. 33–58.

Fritz, Jean. *Homesick: My Own Story.* New York: Penguin Putnam, 1982.

Fuse, Montye P. "Richard E. Kim (1932–)." *Asian American Autobiographers: A Bio-Bibliographical Critical Sourcebook.* Ed. Guiyou Huang. Westport, CT: Greenwood Press, 2001. 159–164.

Gilbert, Kate. "Children of the Revolution." *The Women's Review of Books* 15.8 (May 1998): 1.

Gilmore, Leigh. "Limit-Cases: Trauma, Self-Representation, and the Jurisdictions of Identity." *Biography: An Interdisciplinary Quarterly* 24.1 (Winter 2001): 128–139.

————. *The Limits of Autobiography: Trauma and Testimony.* Ithaca, NY: Cornell University Press, 2001.

Goar, Robert. J. "The Humanism of Richard Kim." *Midwest Quarterly: A Journal of Contemporary Thought* 21.4 (Summer 1980): 450–469.

Goellnicht, Donald C. "Blurring Boundaries: Asian American Literature as Theory." *An Interethnic Companion to Asian American Literature.* Ed. King-Kok Cheung. New York: Cambridge University Press, 1997. 338–365.

————. "A Long Labour: The Protracted Birth of Asian Canadian Literature." *Essays on Canadian Writing* 72 (2000): 1–41.

Goodyear, Sara Suleri. *Boys Will Be Boys: A Daughter's Elegy.* Chicago: University of Chicago Press, 2003.

Gordon, Avery. *Ghostly Matters: Haunting and the Sociological Imagination*. Minneapolis: University of Minnesota Press, 1997.

Grice, Helena. "Face-ing/De-Face-ing Racism: Physiognomy as Ethnic Marker in Early Eurasian/Amerasian Women's Texts." *Re/Collecting Early Asian America: Essays in Cultural History*. Ed. Josephine Lee, Imogene L. Lim, and Yuko Matsukawa. Philadelphia: Temple University Press, 2002. 255–270.

———. *Negotiating Identities: An Introduction to Asian American Women's Writings*. Manchester, England: University of Manchester Press, 2002.

Gullestad, Marianne. "Modernity, Self, and Childhood in the Analysis of Life Stories." *Imagined Childhoods: Self and Society in Autobiographical Accounts*. Ed. Marianne Gullestad. Oslo: Scandinavian University Press, 1996. 1–39.

Gunn, Janet Varner. *Autobiography: Towards a Poetics of Experience*. Philadelphia: University of Pennsylvania Press, 1982.

Gusdorf, Georges. "Conditions and Limits of Autobiography." Trans. James Olney. *Autobiography: Essays Theoretical and Critical*. Ed. James Olney. Princeton, NJ: Princeton University Press, 1980. 28–47.

Hall, Stuart. "Cultural Identity and Diaspora." *Identity: Community, Culture, Difference*. Ed. Jonathan Rutherford. London: Lawrence & Wishart, 1990. 222–237.

Hamilton, Paula. "The Knife Edge: Debates about Memory and History." *Memory and History in Twentieth-Century Australia*. Ed. Kate Darian-Smith and Paula Hamilton. New York: Oxford University Press, 1994. 9–32.

Hazlett, John Downton. *My Generation: Collective Autobiography and Identity Politics*. Madison: University of Wisconsin Press, 1998.

Heng, Liang, and Judith Shapiro. *Son of the Revolution*. New York: Vintage, 1984.

Henke, Suzette. *Shattered Subjects: Trauma and Testimony in Women's Life-Writing*. New York: St. Martin's Press, 1998.

Heywood, Leslie. *Dedication to Hunger: The Anorexic Aesthetic in Modern Culture*. Berkeley: University of California Press, 1996.

Higa, Tomiko. *The Girl with the White Flag*. Trans. Dorothy Britton. Tokyo: Kodansha International, 1995.

Him, Chanrithy. *When Broken Glass Floats: Growing Up under the Khmer Rouge*. New York: Norton, 2000.

Hinz, Evelyn J. "Introduction: Diet Consciousness and Current Literary Trends." *Mosaic* 24.3/4 (Summer/Fall 1991): v–xiii.

Hirsch, Marianne. *Family Frames: Photography, Narrative, and Postmemory*. Cambridge, MA: Harvard University Press, 1997.

Hongo, Garrett. *Volcano: A Memoir of Hawaii*. New York: Vintage Departures, 1995.

Houston, Jeanne Wakatsuki, and James Houston. *Farewell to Manzanar*. 1973. New York: Bantam, 1995.

Houston, Velina Hasu, and Teresa K. Williams, eds. "No Passing Zone: The Artistic and Discursive Voices of Asian-Descent Multiracials." Special issue. *Amerasia Journal* 23.1 (1997).

Hutcheon, Linda. "Crypto-Ethnicity." *PMLA: Publications of the Modern Language Association of America* 113.1 (January 1998): 28–33.

Huynh, Quang Nhoung. *The Land I Lost: Adventures of a Boy in Vietnam.* New York: Harper Trophy, 1982.

Hynes, Samuel. "Personal Narratives and Commemoration." *War and Remembrance in the Twentieth Century.* Ed. Jay Winter and Emmanuel Sivan. New York: Cambridge University Press, 1999. 205–220.

Ibarraran, Amaia. "One Image, A Thousand Words: Revealing and Concealing in Aimee Liu's *Face.*" *Evolving Origins, Transplanting Cultures: Literary Legacies of the New Americans.* Ed. Laura Alonso Gallo and Antonia Dominguez Miguela. Huelva, Spain: Universidad de Huelva, 2002. 109–113.

Igloria, Luisa A., ed. *Not Home, But Here: Writing from the Filipino Diaspora.* Manila, Philippines: Anvil Press, 2003.

Italie, Hillel. "Fact or Fiction of a Memoir." *AsianWeek* (November 3–9, 2000). Available at http://www.asianweek.com/2000_11_03/ae4_tenthousandsorrows.html.

Jackson, Michael. *Minima Ethnographica: Intersubjectivity and the Anthropological Subject.* Chicago: University of Chicago Press, 1998.

Jiang, Ji-Li. *Red Scarf Girl: A Memoir of the Cultural Revolution.* New York: Harper Trophy, 1997.

Kang, K. Connie. *Home Was the Land of Morning Calm: The Saga of a Korean-American Family.* Reading, MA: Addison-Wesley Publishing, 1995.

Kang, Hyok, with Philippe Grangereau. *This is Paradise!* Trans. Shaun Whiteside. Boston: Little, Brown, 2005.

Kang, Younghill. *East Goes West: The Making of an Oriental Yankee.* New York: Scribner's, 1937.

———. *The Grass Roof.* New York: Scribner's, 1931.

———. *The Happy Grove.* New York: Scribner's, 1933.

Kapai, Leela. "Yoshiko Uchida (1921–1992)." *Asian American Autobiographies: A Bio-Bibliographical Critical Sourcebook.* Ed. Guiyou Huang. Westport, CT: Greenwood Press, 2001. 375–381.

Kaplan, Caren. "Resisting Autobiography: Out-Law Genres and Transnational Feminist Subjects." *De/Colonizing the Subject: The Politics of Gender in Women's Autobiography.* Ed. Sidonie Smith and Julia Watson. Minneapolis: University of Minnesota Press, 1992. 115–138.

Kim, Elaine H. *Asian American Literature: An Introduction to the Writings and Their Social Context.* Philadelphia: Temple University Press, 1982.

———. "Myth, Memory, and Desire: Homeland and History in Contemporary Korean American Writing and Visual Art." *Holding Their Own: Perspectives on the Multi-Ethnic Literatures of the United States.* Ed. Dorothea Fischer-Hornung and Heike Raphael-Hernandez. Tübingen, Germany: Stauffenburg Verlag, 2000. 79–91.

Kim, Elizabeth. *Ten Thousand Sorrows: The Extraordinary Journey of a Korean War Orphan.* New York: Doubleday, 2000.

Kim, Richard E. *The Innocent*. Boston: Houghton Mifflin, 1968.

———. *Lost Names: Scenes from a Korean Boyhood*. New York: Praeger, 1970.

———. *The Martyred*. New York: George Brazilier, 1964.

Kingston, Maxine Hong. *The Woman Warrior: Memoir of a Girlhood among Ghosts*. 1975. New York: Vintage Random House, 1989.

Kogawa, Joy. *Naomi's Road*. Toronto: Stoddart, 1995.

———. *Obasan*. Boston: David R. Godine, 1981.

Kornreich, Jennifer. "Selling Her Body, Selling Her Soul." *Women's Review of Books* 13.6 (1996): 17–18.

Koul, Sudha. *The Tiger Ladies: A Memoir of Kashmir*. Boston: Beacon Press, 2002.

Kröller, Eva-Marie. "In-Between Souls." Review of *Paper Shadows*, by Wayson Choy. *Canadian Literature* 163 (Winter 1999): 179–180.

Kuramoto, Kazuko. *Manchurian Legacy: Memoirs of a Japanese Colonist*. East Lansing: Michigan State University Press, 1999.

Kwan, Michael David. *Broken Portraits: Personal Encounters with Chinese Students*. San Francisco: China Books, 1990.

———. *The Chinese Storyteller's Book: Supernatural Tales*. Boston: Tuttle, 2001.

———. *Things That Must Not Be Forgotten: A Childhood in Wartime China*. Toronto: Macfarlane, Walter and Ross, 2000.

Kwan, Michelle, and Laura M. James. *Michelle Kwan Autobiography*. New York: Scholastic, 1998.

Lau, Evelyn. *Fresh Girls and Other Stories*. Toronto: HarperCollins, 1993.

———. *In the House of Slaves*. Toronto: Coach House Press, 1994.

———. *Inside Out: Reflections on a Life So Far*. Vancouver: Anchor Canada, 2001.

———. *Runaway: Diary of a Street Kid*. Toronto: HarperCollins, 1989.

———. *You Are Not Who You Claim*. Victoria: Porcépic Books, 1990.

Lee, Helie. *Still Life with Rice*. New York: Touchstone, 1996.

Lee, Kyhan. "Younghill Kang and the Genesis of Korean-American Literature." *Korea Journal* 31.4 (Winter 1991): 63–78.

Lee, Rachel C. *The Americas of Asian American Literature: Gendered Fictions of Nation and Transnation*. Princeton, NJ: Princeton University Press, 1999.

Lee, Sue-Im. "The Aesthetic in Asian American Literary Discourse." *Literary Gestures: The Aesthetic in Asian American Writing*. Ed. Rocío G. Davis and Sue-Im Lee. Philadelphia: Temple University Press, 2005. 1–14.

Lee, Yan Phou. *When I Was a Boy in China*. Boston: Lothrop, Lee, & Shepard, 1887.

Lejeune, Philippe. "The Autobiographical Pact." *On Autobiography*. Ed. Paul John Eakin. Trans. Katherine Leary. Minneapolis: University of Minnesota Press, 1989. 3–30.

———. "The Autobiography of Those Who Do Not Write." *On Autobiography*. Ed. Paul John Eakin. Trans. Katherine Leary. Minneapolis: University of Minnesota Press, 1989. 185–215.

Lim, Shirley Geok-lin. "The Tradition of Chinese American Women's Life Stories: Thematics of Race and Gender in Jade Snow Wong's *Fifth Chinese Daughter* and Maxine Hong Kingston's *The Woman Warrior*." *American Women's Auto-*

biography: Fea(s)ts of Memory. Ed. Margo Culley. Madison: University of Wisconsin Press, 1992. 252–267.

———, ed. *Approaches to Teaching Kingston's* The Woman Warrior. New York: Modern Language Association, 1991.

Lim, Sing. *West Coast Chinese Boy.* 1979. Montreal: Tundra Books, 1991.

Lin Yutang. *My Country and My People.* New York: John Day, 1937.

Ling, Amy. *Between Worlds: Women Writers of Chinese Ancestry.* New York: Pergamon Press, 1990.

———. "Reading Her/Stories against His/Stories in Early Chinese American Literature." *American Realism and the Canon.* Ed. Tom Quirk and Gary Scharnhorst. Newark: University of Delaware Press, 1994. 69–86.

———. "Yan Phou Lee on the Asian American Frontier." *Re/Collecting Early Asian America: Essays in Cultural History.* Ed. Josephine Lee, Imogen Lim, and Yuko Matsukawa. Philadelphia: Temple University Press, 2002. 273–287.

Lionnet, Françoise. *Autobiographical Voices: Race, Gender, Self-Portraiture.* Ithaca, NY: Cornell University Press, 1989.

Liu, Aimee. *Cloud Mountain.* New York: Warner Books, 1997.

———. *Face.* New York: Warner Books, 1994.

———. *Flash House.* New York: Warner Books, 2003.

———. *Solitaire.* 1979. New York: iuniverse, 2000.

Liu Binyan. *A Higher Kind of Loyalty.* New York: Pantheon Books, 1994.

Lo, Marie. "The Currency of Visibility and the Paratext of 'Evelyn Lau.'" *Essays on Canadian Writing* 85 (forthcoming).

———. "Native-Born Asian Canadian Model Minorities." *Between, Among: English Language Fiction in the Chinese Diaspora.* Ed. Dorothy Wang (forthcoming).

Lowe, Lisa. *Immigrant Acts: On Asian American Cultural Politics.* Durham, NC: Duke University Press, 1996.

Lu, Mei-Yu. "Multicultural Children's Literature in the Elementary Classroom." *ERIC Digest* (1998). Available online at http://www.ericdigests.org/1999-2/literature.htm.

Lu Chi Fa and Becky White. *Double Luck: Memoirs of a Chinese Orphan.* New York: Holiday House, 2001.

Lloyd, Rosemary. *The Land of Lost Content: Children and Childhood in Nineteenth-Century French Literature.* Oxford: Clarendon Press, 1992.

Mah, Adeline Yen. *Chinese Cinderella.* New York: Dell Laurel-Leaf, 1999.

———. *Falling Leaves: The True Story of an Unwanted Chinese Daughter.* New York: John Wiley & Sons, 1998.

Mar, M. Elaine. *Paper Daughter.* New York: HarperCollins, 1999.

Marcus, Laura. *Auto/biographical Discourses: Theory, Criticism, Practice.* Manchester: Manchester University Press, 1994.

Masalski, Kathleen Woods. "Interview with Richard Kim." Available online at http://www.aasianst.org/EAA/lostname.htm (accessed March 2, 2005).

McCloud, Scott. *Understanding Comics: The Invisible Art.* New York: Harper Perennial, 1994.

McKelvey, Robert S. *The Dust of Life: America's Children Abandoned in Vietnam.* Seattle: University of Washington Press, 1999.

———. "Vietnamese Amerasians: The Children We Left Behind." *Mots Plureils* 7 (1998). Available at http://www.arts.uwa.edu.au/MotsPluriels/MP798rmk.html.

Mehta, Ved. *All for Love.* New York: Nation Books, 2001.

———. *Daddyji.* New York: Farrar, Straus, Giroux, 1972.

———. *Dark Harbor: Building House and Home on an Enchanted Island.* New York: Nation Books, 2003.

———. *Face to Face: An Autobiography.* 1957. New York: Oxford University Press, 1976.

———. *The Ledge between the Streams.* New York: Norton, 1984.

———. *Mamaji.* New York: Oxford University Press, 1979.

———. *The Red Letters: My Father's Enchanted Period.* New York: Nation Books, 2004.

———. *Remembering Mr. Shawn's New Yorker: The Invisible Art of Editing.* Woodstock: Overlook Press, 1998.

———. *Sound-Shadows of the New World.* New York: Norton, 1986.

———. *The Stolen Light.* New York: Norton, 1989.

———. *Up at Oxford.* New York: Norton, 1993.

———. *Vedi.* New York: Norton, 1982.

Miki, Roy. "Altered States: Global Currents, the Spectral Nation and the Production of 'Asian Canadian.'" *Journal of Canadian Studies* 35.3 (Fall 2000): 43–72.

———. *Broken Entries: Race, Subjectivity, Writing.* Toronto: Mercury Press, 1998.

———. "Can Asian Adian? Reading the Scenes of 'Asian Canadian.'" *West Coast Line* 34.3 (Winter 2001): 56–77.

Min, Anchee. *Red Azalea: Life and Love in China.* New York: Pantheon Books, 1994.

Moser, Linda Trinh. "Jeanne Wakatsuki and James D. Houston." *Asian American Autobiographers: A Bio-Bibliographical Critical Sourcebook.* Ed. Guiyou Huang. Westport, CT: Greenwood Press, 2001. 127–133.

Murayama, Milton. *Five Years on a Rock.* Honolulu: University of Hawai'i Press, 1994.

Myers, Mitzi. "Missed Opportunities and Critical Malpractice: New Historicism and Children's Literature." *Children's Literature Association Quarterly* 13.1 (1988): 41–43.

Myracle, Lauren. "Molding the Minds of the Young: The History of Bibliotherapy as Applied to Children and Adolescents." *The Alan Review* 22.2 (1995). Available at http://scholar.lib.vt.edu/ejournals/ALAN/winter95/Myracle.html.

Nakashima, Daniel A. "A Rose by Any Other Name: Names, Multiracial/Multiethnic People, and the Politics of Identity." *The Sum of Our Parts: Mixed-Heritage Asian Americans.* Ed. Teresa Williams-León and Cynthia Nakashima. Philadelphia: Temple University Press, 2000. 111–119.

Nam, Vickie, ed. *Yell-Oh Girls: Emerging Voices Explore Culture, Identity, and Growing Up Asian American.* New York: HarperCollins, 2001.

Neuman, Shirley. "Autobiography: From Different Poetics to a Poetics of Difference." *Essays on Life Writing: From Genre to Critical Practice.* Ed. Marlene Kadar. Toronto: University of Toronto Press, 1992. 213–230.

New, Ilhan. *When I Was a Boy in Korea.* Boston: Lothrop, Lee, & Shepard, 1928.

Ngor, Haing, and Roger Warner. *Survival in the Killing Fields.* Berkeley: Carroll & Graf Publishers, 2003.

Nguyen, Kien. *Le Colonial: A Novel.* Boston: Little, Brown, 2004.

———. *The Tapestries.* Boston: Little, Brown, 2002.

———. *The Unwanted.* Boston: Little, Brown, 2001.

Nunez, Sigrid. *A Feather on the Breath of God.* New York: HarperCollins, 1995.

Nussbaum, Felicity A. "Toward Conceptualizing Diary." *Studies in Autobiography.* Ed. James Olney. New York: Oxford University Press, 1988. 128–140.

Oh, Seiwoong. "Chinese Opera and Cowboys: Ethnic Markers in Wayson Choy's *Paper Shadows.*" Unpublished paper presented at the MESEA Conference, Thessaloniki, Greece, May 20–24, 2004.

———. "Ilhan New (1895–1971)." *Asian American Autobiographers: A Bio-Bibliographical Critical Sourcebook.* Ed. Guiyou Huang. Westport, CT: Greenwood Press, 2001. 281–285.

———. "Younghill Kang (1903–1972)." *Asian American Autobiographers: A Bio-Bibliographical Critical Sourcebook.* Ed. Guiyou Huang. Westport, CT: Greenwood Press, 2001. 149–158.

Olney, James. "On Telling One's Own Story; or, Memory and Narrative in Early Life-Writing." *Imagined Childhoods: Self and Society in Autobiographical Accounts.* Ed. Marianne Gullestad. Oslo, Norway: Scandinavian University Press, 1996. 41–61.

Olson, Greta. *Reading Eating Disorders: Writings on Bulimia and Anorexia as Confessions of American Culture.* Frankfurt, Germany: Peter Lang, 2003.

Omi, Michael, and Howard Winnat. *Racial Formation in the United States: From the 1960s to the 1990s.* 2nd ed. New York: Routledge, 1994.

Ondaatje, Michael. *Running in the Family.* New York: Penguin, 1982.

Otano, Alicia. *Speaking the Past: Child Perspective in the Asian American Bildungsroman.* Hamburg, Germany: LIT Verlag, 2004.

Pardeck, John T. "Using Bibliotherapy in Clinical Practice with Children." *Psychological Reports* 67 (1990): 1043–1049.

Park, Frances, and Ginger Park. *To Swim across the World.* New York: Miramax, 2002.

Pataray-Ching, Jann, and Stuart Ching. "Talking about Books: Supporting and Questioning Representation." *Language Arts* 78.5 (2001): 476–484.

Pelaud, Isabelle Thuy. "*Metisse Blanche:* Kim Lefebre and Transnational Space." *Mixed Race Literature.* Ed. Jonathan Brennan. Stanford: Stanford University Press, 2002. 122–136.

Popkin, Jeremy D. "Coordinated Lives: Between Autobiography and Scholarship." *Biography: An Interdisciplinary Quarterly* 24.4 (Fall 2001): 781–806.

Porter, Roger J. *Self-Same Songs: Autobiographical Performances and Reflections*. Lincoln: University of Nebraska Press, 2002.

Pran, Dith, and Kim DePaul, eds. *Children of Cambodia's Killing Fields: Memoirs by Survivors*. New Haven, CT: Yale University Press, 1999.

Pratt, Mary Louise. *Imperial Eyes: Travel Writing and Transculturation*. New York: Routledge, 1992.

Reyes, Norman. *Child of Two Worlds: An Autobiography of a Filipino-American, or Vice Versa*. 1995. Pasig City, Philippines: Anvil Publications, 1996.

Robbins, Trina. *From Girls to Grrrlz: A History of Women's Comics from Teens to Zines*. San Francisco: Chronicle Books, 1999.

Rodríguez, Richard. *Hunger of Memory: The Autobiography of Richard Rodríguez*. New York: Bantam Books, 1982.

Roh-Spaulding, Carol. "Beyond Biraciality: 'Race' as Process in the Work of Edith Eaton/Sui Sin Far and Winnifred Eaton/Onoto Watanna." *Asian American Literature in the International Context: Readings on Fiction, Poetry, and Performance*. Ed. Rocío G. Davis and Sämi Ludwig. Hamburg, Germany: LIT Verlag, 2002. 21–36.

———. "'Wavering Images': Mixed-Race Identity in the Stories of Edith Eaton/Sui Sin Far." *Ethnicity and the American Short Story*. Ed. Julie Brown. New York: Garland, 1997. 155–176.

Roley, Brian Ascalon. *American Son*. New York: Norton, 2001.

Root, Maria P. P. "Multiracial Asians: Models of Ethnic Identity." *Amerasia Journal* 23.1 (1997): 29–41.

Ropp, Steven Masami. "Do Multiracial Subjects Really Challenge Race? Mixed-Race Asians in the United States and the Caribbean." *Amerasia Journal* 23.1 (1997): 1–16.

Sakurai, Patricia A. "The Politics of Possession: The Negotiation of Identity in *American in Disguise, Homebase*, and *Farewell to Manzanar*." *Privileging Positions: The Sites of Asian American Studies*. Ed. Gary Y. Okihiro et al. Pullman: Washington State University Press, 1995. 157–170.

Santa Ana, Jeffrey J. "Affect-Identity: The Emotions of Assimilation, Multiraciality, and Asian American Subjectivity." *Asian North American Identities beyond the Hyphen*. Ed. Eleanor Ty and Donald C. Goellnicht. Bloomington: Indiana University Press, 2004. 15–42.

Silliman, Jael. *Jewish Portraits, Indian Frames: Women's Narratives from a Diaspora of Hope*. Hanover, NH: Brandeis University Press/University Press of New England, 2001.

Simal González, Begoña. "Ostracism and Emplacement in Nunez's *A Feather on the Breath of God* and Liu's *Face*." *Atlantic Literary Review* 2.4 (2001): 113–131.

Singh, Amritjit, Joseph T. Skerrett, Jr., and Robert E. Hogan, eds. *Memory, Narrative, and Identity: New Essays in Ethnic American Literatures*. Boston: Northeastern University Press, 1994.

Slatin, John M. "Blindness and Self-Perception: The Autobiographies of Ved Mehta." *Mosaic* 19.4 (Fall 1986): 173–193.

Slemon, Stephen. "Post-Colonial Allegory and the Transformation of History." *Journal of Commonwealth Literature* 23.1 (1988): 157–168.

Smith, Katharine Capshaw. "Introduction: The Landscape of Ethnic American Children's Literature." *MELUS* 27.2 (Summer 2002): 3–8.

Smith, Paul. *Discerning the Subject*. Minneapolis: University of Minnesota Press, 1988.

Smith, Sidonie. "Performativity, Autobiographical Practice, Resistance." *Women, Autobiography, Theory: A Reader*. Ed. Sidonie Smith and Julia Watson. Madison: University of Wisconsin Press, 1998. 108–125.

———. *Subjectivity, Identity, and the Body: Women's Autobiographical Practices in the Twentieth Century*. Bloomington: Indiana University Press, 1993.

Smith, Sidonie, and Julia Watson. *Reading Autobiography: A Guide for Interpreting Narratives*. Minneapolis: University of Minnesota Press, 2001.

Sollors, Werner. *Neither Black nor White Yet Both: Thematic Explorations of Interracial Literature*. New York: Oxford University Press, 1997.

Sone, Monica. *Nisei Daughter*. 1953. Seattle: University of Washington Press, 1991.

Spickard, Paul R. "What Must I Be? Asian Americans and the Question of Multiethnic Identity." *Amerasia Journal* 23.1 (1997): 43–60.

Spiegelman, Art. "Commix: An Idiosyncratic Historical and Aesthetic Overview." *Print* 42.7 (1988): 61–73, 195–196.

———. *Maus: A Survivor's Tale*. New York: Pantheon Books, 1993.

Stanley, Liz. "Is There Life in the Contact Zone? Auto/Biographical Practices and the Field of Representation in Writing Past Lives." *Representing Lives: Women and Auto/biography*. Ed. Alison Donnell and Pauline Polkey. London: Macmillan, 2000. 3–30.

Steedman, Carolyn. "Enforced Narratives: Stories of Another Self." *Feminism and Autobiography: Texts, Theories, Methods*. Ed. Tess Cosslett, Celia Lury, and Penny Summerfield. New York: Routledge, 2000. 25–39.

Stone, Albert E. *Autobiographical Occasions and Original Acts: Versions of American Identity from Henry Adams to Nate Shaw*. Philadelphia: University of Pennsylvania Press, 1982.

Stotesbury, John A. "Blind Visions of Childhood: Autobiography and Unseen Worlds." *Small Worlds: Transcultural Visions of Childhood*. Ed. Rocío G. Davis and Rosalia Baena. Pamplona, Spain: University of Navarra Press, 2001. 133–141.

Sturken, Marita. "Personal Stories and National Meanings: Memory, Reenactment, and the Image." *The Seductions of Biography*. Ed. Mary Rhiel and David Suchoff. New York: Routledge, 1996. 31–41.

Su, Karen. "Jade Snow Wong's Badge of Distinction in the 1990s." *Critical Mass: A Journal of Asian American Cultural Criticism* 2.1 (Winter 1994): 3–52.

Sugimoto, Etsu. *A Daughter of the Samurai*. 1925. New York: Doubleday, 1966.

Sui Sin Far. "Leaves from the Mental Portfolio of an Eurasian." *Independent* (January 7, 1909): 125–132.

Sun-Childers, Jaia, and Douglas Childers. *The White-Haired Girl: Bittersweet Adventures of a Little Red Soldier*. New York: Pica Books, 1997.

Suleri, Sara. *Meatless Days*. Chicago: University of Chicago Press, 1989.

Szymusiak, Molyda. *The Stones Cry Out: A Cambodian Childhood, 1975–1980*. Bloomington: Indiana University Press, 1999.

Takashima, Shichan. *A Child in Prison Camp*. 1971. Toronto: Tundra Books, 1998.

Takei, George. *To the Stars: The Autobiography of George Takei, Star Trek's Mr. Sulu*. New York: Pocket Books, 1994.

Tal, Kalí. *Worlds of Hurt: Reading the Literatures of Trauma*. New York: Cambridge University Press, 1996.

Tausky, Thomas E. "'A Passion to Live in this Splendid Past': Canadian and Australian Autobiographies of Childhood." *Ariel* 17.3 (July 1986): 40–62.

Tham, Hilary. "Finding Your Voice." Available online at http://www.geocities.com/Hilarytham/essays.html#voice (accessed February 19, 2005).

———. *Lane with No Name: Memoirs and Poems of a Malaysian-Chinese Girlhood*. London: Three Continents Book/Lynne Reinner Publishers, 1997.

Thompson, Becky W. *A Hunger So Wide and So Deep: American Women Speak Out on Eating Problems*. Minneapolis: University of Minnesota Press, 1998.

Todorov, Tzevetan. "The Origin of Genres." *New Literary History* 8 (Autumn 1976): 159–170.

Trites, Roberta Seelinger. "Multiculturalism in Children's Literature." *Children's Literature Association Quarterly* 28.2 (Summer 2003): 66–67.

Ty, Eleanor. "Abjection, Masculinity and Violence in Brian Ascalon Roley's *American Son* and Han Ong's *Fixer Chao*." *MELUS* 29.1 (Spring 2004): 119–136.

———. *The Politics of the Visible in Asian North American Narratives*. Toronto: University of Toronto Press, 2004.

Uchida, Yoshiko. *Desert Exile: The Uprooting of a Japanese-American Family*. 1982. Seattle: University of Washington Press, 1989.

———. *The Invisible Thread*. 1991. New York: Beech Tree Books, 1995.

Ung, Loung. *First They Killed My Father: A Daughter of Cambodia Remembers*. New York: HarperCollins, 2000.

———. *Lucky Child: A Daughter of Cambodia Reunites with the Sister She Left Behind*. New York: HarperCollins, 2005.

Uno, Kathleen. "Afterword." *Manchurian Legacy: Memoirs of a Japanese Colonist*, by Kazuko Kuramoto. East Lansing: Michigan State University Press, 1999. 177–189.

Wah, Fred. *Diamond Grill*. Edmonton: NeWest Press, 1996.

Watanna, Onoto (Winnifred Eaton). *Me, A Book of Remembrance*. New York: Century, 1915.

Watkins, Yoko Kawashima. *My Brother, My Sister, and I*. 1994. New York: Simon Pulse, 2002.

———. *So Far from the Bamboo Grove*. New York: Beech Tree Books, 1986.

———. *Tales from the Bamboo Grove*. New York: Simon & Schuster, 1992.

Wertsch, James V. *Voices of Collective Remembering*. New York: Cambridge University Press, 2002.

Whitlock, Gillian. *The Intimate Empire: Reading Women's Autobiography*. London: Cassell, 2000.

Winter, Jay, and Emmanuel Sivan. "Setting the Framework." *War and Remembrance in the Twentieth Century.* Ed. Jay Winter and Emmanuel Sivan. New York: Cambridge University Press, 1999. 6–39.

Witek, Joseph. "From Genre to Medium: Comics and Contemporary American Culture." *Rejuvenating the Humanities.* Ed. Ray B. Browne and Marshall W. Fishwick. Bowling Green, OH: Bowling Green State University Press, 1992. 71–79.

Wong, Jade Snow. *Fifth Chinese Daughter.* 1945. Seattle: University of Washington Press, 1989.

———. *No Chinese Stranger.* New York: Harper and Row, 1975.

Wong, Rita. "Market Forces and Powerful Desires: Reading Evelyn Lau's Cultural Labour." *Essays on Canadian Writing* 73 (Spring 2001): 122–140.

Wong, Sau-ling Cynthia. "Autobiography as Guided Chinatown Tour? Maxine Hong Kingston's *The Woman Warrior* and the Chinese-American Autobiographical Controversy." *Multicultural Autobiography: American Lives.* Ed. James Robert Payne. Knoxville: University of Tennessee Press, 1992. 248–279.

———. "Ethnic Dimensions of Postmodern Indeterminacy: Maxine Hong Kingston's *The Woman Warrior* as Avant-Garde Autobiography." *Autobiographie & Avant-Garde.* Ed. Alfred Hornung and Ernspeter Ruhe. Tübingen, Germany: Gunter Narr Verlag, 1992. 273–284.

———. "Ethnic Subject, Ethnic Sign, and the Difficulty of Rehabilitative Representation: Chinatown in Some Works of Chinese American Fiction." *The Yearbook of English Studies* 24 (1994): 251–262.

———. *Reading Asian American Literature: From Necessity to Extravagance.* Princeton, NJ: Princeton University Press, 1993.

Wong, Sau-ling, and Jeffrey J. Santa Ana. "Gender and Sexuality in Asian American Literature." *Signs* 25.1 (Autumn 1999): 171–221.

Wong, Shawn. *American Knees.* New York: Simon & Schuster, 1995.

Yamada, Teri Shaffer. "Cambodian American Autobiography: Testimonial Discourse." *Form and Transformation in Asian American Literature.* Ed. Zhou Xiaojing and Samina Namji. Seattle: University of Washington Press, 2005. 144–167.

Yamamoto, Traise. *Masking Selves, Making Subjects: Japanese American Women, Identity, and the Body.* Berkeley: University of California Press, 1999.

Yang, Rae. *Spider Eaters: A Memoir.* Berkeley: University of California Press, 1997.

Yep, Laurence. *The Lost Garden.* New York: Simon & Schuster, 1991.

Yun, Charse. "Fact or Fiction?" *Koream Journal* 11.11 (November 2000): 12–13.

Zhang, Song Nan. *A Little Tiger in the Chinese Night: An Autobiography in Art.* Toronto: Tundra Books, 1993.

Zhou Xiaojing. "Hilary Tham (1946–)." *Asian American Autobiographers: A Bio-Bibliographical Critical Sourcebook.* Ed. Guiyou Huang. Westport, CT: Greenwood Press, 2001. 363–369.

Index

Abel, Jessica, 144
abuse, Mah's experience of, 160–161
Accomando, Claire Hsu, *Love and Rutabaga,* 84
Adams, Henry, 9–10
adolescence: Lau's diary of, 140–143. *See also* anorexia
adoptions, 123, 126, 150–151
agency: of autobiographers, 13–14, 81, 109; of readers and writers, 26
alimentary images. *See* food
Amerasians, 88, 99–100, 198n. 17. *See also* biracial individuals; Eurasians
Americanization: individuality of process, 159; tropes of, 127. *See also* North Americanization
Anderson, Linda, 24–25
anorexia, 130, 134, 139, 140
Anzaldua, Gloria, 39
artists, autobiographies of, 168–169, 179–180. *See also* comics; *künstlerroman*
Asian American literary criticism, 3, 187n. 3
Asian American literature: bildungsroman, 20; differences from Asian Canadian writing, 13, 187n. 3; early, 41; food trope, 128; founding text, 39
Asian Americans: athletes, 178–179, 205n. 16; culture, 183; identities, 20–21, 27; immigrant writers, 16; names, 132; subjectivity, 20. *See also* Asian North Americans; Cam-

bodian Americans; Chinese Americans; Filipino Americans; Japanese Americans; Korean Americans
Asian Canadian literary criticism, 187–188n. 3
Asian Canadian literature: differences from Asian American writing, 13, 187n. 3
Asian Canadians. *See* Asian North Americans; Chinese Canadians; Japanese Canadians
Asian North American autobiographies of childhood. *See* Childhoods, Asian North American
Asian North American children's literature, 156–158
Asian North Americans: bildungsroman, 8; marginalization, 18; myths of childhood, 14; participation in history, 171–178; racial discrimination, 18; writing, 3. *See also* Asian Americans; Asian Canadians
authenticity, 41, 157
autobiofictionalography, 144
autobiographical inscription, 109, 149
autobiographies of childhood. *See* Childhoods
autobiography: change metaphors, 14–15; chronotopic position of subjects, 19, 34, 87; collective readings, 66–68; cultural contexts, 3–4, 32; diasporic, 24; Euro-American, 8, 9–10, 12, 14, 20, 21; generational, 66–67, 203n. 13; healing

potential, 81, 140, 152; interaction of theme and form, 136–137; meaning of term, 187n. 2; performative aspects, 2, 10, 27–31, 32, 189–190n. 3; postmodern, 9; relational, 28, 137, 148–151, 203n. 13; self-representation in, 15, 137, 140; structures, 10–11, 136–138, 184; subjects, 10; *testimonio*, 142; traumatic experiences, 75; voices, 24; of White males, 9–10, 14; of women, 26; writer-reader relationship, 23–26. *See also* ethnic autobiography

autobiography for children. *See* Childhoods, for children

Bader, Barbara, 203n. 1
Baena, Rosalia, 101, 124–125
Bakhtin, M. M., 19, 34
Bal, Mieke, 29
Barros, Carolyn A., 14
Barry, Lynda: career as graphic artist, 143, 194n. 19; *One Hundred Demons*, 11, 136, 143, 144, 145–148; style, 145; use of comics, 143, 144
Beauregard, Guy, 187n. 3
Benjamin, Jessica, 152
Bergland, Betty, 9, 15, 16, 31, 34, 114
Bhabha, Homi K., 18, 87, 113
bibliotherapy, 158–159
bildungsroman, 8, 20, 111–112
biracial Childhoods: America as structuring frame, 108; audiences, 87; book covers, 101; closure strategies, 108–109; controversial, 197n. 5; of Delman, 84–86; differences from other immigrant autobiographies, 108–109; of Fenkl, 93–98; of Kwan, 103–108; liminality, 82; meaning of biraciality, 84; of Nguyen, 98–103; of Reyes, 88–93; set in Asia, 86–87, 88–108. *See also* Barry, Lynda
biracial individuals: Americanization processes, 108–109; Asian views of, 88; autobiographies, 83; bicultural-

ity, 91, 102; classification difficulties, 85; ethnic identities, 83; Eurasians, 83, 88, 106; fictional treatments, 196n. 2; identities, 86, 87–88, 90, 91–93, 95–96, 102, 197n. 8; liminal positions, 82, 87–88, 89, 90, 95, 97; literature of, 86; names, 95–96; in Philippines, 88–93; physical appearances, 88, 98, 100–102, 106–107; positioning of, 83, 86, 87–88; self-rejection, 100, 107; social statuses, 87, 88, 90, 93, 100; stereotypes of, 83, 90; terms for, 90, 100, 106, 107, 196n. 1, 198n. 17; in Vietnam, 88, 99, 198n. 17

Blaise, Clark, and Bharati Mukherjee, *Days and Nights in Calcutta*, 203n. 13

blind individuals: autobiographies, 46; facial vision, 50; schools, 46, 47–49, 51. *See also* Mehta, Ved

Boelhower, William, 9, 10, 17, 111, 112, 118, 120, 127, 191n. 16, 199n. 1

book covers, 73, 101, 195n. 6

Bordo, Susan, 139–140

Brainard, Cecilia Manguerra, 197n. 11

Brennan, Jonathan, 82, 86

Browdy de Hernandez, Jennifer, 45

Brown, James W., 128

Brown, Wesley, 67

Bruss, Elizabeth W., 8

Bulosan, Carlos, 41, 193n. 9

Buss, Helen, 189n. 3

Cambodia: Childhoods set in, 68, 74, 75–81, 195n. 7; Communist/Khmer Rouge takeover, 35, 68, 74–81, 151, 152; cultural practices, 80; invasions of, 77, 78; memoirs of survivors, 74–75

Cambodian Americans: adopted children, 150–151. *See also* Asian Americans; Him, Chanrithy; Ung, Loung

Campaign for a Landmine-Free World, 78, 81

Canada: First Nations peoples, 179;

internment of Japanese Canadians, 175–176; multiculturality, 198n. 15; racism in, 18, 179; visible minority discourse, 21, 25

Canadian Childhoods, 123–124. *See also* Childhoods, Asian North American; Chinese Canadians; Japanese Canadians

Carpenter, Carole H., 157

Caskey, Noelle, 140

Chai, May-lee and Winberg, *The Girl from Purple Mountain,* 203n. 13

Chang, Elaine K., 142, 201n. 4

Chang, Jung, *Wild Swans,* 69

Chao, Lien, 142, 202nn. 7–8

Chen, Da: *China's Son,* 158, 163, 170, 171; *Colors of the Mountain,* 35, 67, 68, 72–74, 170, 195n. 6; *Sounds of the River,* 195n. 4

Chen, Fu-jen, 200nn. 3, 5

Cheng, Nien, *Life and Death in Shanghai,* 69

Cheung, Floyd, 38, 39–40, 190n. 7, 191n. 12, 192n. 5

Childers, Douglas, 69

Childhoods: advantages, 11; as beginnings, 2; Coe on, 2, 5, 7, 8, 11; construction of cultural memory, 30–31; definition, 7; endings, 7, 11, 35–36, 81, 192n. 3; Euro-American, 21, 36, 86, 112; explanations of present, 11–12; identity formation and, 2, 11–12; imaginative restructurings of past history in, 110–111; myths of childhood in, 12–13, 14, 103, 108; role of community, 112; socialization processes, 14, 20–22, 114; solitude of writers, 105–106

Childhoods, Asian North American: anthologies, 67; appropriation of genre, 8–9, 12, 21, 112; audiences, 25; community-building function, 3, 4; cultural aims, 1, 4, 22–23, 27, 156, 185; cultural ambassador function, 114–115, 117; didactic purposes, 12, 13, 184; differences between Canadian and American,

13; early, 15–16; endings, 21, 22, 114; ethnic identities explored in, 16–20; future-directedness, 184–185; historical events described, 4, 21–22, 35, 110; immigrant socialization stories, 110–135; influence of, 183–184; reconstruction of past, 3, 112; relationship between past and present in, 33–34; relationship to history, 4–5; socialization processes, 110–111; structural evolution, 184; subversive potential, 14; as writerly acts, 183; writer-reader relationship, 22, 28. *See also* biracial Childhoods

Childhoods, for children: adult autobiographies rewritten for children, 158, 170, 171, 176; audiences, 159, 182; challenges to stereotypes, 159; as cultural products, 156, 158; customs described, 160, 161, 163, 179; didactic purposes, 157–158, 160, 165, 182; empowerment of readers, 159; functions, 182; historical events described, 157, 163, 171; roles of Asians in American and Canadian history, 171–178; set in Asia, 159–171; set in North America, 171–181

Childhoods, set outside North America: ambivalence about homelands, 18, 37, 39; of biracial individuals, 86–87, 88–108; in Cambodia, 68, 74, 75–81, 195n. 7; challenges to North American myths, 17–18; changes in 1960s, 45; children's literature, 159–171; in China, 36–41, 67–68, 103–108, 160–162, 168–171; colonial childhoods, 57–64; cultural ambassador function, 15–16, 35, 89–90; customs described, 16, 41–44, 52, 57, 80, 89–90, 92; didactic purposes, 12, 32–33, 36–37, 61–62, 76; early, 16, 26, 34–35, 36–41; endings, 17, 35–36; historical events described, 35, 44, 49–50, 56, 57–58, 66, 87,

163; immigration as conclusion, 17, 35–36, 44, 57, 93, 108; in India, 46–51; information provided to readers, 32–33; in Kashmir, 55–57; in Korea, 36–38, 41–45, 93–98, 164–168, 195n. 7; in Malaysia, 51–55; palimpsestic function, 17–18, 29, 33, 159; in Philippines, 88–93; readers, 40; subversive potential, 39–41, 43

children's literature: Asian North American, 156–158; audiences, 156–158; autobiography, 156; ethnic, 156, 171; new historicism, 157; use in bibliotherapy, 158–159

Chin, Frank, 119

China: attitudes toward biracial individuals, 106; Childhoods set in, 36–41, 103–108, 160–162, 168–171; events of 1930s and 1940s, 103–108; Japanese colonial rule, 35, 57–58, 59–62; Japanese invasion, 105, 168. *See also* Cultural Revolution; Manchuria

Chinatown bachelors, 125, 200–201n. 7

Chinatowns: roles in Childhoods, 112–113; San Francisco, 116, 120; as trope, 120–122; Vancouver, 120, 122, 123, 124, 179

Chinese, in Malaysia, 51–55

Chinese Americans: biracial Childhoods, 103–108; Childhoods for children, 160–162, 169–171, 178–179, 180–181; Childhoods set during Cultural Revolution, 67–68, 69–74, 170–171; Childhoods set in Malaysia, 51–55; Childhoods set in United States, 114–122, 127–134, 138–140, 178–179, 180–181; earliest Childhood, 16, 34–35, 36–41; expectations of children, 115–116, 141; identities, 27, 40; liminal positions, 180, 181. *See also* Asian Americans; Kingston, Maxine Hong; Wong, Jade Snow

Chinese Canadians: Childhoods, 122–127; Childhoods for children, 168–169, 179–180; ethnic identi-

ties, 124; Vancouver Chinatown, 120, 122, 123, 124, 179. *See also* Lau, Evelyn

Chinese Exclusion Act of 1882, 40

Chinese restaurants, 129–130

Ching, Stuart, 158

Choi, Sook Nyul: *Echoes of the White Giraffe,* 165, 166–167; *Gathering of Pearls,* 165, 167; historical events in autobiographies, 163; use of third person, 168; *Year of Impossible Goodbyes,* 165–166

Choy, Wayson: as adult, 22; *The Jade Peony,* 122–123, 194n. 19, 201n. 8; name, 19; *Paper Shadows,* 10, 19, 110, 112–113, 120, 121, 122–127, 135; sexual orientation, 201n. 8

chronotopic position, 19, 34, 87

Chu, Patricia P., 8, 20, 111, 112

Chun, Gloria Heyung, 120, 200n. 6

Cinderella, 160, 161

Coe, Richard N.: on Childhoods, 2, 5, 7, 8, 11, 22, 75; on endings of Childhoods, 7, 35–36, 81, 192n. 3; "exotic-schizophrenic childhood," 190n. 6; on loss of religious faith, 21; on myths of childhood, 12–13, 14, 103, 108, 190n. 5; on North American Childhoods, 112; on paradigms of Childhoods, 7, 12, 106, 114; on role of school in child's development, 106; on solitude of Childhood writers, 105–106; *When the Grass Was Taller,* 2, 7; on writing of Childhoods, 17

collective identities, 172, 199–200n. 2

collective memory, 28–29, 30–31, 58, 150, 185

colonial childhoods, 57–64

colonial mentality, 90, 197n. 10

comics: autobiographical, 143, 144, 145; interaction of drawing and language, 144–145; as medium, 143–145; use of term, 202n. 9. *See also* Barry, Lynda

community: building in Childhoods, 3, 4; role in Childhoods, 112; writing stories of, 137

connected reading, 29
consent, strategies of, 111, 199n. 1
contact zone, 34, 40–41
cooking. *See* food
Coveney, Peter, 11
Crewe, Jonathan, 29
criticism. *See* Asian American literary criticism
crypto-ethnicity, 95, 198n. 15
cultural memory, 22–23, 29–30, 33, 58
Cultural Revolution: autobiographies set during, 69; Childhoods set during, 67–68, 69–74, 169–171; fictional works on, 69; historical importance, 68; names reflecting, 132; Red Guards, 67–68, 69, 71; victims, 68, 72–74
cultural survival, 138

Davis, Rocío G., 3, 188n. 6, 189n. 2, 193n. 15, 196n. 2, 201n. 3, 203nn. 1, 13, 204n. 13, 205n. 15
Day, Iyko, 187n. 3
De Jesús, Melinda, 146, 203n. 10
Delman, Carmit, *Burnt Bread and Chutney,* 84–86, 197n. 7
de Man, Paul, 136
de Manuel, Dolores, 203n. 1
descent, strategies of, 111, 199n. 1
diaries: of children in wartime, 176; of Lau, 140–143; of Takashima, 175–176; therapeutic writing, 141
diaspora, autobiographies of, 24. *See also* immigration
diasporic identities, 14, 15
disabilities. *See* blind individuals
disability studies, 14
Dodge, Georgina, 191n. 12
double narratives, 103, 137, 148, 150–151
Doucet, Julie, 144
Douglas, Kate, 5, 101, 191n. 15
Duan Chengshi, 160

Eakin, Paul John, 2, 28, 144, 149, 150, 175, 191nn. 13–14
eating. *See* food

eating disorders, 139–140. *See also* anorexia
Eaton, Edith Maud (Sui Sin Far), 83, 196n. 3
Eaton, Winifred (Onoto Watanna), 83, 196n. 3
education: as goal of Childhood writers, 44, 51, 72, 73, 170; of immigrant children, 134, 201n. 9; role in Childhoods, 106; schools for blind children, 46, 47–49, 51. *See also* English language
Egan, Susanna, 23–24, 52, 144, 149, 191n. 13
Eidse, Faith, 67
Eisner, Will, 144, 202n. 9
Elbaz, Robert, 102
Elliot, Doung Van Mai, *The Sacred Willow,* 203n. 13
empowerment, 159, 170. *See also* agency
English language: acquisition by children of immigrant families, 113, 125, 126, 127, 131, 132, 133; learning in Asia, 50, 54, 73, 95, 102–103; as trope, 127, 131, 135
Espiritu, Yen Le, 88
ethnic autobiography: diasporic, 24; expansion of autobiography genre, 1–2; external expectations of, 23; of immigrants, 17, 111, 115–116; political nature, 189n. 9; as reflection of culture, 183; relational approaches, 148–150; role of community and family, 112; scholarship on, 9, 10, 17; self-representation, 31; structures, 137–138; tropes, 111–112
ethnic children's literature, 156, 171
ethnic identities: of autobiographers, 16–20; of biracial individuals, 83; of Chinese Canadians, 124; in United States, 10. *See also* identities
ethnicity: affiliation, 14, 16–20; in American society, 10; crypto-, 95, 198n. 15; reinventions, 20; self-representation, 10, 13–14, 15, 31; situational, 83

ethnic studies, 9, 14
ethnic writing: emancipatory project, 24–25; food trope, 119, 128; relationality, 28
Eurasians: in China, 104, 106; literary stereotypes of, 83; in Vietnam, 88. *See also* biracial individuals
Euro-American autobiography, 8, 9–10, 12, 14, 20, 21
Euro-American Childhoods, 21, 36, 86, 112

families: in Chinese society, 53, 54, 115; father-son relationships, 95–97; generational autobiographies, 66–67, 203n. 13; Kashmiri customs, 56; mother-daughter relationships, 55, 133–134; patriarchal, 54; roles in ethnic autobiography, 112
father-son relationships, 95–97
Feldman, Carol Fleisher, 137, 138
feminism, 52, 53, 54
feminist studies, 9, 14, 115
Fenkl, Heinz Insu: *Memories of My Ghost Brother,* 17, 82, 87, 93–98, 101, 102, 108, 198n. 13; name, 19
Fifield, Adam, *A Blessing over Ashes,* 150–151
Filipino Americans, 41. *See also* Asian Americans; Barry, Lynda; Bulosan, Carlos; Reyes, Norman
films: cowboy movies, 124; *The Killing Fields,* 74, 153
First Nations peoples, 179
Fischer, Michael M. J., 13, 19–20, 24, 183, 203n. 12
food: Chinese restaurants, 129–130; ethnic feast trope, 119; in ethnic writing, 128; trope of, 85, 113–114, 118, 119, 127–131, 134–135. *See also* anorexia
food pornographers, 119
France: biracial Childhoods set in, 84; colonial rule of Vietnam, 88
Frank, Anne, 176
Friedman, Susan Stanford, 112
Fritz, Jean, 164; *Homesick,* 204n. 5
Fuse, Montye P., 64, 194n. 21

gender. *See* women
generational autobiography, 66–67, 203n. 13
generic choices, 8
Gilbert, Kate, 70
Gilmore, Leigh, 26, 75, 195n. 8
Goar, Robert J., 63–64, 194n. 22
Goellnicht, Donald C., 9, 187n. 3, 190–191n. 10
Gordon, Avery, 94
Gramsci, Antonio, 189n. 9
graphic narratives. *See* comics
Grice, Helena, 83, 101, 196nn. 1, 3
Gullestad, Marianne, 3–4, 12, 26, 189n. 1
Gunn, Janet Varner, 32, 137
Gusdorf, Georges, 2

Hakuin Ekaku, 145
Hall, Stuart, 15, 110
Hamilton, Paula, 192n. 18
haunting, 94–95, 98
Hazlett, John Downton, 66
healing: autobiography's potential for, 81, 140, 152; bibliotherapy, 158–159; role of writing, 140, 175
Heng, Liang, *Son of the Revolution,* 69
Higa, Tomiko, *The Girl with the White Flag,* 204n. 11
Him, Chanrithy, *When Broken Glass Floats,* 68, 74, 76, 78–81
Hirsch, Marianne, 191–192n. 17
historical events: children's awareness of, 21–22, 35; in children's literature, 157; described in Childhoods, 4, 21–22, 35, 110–111; described in Childhoods for children, 157, 163, 171; described in Childhoods set in Asia, 35, 44, 49–50, 56, 57–58, 66, 87, 163; reclamation of, 3; roles of Asian North Americans, 171–178. *See also* Cultural Revolution; wars
Holland, Patricia, 101
home, as contested site, 45
Hongo, Garrett, *Volcano,* 203n. 13
Houston, Jeanne Wakatsuki, *Farewell to Manzanar,* 1, 172–175, 199n. 2
Houston, Vera Hasu, 197n. 6

Hutcheon, Linda, 95, 198n. 15
Huynh, Quang Nhoung, *The Land I Lost,* 162–163
Hwang, David Henry, 170
Hynes, Samuel, 30, 191–192n. 17

Ibarraran, Amaia, 196n. 2
identities: of biracial individuals, 86, 87–88, 90, 91–93, 95–96, 102, 197n. 8; collective, 172, 199–200n. 2; construction in autobiography, 32; double, 120; formation of and Childhoods, 2, 11–12; of immigrants, 118, 127; of Japanese colonists, 60; roles of family and clan in Chinese, 53. *See also* ethnic identities
Igloria, Luisa A., 67
illustrations: of Lim, 179–180; of Takashima, 175–176; of Zhang, 168–169. *See also* photographs
immigrant autobiography: Childhoods, 110–135; macrotext of, 17
immigrants: ambivalence about homelands, 18; Amerasians from Vietnam, 103; assimilation, 20, 112, 119–120, 125; attitudes toward homelands, 171; conflicts with children, 20, 115–116, 117–118, 133; denizens or sojourners, 41, 44, 111, 112; educations, 134, 201n. 9; foods, 85, 119, 128–129; identities, 118, 127; languages, 113, 131, 133; liminal positions, 116–117, 132; name changes, 19, 132; social classes, 38, 44; socialization of, 110–111; values conflicts, 167, 190n. 6
immigration: American dream and, 73, 87, 103, 134; at conclusion of Childhoods, 17, 35–36, 44, 57, 93, 108; debates on U.S. laws, 40
India: Bene Israel community, 84, 86; independence, 49–50; partition, 51, 56. *See also* Delman, Carmit; Kashmir; Mehta, Ved
individual, relationship to collective, 67, 68–69, 116, 149

individualism, American, 116, 167
intermarriage. *See* biracial individuals
internment camps, 1, 172–177, 199–200n. 2
intersubjectivity, 28, 148–150, 152

Jackson, Michael, 149
James, Laura M., 178
Japan: colonization of Korea, 35, 44, 57–58, 62–64, 164, 165–166, 194n. 21; colonization of Manchuria, 58, 59–62, 164; invasion of China, 105, 168; occupation of China, 35, 57–58, 59–62; returnees from Manchuria and Korea, 59, 61, 168; surrender in World War II, 61, 63, 166
Japanese Americans: Childhoods for children, 164–165, 172–175, 176–177; Childhoods set in Manchuria and Korea, 57–62, 164–165; Childhoods set in United States, 172–175, 176–177; internment of, 1, 172–175, 176–177, 199–200n. 2; racist attitudes toward, 172, 173, 174, 177; stereotypes of, 174; women's narratives, 13–14. *See also* Asian Americans
Japanese Canadian Cultural Center, 175
Japanese Canadians: Childhoods, 175–176; government apology to, 175, 176; internment during World War II, 175–176
Jews, 84–86, 144
Jiang, Ji-Li, *Red Scarf Girl,* 69, 163, 169–171

Kang, Connie, *Home Was the Land of Morning Calm,* 203n. 13
Kang, Hyok, *This is Paradise!,* 195n. 7
Kang, Younghill: autobiography for children, 158; *East Goes West,* 41; *The Grass Roof,* 17, 35, 41–45, 193n. 8; social status, 44
Kaplan, Caren, 138
Kashmir, Childhoods set in, 55–57
Keller, Helen, 48
Khmer Adolescent Project, 81

Khmer Rouge, 35, 68, 74–81, 151, 152, 153

Killing Fields, The (film), 74, 153

Kim, Elaine H., 15, 37, 39, 41, 44, 83, 96, 117–118, 121, 173, 174, 192n. 2, 193nn. 9, 11, 200n. 5, 200–201n. 7

Kim, Elizabeth, *Ten Thousand Sorrows,* 197n. 5

Kim, Richard, *Lost Names,* 17, 18, 57–58, 62–64, 184, 194nn. 20–21

Kingston, Maxine Hong, *The Woman Warrior,* 4, 10, 23, 27, 55, 136, 149, 188n. 7, 189n. 1

Kogawa, Joy, 189n. 1, 204n. 3

Kominsky, Aline, 144

Korea: attitudes toward biracial children, 97–98; Childhoods set in, 36–38, 41–45, 62–64, 93–98, 164–168, 195n. 7; Japanese colonial rule, 35, 44, 57–58, 62–64, 164, 165–166, 194n. 21; legends and fables, 94; missionaries, 43; name changes, 18, 63, 64, 166; Russian troops in, 164, 166; Western influences, 43–44; World War II in, 164, 165

Korean Americans: biracial Childhoods, 93–98; Childhoods for children, 164–168; Childhoods set in Korea, 36–38, 41–45, 62–64, 93–98, 164–168, 197n. 5; connection to homeland, 194n. 21; earliest Childhood, 16, 34–35, 36–38, 39, 41; immigrants, 41; writers, 41. *See also* Asian Americans

Korean War, 166–167

Kornreich, Jennifer, 201n. 4

Koul, Sudha, *The Tiger Ladies,* 35, 55–57

Kröller, Eva-Marie, 124

künstlerroman: comics as, 145; of Lim, 179–180; of Uchida, 176–178

Kuramoto, Kazuko, *Manchurian Legacy,* 17, 57–58, 59–62

Kwan, Michael David: as adult, 22, 103, 194n. 19; *Things That Must Not Be Forgotten,* 17, 82, 87, 101, 103–108

Kwan, Michelle, and Laura M. James, *Michelle Kwan Autobiography,* 178–179

language: in immigrant families, 113, 131, 133; interaction with drawing in comics, 144–145; loss of, 64, 113; as trope, 113; untranslatable cultural concepts, 131. *See also* English language

Lau, Evelyn: as adult, 202n. 8; *Inside Out,* 142–143; poetry, 202n. 8; *Runaway,* 136, 138, 140–143

Lee, Helie, *Still Life with Rice,* 203n. 13

Lee, Kyhan, 39

Lee, Sue-Im, 3

Lee, Yan Phou: involvement in immigration debate, 40; social status, 38; *When I Was a Boy in China,* 16, 34–35, 36–41, 192n. 5

Lejeune, Philippe, 149, 187n. 2

Lim, Shirley Geok-lin, 115, 188n. 7, 191n. 12, 200n. 5

Lim, Sing, *West Coast Chinese Boy,* 179–180

liminal positions: of biracial individuals, 82, 87–88, 89, 90, 95, 97; of Chinatown, 120; of Chinese Americans, 180, 181; of immigrants, 116–117, 132

Ling, Amy, 38, 39–41, 67, 83, 190n. 7, 191n. 12, 192n. 5, 192–193n. 7, 196n. 3

Lin Yutang, 38, 192n. 2

Lionnet, Françoise, 84, 189n. 10

literary criticism: Asian American, 3, 187n. 3; Asian Canadian, 187–188n. 3; *métissage* concept, 84

literature of trauma, 75–76

Litton, Edmund, 197n. 11

Liu, Aimee: novels, 196n. 2, 201n. 3; *Solitaire,* 136, 137, 138–140, 143

Liu Binyan, *A Higher Kind of Loyalty,* 69

Lloyd, Rosemary, 2

Lo, Marie, 141, 187–188n. 3, 190n. 9, 202n. 6

Lopez, Erika, 144

Lothrop, Lee, and Shephard Publishing

Company, "Children of Other Lands Books," 36, 62
Lowe, Lisa, 20–21, 183
Lu Chi Fa, and Becky White, *Double Luck,* 160, 161–162
Lu Xun, 71

Mah, Adeline Yen: *Chinese Cinderella,* 158, 160–161; *Falling Leaves,* 204n. 6
Malaysia: Childhoods set in, 51–55; ethnic groups, 52–53, 54
Manchuria: Childhoods set in, 59–62; Japanese occupation, 58, 59–62, 164; Koreans in, 62; World War II in, 61
Manzanar, 1, 172–175
Mao Zedong, 69, 71, 73, 169, 170. *See also* Cultural Revolution
Mar, M. Elaine: as adult, 22; name, 19, 132; *Paper Daughter,* 19, 110, 127–134, 135
Mass, Amy Iwasaki, 83
McCloud, Scott, 145, 202n. 9
McKelvey, Robert S., 99, 198n. 16
meals. *See* food
Mehta, Ved: as adult, 22; autobiographies, 46, 193n. 13; blindness, 46–49, 50; *Face to Face,* 45–46; *The Ledge between the Streams,* 35, 46–47, 49–51; *Sound Shadows of the New World,* 193n. 14; *Vedi,* 35, 46–49
memory: autobiography as performance of, 27–31; collective, 28–29, 30–31, 58, 150, 185; cultural, 22–23, 29–30, 33, 58; nonlinearity, 51
mental illness. *See* anorexia
métissage, 84
Miki, Roy, 187n. 3
Min, Anchee, *Red Azalea,* 69
mirror talk, 149
mixed race individuals. *See* biracial individuals
model minority discourse, 21, 25, 114, 141
Moser, Linda Trinh, 174

mother-daughter relationships, 55, 133–134
Murayama, Milton, *Five Years on a Rock,* 203n. 14
Myers, Mitzi, 157
myths: of childhood, 12–13, 14, 103, 108; collective memory and, 30

Nakashima, Daniel A., 18, 96
Nam, Vickie, 67
names: of biracial individuals, 95–96; of immigrants, 19, 132; importance, 18–19; in Japanese-occupied Korea, 18, 63, 64, 166
national affiliation, 14
Neuman, Shirley, 4
New, Ilhan: social status, 39; *When I Was a Boy in Korea,* 16, 34–35, 36–38, 39, 41
Ngor, Haing, 74–75
Nguyen, Kien: historical novels, 199n. 18, 203n. 14; *The Unwanted,* 17, 82, 87, 98–103, 108
North Americanization, 18, 110–111, 113
North Korea: Childhoods set in, 195n. 7; Russian troops in, 164, 166. *See also* Korea
Nunez, Sigrid, 196n. 2
Nussbaum, Felicity A., 141

Oh, Seiwoong, 39, 41, 192n. 6, 193nn. 10–11
Olney, James, 33
Omi, Michael, 196n. 1
Ondaatje, Michael, *Running in the Family,* 10–11
orphans, 160, 161–162
Ortega y Gasset, José, 66–67
Otano, Alicia, 94, 190n. 4

Park, Frances and Ginger, *To Swim across the World,* 203n. 14
Pataray-Ching, Jann, 158
Pelaud, Isabelle Thuy, 100
performance: in autobiography, 2, 10, 27–31, 32, 189–190n. 3; in comics, 145; of memory, 27–31

Philippines: American colonial rule, 88–89, 91; biracial individuals, 88–93; Childhoods set in, 88–93; folktales, 147; *mestizos,* 88–93, 147; Spanish colonial rule, 88, 91; World War II in, 92–93, 147, 198n. 12. *See also* Filipino Americans

photographs: in autobiographies, 124–125; on book covers, 73, 101, 195n. 6; in Childhoods set in Asia, 37, 101; in *Paper Shadows* (Choy), 124–125

pluralism, 13

political history. *See* Cultural Revolution; historical events; wars

Pol Pot, 77. *See also* Khmer Rouge

Popkin, Jeremy D., 67

Porter, Roger, 189–190n. 3

poststructuralism, 15, 136

post-traumatic stress disorder, 81

Pran, Dith, 74

Pratt, Mary Louise, 34, 192n. 1

race: Asian views of, 88; links to class, 88, 93; social construction of, 82; theories, 196n. 1. *See also* biracial individuals

racial discrimination: against biracial individuals, 88, 99–100; in North America, 18

racism: in Canada, 18, 179; effects on Japanese Americans, 172, 173, 174, 177; in Malaysia, 53

relational autobiography: Asian North American, 203n. 13; *A Blessing over Ashes* (Fifield), 150–151; by ethnic subjects, 148–150; experiments, 150–151; *Lucky Child* (Ung), 136, 137, 148, 151–154; scholarship on, 28

restaurants, Chinese, 129–130

Reyes, Norman, *Child of Two Worlds,* 82, 87, 88–93, 102, 108, 198n. 12

Robbins, Trina, 144, 203n. 11

Rodriguez, Richard, *Hunger of Memory,* 201n. 9

Roh-Spaulding, Carol, 196n. 3

Roley, Brian Ascalon, 196n. 2

Root, Maria P., 97, 98–99, 197n. 8

Ropp, Stephen, 196n. 1

Sakurai, Patricia A., 174–175

San Francisco Chinatown, 116, 120

Santa Ana, Jeffrey, 197n. 6, 202n. 5

scriptotherapy, 140

Shapiro, Judith, 69

short stories. *See* story cycles

Sichel, Nina, 67

Silliman, Jael, 197n. 7

Simal González, Begoña, 196n. 2

situational ethnicity, 83

Sivan, Emmanuel, 30, 58, 191–192n. 17

Slatin, John M., 46, 193n. 12

Slemon, Stephen, 171

Smith, Katharine Capshaw, 156, 172, 203n. 1

Smith, Sidonie, 5, 27–28, 29, 189n. 3

social classes: biraciality and, 87, 88, 90, 93, 100; of immigrants, 38, 44; link to race, 88, 93; of writers of Childhoods, 38

socialization: of biracial individuals, 87; in Childhoods, 14, 20–22, 114; of immigrants, 110–111; truncated, 14, 21. *See also* North Americanization

Sollors, Werner, 82–83

Sone, Monica, 18–19, 199n. 2

South Korea. *See* Korea

Spain, rule of Philippines, 88, 91

Spickard, Paul R., 83, 196n. 4

Spiegelman, Art: "commix" term, 202n. 9; *Maus,* 144

Spitzer, Leo, 29

sports. *See* athletes

Stanley, Liz, 34, 40, 192n. 1

Steedman, Carolyn, 27, 185

stereotypes: of Asians, 119; of biracial individuals, 83, 90; challenges to in children's literature, 159; in ethnic writing, 111, 118–119; of Japanese, 174

Stone, Albert E., 4, 188–189n. 8

story cycles: *Lane with No Name* (Tham), 51–55; *Lost Names* (Kim), 62–64

Stotesbury, John A., 46, 193n. 12
Sturken, Marita, 30, 33
Su, Karen, 119, 120, 200nn. 3, 5
subjectivity: Asian American, 8, 20; in
    Asian North American Childhoods,
    14, 15–16; of autobiographer, 13,
    114; of biracial individuals, 87–88;
    inter-, 28, 148–150, 152; multiple,
    114; processes, 14–16
Sugimoto, Etsu, *A Daughter of the Samu-
    rai,* 10, 38, 192n. 2
Suleri (Goodyear), Sara: *Boys Will Be
    Boys,* 203n. 13; *Meatless Days,* 55,
    203n. 13
Sun-Childers, Jaia, and Douglas
    Childers, *The White-Haired Girl,* 69
Szymusiak, Molyda, *The Stones Cry Out,*
    195n. 7

Taft, William Howard, 89
Takashima, Shichan, *A Child in Prison
    Camp,* 172, 175–176
Takei, George, 199n. 2
Tal, Kali, 75, 195nn. 8–9
Tausky, Thomas E., 123
testimonio, 142
Tham, Hilary: development as poet, 52,
    54, 193–194n. 16; *Lane with No
    Name,* 35, 51–55; poetry, 51–52,
    194n. 19
third person narratives, 115–116, 168
Thompson, Becky W., 139
Todorov, Tzevetan, 8
Tokyo Rose (Iva Ikuko Toguri), 198n.
    12
transculturality: borderlands, 39; con-
    tact zone, 34, 40–41; as metaphor,
    17; photographic discourse and,
    124–125; revisionary models, 16
traumatic experiences: abuse, 160–161;
    in adolescence, 140, 143; in Child-
    hoods, 21, 81, 138, 160–161;
    children's responses, 74, 168; liter-
    ature of, 75–76; post-traumatic
    stress disorder, 81; therapeutic
    writing, 140. *See also* wars
travel and displacement, 67. *See also*
    immigration

Trites, Roberta Seelinger, 203n. 1
tropes: of Americanization, 127; bil-
    dungsroman structure, 111–112;
    Chinatown, 120–122; English
    language, 127, 131; in ethnic auto-
    biography, 111–112; ethnic feast,
    119; food, 85, 113–114, 118, 119,
    127–131, 134–135; language, 113;
    meanings, 111; subversion of,
    113–114, 135; writing, 127, 134
Twain, Mark, *Huckleberry Finn,* 42, 92
Ty, Eleanor, 190n. 9, 196n. 2

Uchida, Yoshiko: as adult, 22, 194n. 19;
    Desert Exile, 176, 199n. 2; *The
    Invisible Thread,* 19, 25, 158, 172,
    176–178, 199n. 2; name, 19
Ung, Loung: as adult, 78, 81; *First They
    Killed My Father,* 17, 68, 74, 75–78,
    80–81, 148, 153–154; *Lucky Child,*
    136, 137, 148, 151–154
United States: individualism, 116, 167;
    internment of Japanese Americans,
    1, 172–175, 176–177, 199–200n.
    2; model minority discourse, 21,
    25, 114, 141; racial discrimination
    in, 18; rule of Philippines, 88–89,
    91. *See also* Asian Americans;
    immigration
Uno, Katherine, 194n. 17

Vancouver Chinatown, 120, 122, 123,
    124, 179
Vietnam: biracial children, 88, 99–100,
    198n. 17; Childhoods set in,
    98–103, 162–163; Communist
    takeover, 99; French colonial rule,
    88; invasion of Cambodia, 77;
    Orderly Departure Program for
    Amerasians, 103
Vietnam Veterans of America Founda-
    tion, 81
Vietnam War: children's experiences,
    163; end of, 99; invasion of
    Cambodia, 78
visible minority discourse, 21, 25

Wah, Fred, *Diamond Grill,* 11

About the Author

Rocío G. Davis has degrees from the Ateneo de Manila University and the University of Navarra, where she is currently associate professor of American and postcolonial literatures. Her publications include *Transcultural Reinventions: Asian American and Asian Canadian Short Story Cycles* (2001), *Sites of Ethnicity: Europe and the Americas* (co-edited with William Boelhower and Carmen Birkle, 2004), *Asian American Literature in the International Context: Readings on Fiction, Poetry, and Performance* (co-edited with Sämi Ludwig, 2002), and *Tricks with a Glass: Writing Ethnicity in Canada* (co-edited with Rosalía Baena, 2000). She has edited a special issue of the journal *MELUS* on Filipino American literature.

Production Notes for *Davis / Begin Here*

Cover and interior designed by University of Hawai'i Press
production staff in Berkeley and Gill Sans

Composition by Josie Herr

Printing and binding by The Maple-Vail Book
Manufacturing Group

Printed on 60 lb. Glat Offset B18, 420 ppi